INDIVIDUALISM, by Ronald Gross and Paul Osterman brings together a series of essays that address themselves to a central issue of American life—the individual's role in an increasingly complex society.

RONALD GROSS is vice-president and editor-in-chief of the Academy for Educational Development, a non-profit consulting firm. His previous books include *Radical School Reform, The Teacher and the Taught, Learning by Television,* and *The Revolution in the Schools.* Mr. Gross' articles and essays have appeared in *Harper's, Saturday Review,* and *The New York Times Magazine.* He is also widely known for his experimental poetry and literary criticism.

PAUL OSTERMAN, a former New York City teacher, is also with the Academy for Educational Development. He has been a consultant for the Ford Foundation, the United States Office of Education, and the Commonwealth of Massachusetts, and his articles and essays have appeared in *The New Republic* and *Commonweal.* Mr. Osterman is co-editor of *High School,* an anthology on the future of secondary education.

INDIVIDUALISM
Man in Modern Society

RONALD GROSS
and
PAUL OSTERMAN

A LAUREL ORIGINAL

Published by
Dell Publishing Co., Inc.
750 Third Avenue
New York, New York 10017
Copyright © 1971 by Ronald Gross
All rights reserved. No part of this book may be
reproduced in any form or by any means without the
prior written permission of the Publisher, excepting
brief quotes used in connection
with reviews written specifically for inclusion
in a magazine or newspaper.
Laurel ® TM 674623, Dell Publishing Co., Inc.
Printed in the United States of America
First printing—April 1971
Second printing—September 1972

Acknowledgments for copyrighted material
appear on pages V and VI and constitute an
extension of this page.

ACKNOWLEDGMENTS

"The Role of Individuality" by Bertrand Russell: Copyright ©
1949 by Bertrand Russell. Reprinted by permission of Simon
& Schuster . . . and George Allen & Unwin Ltd. . . . from
AUTHORITY AND THE INDIVIDUAL by Bertrand Russell.

"Individuality and Its Limits" by John W. Gardner: From SELF-
RENEWAL by John W. Gardner. Copyright © 1964 by John
W. Gardner. Reprinted by permission of Harper & Row,
Publishers.

"American Individualism in the Twentieth Century" by David
M. Potter: From INNOCENCE AND POWER, ed. Gordon Mills
(University of Texas Press, 1965). Reprinted by permission.

"Individualism Reconsidered" by David Riesman: Reprinted
with permission of The Macmillan Company from INDIVIDU-
ALISM RECONSIDERED by David Riesman. Copyright 1954 by
the Free Press of Glencoe.

"One-Dimensional Man" by Herbert Marcuse: Reprinted by
permission of the Beacon Press. Copyright © 1964 by Herbert Marcuse. From ONE-DIMENSIONAL MAN by Herbert Marcuse.

"Black Manhood" by William H. Grier and Price M. Cobbs:
Excerpted from Chapter IV of BLACK RAGE by William H.
Grier and Price M. Cobbs. Copyright © 1968 by William H.
Grier and Price M. Cobbs, Basic Books, Inc., Publishers,
New York.

"The Individual and the Technocracy" by John Kenneth Galbraith: From THE NEW INDUSTRIAL STATE. Copyright © 1967
by John Kenneth Galbraith. Reprinted by permission of the
publisher, Houghton Mifflin Company.

"Schooling and the Individual" by Edgar Z. Friedenberg: From
COMING OF AGE IN AMERICA by Edgar Z. Friedenberg. Copyright © 1965 by Edgar Z. Friedenberg. Reprinted by permission of Random House, Inc.

"Individualism in Suburbia" by William H. Whyte, Jr.: Reprinted by permission of the author.

09226

This book is dedicated to
Basil O'Connor, an individual
in an age of conformity.

We would like to acknowledge
Leslie Shalen, who contributed time
and intelligence to this book.

CONTENTS

INTRODUCTION

Much of contemporary American social and political thought can be seen as a continuing debate over the problems and prospects of individualism in our national life. From anarchist appeals for ultimate decentralization of all our major social enterprises to demands for a return to classical laissez-faire, the debate rages in major key. And in minor key it echoes through the civil-rights and youth movements of the past twenty years, in which the rights of the individual have been pitted against the rights of property holders, or states rights, or the rights of the federal government itself.

Similarly, one can trace the changing attitudes toward the individual in American literature, philosophy, sociology, history, economics, and political science. For so basic is the concept of individualism to American society that every major issue which faces us as a nation invariably poses itself in these terms.

There is no single acceptable definition of "individualism." The term has signified many different ideas throughout American history. The purpose of this book is to explore the background and present status of the individual and of the idea of individualism, and the essays were selected to illustrate what individualism means today.

Winston Smith struggled, but in the end he loved Big Brother. In George Orwell's *1984* the individual was helpless before the Party. Children were thoroughly indoctrinated by the educational system. Adults had no privacy—two-way television spied on them constantly. The government, economy, press, and every other important locus of power was controlled by the Party. Is it any wonder that Winston Smith succumbed to the system?

How near is *1984*? Today, Americans are haunted by antiutopian prophecies because so many of the elements of these fantasies seem to be with us. Schools impose conformity and obedience. The mass media traffic in an indigestible combination of senseless trivia and political palaver. Privacy is threatened by electronic devices, national data banks, and wiretaps. Brush-fire wars and anticommunism keep Americans in a state bordering on paranoia. Finally, historical forces seem to be concentrating enormous power in few hands as Big Business and Big Government merge and become indistinguishable.

Nor is *1984* the only warning of the apocalypse. Pick up any recent work which tries to discern where we are headed, and this theme will likely be there. This pessimistic view of the fate of the individual in modern society has been explicated by many recent writers: Jacques Ellul, Lewis Mumford, Aldous Huxley, Roderick Seidenberg, Herbert Marcuse, etc. One of the clearest, most apocalyptic and least well-known expositions is Roderick Seidenberg's. In his book *Posthistoric Man*,[1] Seidenberg begins by noting a pervasive characteristic of modern life: its high degree of organization. Mankind, he writes, seems to be groping toward new and all-inclusive modes of organization. Today the most advanced nations are corporate societies, dominated by huge national organizations—business corporations, governmental bureaucracies, labor unions, etc. Moreover, as organizations expand and multiply they increase the pressure on their membership. The business corporation, for example, produces the "Organization Man." The compulsion to organize is so all-pervasive that we accept it as a given, just as we accept the necessity of being "scientific."

Why has the urge to organize come to dominate modern life? Seidenberg finds two answers to this question. The simple, surface answer is that, once we begin to organize *something*, we are inevitably driven to organize *everything*. We find an example in the early history of industrial man-

[1] Roderick Seidenberg, *Posthistoric Man* (Chapel Hill: University of North Carolina Press, 1950).

agement. Frederick Taylor, the first "efficiency expert," began his work in the yards of the Bethlehem Steel Company, where day laborers loaded pig iron onto railway cars. Taylor raised the men's productivity by teaching them the most efficient way to bend and use the shovel, just how big a bite to take each time, etc.; this enabled each man to shovel more iron and get less tired. At the same time, however, the new method turned the men into the virtual automatons characteristically produced by overorganization. It also had another effect, which explains why organization tends to spread. Once he had organized and mechanized the movements of the laborers, Taylor found that he had to bring the other phases of the plant up to a comparable level of efficiency. The shipments of iron had to be speeded up, the front office had to be systematized so that it could provide the workmen with the various-size shovels they needed; this required the installation of telephone lines throughout the vast yards. The same phenomenon is occurring today as industry becomes automated: once the factory is automated, it becomes necessary to install a computer in the front office to control production and process orders. The lesson is clear. Organization breeds more organization. A system can only run at top efficiency if the system from which it draws its materials and into which it feeds its products are equally efficient.

A still deeper reason—says Seidenberg—lies behind this increase in organization. Organization is the expression of intelligence in human affairs—the rational adjustment of means to a specific end. The age of organization is the age of intelligence, reason and science. But over what, we must ask, does this intelligence dominate? Not merely over the environment, but over our elemental impulses. In this conflict between intelligence and instinct Seidenberg finds the key to man's nature and history, and through it he traces man's past and projects his future.

According to Seidenberg, man emerged into history when he first began to use his intelligence to differentiate himself from the animals. Man's advantage was culture, through which his achievements in conquering the environment were made cumulative and passed on from generation to generation. Thus the development of the human race followed the development of the individual as Freud had described it: "Where id is, there shall ego be." For the rule of instinct, mankind gradually substituted the guidance of intelligence.

While the voice of intelligence was barely audible at first, it had a decisive advantage in its long-range struggle with instinct. Being cumulative, intelligence could increase its power through each generation, while the force of instinct, which was merely passed on by heredity and could not augment its strength, remained a constant. Seidenberg sees the growing strength of intelligence, as expressed in the power of science to control and mold the world, as a great tidal wave swelling through all of human history, despite the rise and decline of each discrete civilization. (Similarly, Toynbee sees each of the great cultures leaving behind a residue which grows steadily throughout history; but for Toynbee, this residue is the wisdom of the higher religions.)

Where will it all end? Seidenberg has the distinction of being the most pessimistic philosopher of history on the current scene. He is unflinching in his portrayal of the inevitable triumph of intelligence over instinct. Intelligence, as expressed in organization, science mechanization—this is the wave of the future which cannot be held back. Organization pushes always for more organization until everything is unified and coherent; science, having conquered the world, turns its techniques to man himself and will not stop until it has control of his mind, his body and his genes; the machine, that concrete and perfect embodiment of organization, intelligence and science, will not only spread its pall over the entire globe, but will also force its human attendants into ever closer adherence to its mechanical rhythms.

The result, argues Seidenberg, will be posthistory, a period roughly symmetrical with the eons of time we now think of as prehistory, in which individuals had not yet differentiated themselves from the social group. Once the dominance of intelligence over instinct is complete, the individual will again sink into the social mass. But this time it will be intelligence rather than instinct which dictates the fixed rules of social life. Individuality will be dead, and history—which was merely the conflict of instinct and intelligence—will be over. Like the prehistoric era, the posthistoric one will extend indefinitely, making the six-thousand-year period of history seem like a mere lyrical interlude in the somber march music of human evolution.

It has become a cliché to see the present as a transitional period. Seidenberg goes one better: he sees all of history as transitional and atypical. It is the interval during which instinct and intelligence are in a precarious balance; intelligence is just beginning the final push which will culminate in the irrevocable subjugation of instinct. The "natural" state of man is automatism. The course of human history is merely the transition from his primitive state, in which he was a puppet animated from within by the hand of instinct, to his final condition, when he will become a marionette controlled from without by the compulsions of intelligence.

Other social critics, while agreeing with Seidenberg that the spread and perfection of modern technology spells the end of individualism, approach the problem from a different angle. Marshall McLuhan [2] stands out as the thinker who has posited the most decisive, far-reaching and unique implications for the new technology.

Like Seidenberg, McLuhan views recorded history as an interlude between two essentially similar periods. According to McLuhan, the development of phonetic writing and, more dramatically, the invention of movable print wrenched man out of his early tribal environment and forced his thinking and his life into certain linear, rational patterns. It was this disassociation of man from his natural tribal environment which led to the concept of individualism. Today, according to McLuhan, our electronic environment is creating a new tribal culture, and the idea of individualism is on the way out.

Before the advent of print technology, says McLuhan, man lived in a world of sensory balance, where all the senses were active, and—because the primary medium of communication was speech—the ear structured the culture. No man knew much more than any other and "there was

[2] See Marshall McLuhan, *Understanding Media* (New York: Mc-Graw-Hill, 1964), and *Gutenberg Galaxies* (Toronto: University of Toronto, 1962).

little individualism and specialization, the hallmarks of 'civilized' Western man." According to McLuhan, "Audile-tactile tribal man partook of the collective unconscious, lived in a magical integral world patterned by myth and ritual, its values divine and unchallenged."

The invention of print technology led to the domination of man's five senses by his eye. "The new medium of linear, uniform, repeatable type reproduced information in unlimited quantities and at hitherto-impossible speeds, thus assuring the eye a position of total predominance in man's sensorium." This extension of man—for to McLuhan all media are extensions of man's original senses—shaped our environment and was responsible for the entire shape of modern society. The Reformation, perspective in art, the assembly line and narrative chronology in literature all are the offspring of print technology. More important for our purposes, McLuhan believes that "literate mechanical society separated the individual from the group in space, engendering privacy; in thought, engendering point of view; and in work, engendering specialism—thus forging all values associated with individualism."

But, according to McLuhan, this development was not beneficial. Man's separation from the group created an environment that was ". . . fragmented, explicit, logical, specialized, and detached." Separated from his tribal group, the individual became disassociated, rootless, alienated. The individualism we so prize is in fact no blessing: it leaves man without roots, dehumanizes him and leads to a search for identity culminating in mass mind and mass uniformity. "The alphabet shattered the charmed circle and resonating magic of the tribal world, exploding man into an agglomeration of specialized impoverished individuals or units."

However, McLuhan argues, we are moving into a new era, a return to the tribal culture. The new electric media are the source of this revolution, supplanting print as the dominant communications technology and creating a global village. "The electric media are the telegraph, radio, films, telephone, computer and television, all of which have not only extended a single sense or function as the old mechanical media did . . . but have enhanced and externalized our entire central nervous system, thus transforming all aspects of our social and psychic existence." These new media will bring our long neglected audio-tactile senses to the fore and hence will recreate the conditions, emotions and sensibilities of tribal life.

With this revolutionary change will come a return to the ancient concept of the individual, the view of man as a member of a group or a tribe. The entire human family will be sealed into "a single universal membrane." For McLuhan this will be a liberation. Man will no longer be a disassociated unit. He will be part of a group, a group closely knit by electronic media.

Thus, for McLuhan, as for Seidenberg, recent history has simply been an aberration and the future will be radically different from the historic past. For both men, the future holds a similar fate for the individual—a return to his prehistoric situation. To Seidenberg, this means the submergence of individuality. Is McLuhan's vision much different? According to McLuhan, man will no longer feel alienated from himself, from others and from his environment. This is the chief benefit of the new order. Magic will once again be dominant: "Once we are enmeshed in the magical resonance of the tribal echo chamber, the debunking of myths and legends is replaced by their religious study." The day of privacy, of points of view, of special goals will be over. Man will trade his current style of life, with both its exaltation of individual human values and the alienation and despair of rootlessness and insecurity, for a worldwide family which will offer security, but also mythology and conformity.

At the other extreme from the unmitigated gloom of Seidenberg and the radical changes foreseen by McLuhan is the optimism of many American social scientists who describe the United States as a pluralistic, open society which, through compromise and shared beliefs, allows great individual freedom. This vision is dominant among the overwhelming majority of university social scientists. The analysis typically includes a description of the shared American consensus (our general agreement on methods and goals) and a description of the opportunities offered individuals to achieve success and happiness in any of the variety of social and political structures open to him.

The general argument is that modern American society has a high degree of structural differentiation, and that this differentiation offers individuals a wider range of choices than those available in less differentiated societies. In more primitive societies, the social scientists argue, several functions are performed by the same structure, and the performance of one function is tied closely to the performance of another. Hence, to use one of Winston White's [3] examples, on a family farm the family performs several functions: raising the young, controlling the behavior patterns of its members, and carrying out basic economic functions. In a more differentiated society, White argues, the greater structural differentiation allows the individual more choices. Thus, in a highly differentiated society, farming is big business and economic and family functions are handled by two different structures. This allows both for more efficiency of resources (the farm can be run without regard to family concerns: the best individuals can be hired, and resources can be used for increasing production, not for family purposes) and for greater individual freedom (the members of the family are not committed to working on the farm).

This, then, is the key to the optimist's thesis: in a highly differentiated society the individual has a greater range of choices as to the path to follow in his life because in such a society the number of available roles—both occupational and non-occupational—is increased. The worker has greater choice about the kind of industry to enter and the particular employer for whom to work. Moreover, the need for citizen participation in local government and for membership participation in unions and such voluntary associations as clubs and lodges has increased the number of roles available to the individual, thus offering him more choice in determining his destiny.

The views of Seidenberg and McLuhan, on the one hand, and of the optimists, on the other, define the poles in the debate concerning individualism. These theoretical positions are useful in defining the issues and in pointing to key trends.

[3] Winston White's *Beyond Conformity* (Free Press) does an excellent job of explicating the optimistic viewpoints.

Certainly there is much truth in the views of Seidenberg and McLuhan. The rapid growth of organization and rationalization has created huge bureaucracies which deprive man of much of his freedom and individuality. Moreover, the new modes of communication are exerting profound influences on our perception of the world and our attitude toward ourselves and society. Yet both thinkers are much too apocalyptic. It is always dangerous to engage in single-factor analysis, and both do it with a vengeance. Too many variables—such as demography, war, political shifts or scientific progress—can affect the course of history. In addition, it is rather sweeping to assert that men have no free will and that it is totally impossible to reverse or change the course of a development. The example of Marx and his followers should have convinced us of the folly of predicting the "inevitable course of history."

The optimists are correct in asserting that the American social structure is highly differentiated, and there is much surface validity to their belief that the differentiation itself provides more opportunities for the individual. Nor can it be denied that America's economic success has set the stage for the flowering of individualism. Nonetheless, disturbing trends in American society point to the diminution of the individual and support Seidenberg's gloomy views. These trends include political repression, economic inequality, our growing command of the tools of technological control and the continued growth of large-scale bureaucracy.

It would seem, therefore, that the real situation of the individual today lies somewhere between the gloomy analysis of Seidenberg and McLuhan and the optimism of most American social scientists. It is clear that large groups in society—especially the poor and the young—are almost completely excluded from the American Dream. The Kerner Commission Report amply documented the deprivation and inadequate opportunity of our city's ghettos. Individuality and individualism diminish when people do not even have steady jobs or adequate housing.

The issue of the young is somewhat more subtle, but it is becoming increasingly clear that society denies youth adequate opportunities for the expression of individuality. An impressive body of literature has attacked schools for depriving students of basic civil rights. Devices such as hall passes, lunch monitors and bathroom privileges all serve to create a restricted and almost prisonlike atmosphere in the school, and compulsory education gives these edicts the force of law. Certainly, individuality is not encouraged in these circumstances. In *Coming of Age in America*[4] Edgar Friedenberg wrote:

> The elements of the composition—the passes, the tight scheduling, the reliance on threats of detention or suspension as modes of social control—are nearly universal. The complete usurpation of any possible area of student initiative, physical or mental, is about as universal. What is learned in high school, or for that matter anywhere at all, depends far less on what is taught than on what one actually experiences in the place. . . . What is learned most thoroughly by attendance . . . is certain core assumptions that govern the conditions of life of most adolescents in this country and train them to operate as adult, if not as mature, Americans.

The balance of *Coming of Age in America* is devoted to studying what these core assumptions are and what the values are that students learn in school. Not surprisingly, Friedenberg concludes that students learn to value conformity and order, not individuality and creativity.

The optimistic view falls not only on the issues of poverty and schooling. Very few jobs in America permit an individual to express himself or to feel that he is doing anything important. Structural differentiation is not very meaningful to a man when he has a choice of working on an automobile or airplane assembly line. How many exciting and creative jobs are open to the college graduate? This paucity of interesting work is largely responsible for student unrest; what is the point in respecting school when it only prepares you for mindless paper shuffling? Jules Henry made this point well when he wrote: "The young worker enters the occupational system not where he would, but where he can; and his job-dream, so often an expression

---

[4] Edgar Friedenberg, *Coming of Age in America* (New York: Random House, 1963).

of his dearest self, is pushed down with all his other unmet needs to churn among them for the rest of his life. The worker gives up an essential part of himself to take a job, to survive." [5] Because the worker feels no attachment to his job, because it is dull, routine and unimaginative, he must find alternative ways to fulfill his self-esteem. This is the real meaning of America's obsession with material goods and standard of living: the drive for material possessions takes the place of satisfying work.

Concentration of economic and political power in large bureaucracies has also raised serious threats to individual autonomy. In recent years the three dominant centers of power—government, business and unions—have become large, powerful and highly centralized. Ferdinand Lundberg [6] summarized the trend when he wrote, speaking of industrial and trading companies in 1962, "2,632 active corporations, or slightly more than .2 percent of all active corporations (almost always dominantly owned and controlled by less than .1 percent of their stockholders) held nearly 65 percent of net corporate income." The centralization is even more pronounced because these two thousand-odd corporations are not separate from each other but are often linked by mergers, interlocking directorates, etc. The picture that emerges is of a massive industrial empire controlled by an extremely small number of corporate giants.

The same is true for unions and government. The American union movement has become a massive bureaucratic structure dominated, of course, by the AFL-CIO. The federal government's power is pervasive, obvious and centralized. Each locus of power exerts massive influence on the individual and increasingly the individual is losing control over them. Traditionally, Americans have turned to their government to protect them from the excesses of unchecked private power. Today, however, this traditional remedy is not very efficacious. The federal government itself has become large and unresponsive. In many instances, indeed, it has become a source of oppression. Examples

[5] Jules Henry, *Culture Against Man* (New York: Random House, 1963).

[6] Ferdinand Lundberg, *The Rich and the Super-Rich* (New York: Lyle Stuart, 1968).

abound: wiretapping, conspiracy laws, etc. The federal government has grown so rapidly and has centralized so much power that it is often unresponsive to the needs of the people—its titular masters.

In theory, the existence of three great bureaucracies, each centralized and each wielding tremendous power, would be ameliorated by a system of checks and balances. This, ominously, is not the case. The giant bureaucracies which dominate America have moved closely together and cooperate on most issues.

In fact, the distinction between public and private institutions is rapidly disappearing. In what sense is a defense industry private when it receives most of its income from the federal government? When much of a "private" university's scholarship money, research contracts, building money, etc., comes from public sources, what right does that university have to call itself private? When the same personnel work interchangeably for business and government, why should the institutions be regarded as distinct? There are many similar questions because the three giant bureaucracies are growing together so closely that it is becoming accurate to maintain that America is dominated by a single giant bureaucratic structure. Different parts of this structure have different functions, but the entire bureaucracy shares common perceptions and goals, and pools information and resources.

What are the implications of this development for the individual? Because many Americans are employees of the bureaucracy, patterns of bureaucratic behavior condition the ways that many of us behave. The "organization man" syndrome is a familiar one and has been described by many writers. Alan Harrington, in *Life in the Crystal Palace,* wrote of the typical executive:

> He has the talents of a cork. There are great advantages in being an intellectual lightweight. . . . The official, having no ideas to burden him, can bob around like a buoy or a marker in the roughest water while others are dashed against the rocks. . . . The absence of creative ability is a talent in itself. In a corporation it can be a positive asset. . . . No matter how many times the decision is changed the man with-

out ideas remains unaffected. . . . A good administrator has a remarkable talent for staying out of trouble. . . . To avoid blame the corporation bureaucrat always goes by the book. . . . The book is a covenant worked out by mediocre people to frustrate outlaws. The outlaw is the original man.[7]

The picture may be somewhat overdrawn, but the point is valid. The essence of bureaucracy is rationalization—an attempt to fit the tremendous complexities and diversities of life into categories. In order to accomplish its goals, rules must be devised and behavior must be patterned. Even if the bureaucrat has no thought of conforming for the sake of pleasing his superior and protecting himself, he still must limit the range of his behavior in order to function. Limiting behavior is not in itself bad; laws against murder, after all, limit behavior. However, the limitations can be carried to such an extreme that individuality is suppressed. This is exactly the effect of life in large bureaucracy.

Centralization also threatens individuals who do not work for the bureaucracy. A bureaucracy cannot treat clients as individuals; it must devise categories and standard responses. This is the source of much of the impersonality of bureaucracy. A big-city school system, for example, must pretend that all children and all neighborhoods are the same; to behave differently would lead to bureaucratic chaos. Overorganization stifles creativity simply because once placed in the bureaucratic hopper a new idea or artistic endeavor is likely to be denatured by the time it has been processed. Aldous Huxley perceptively wrote: "Physically and mentally each one of us is unique. Any culture which, in the interests of efficiency . . . seeks to standardize the human individual, commits an outrage against man's biological nature." [8]

Perhaps more ominous than the dangers of bureaucracy is the threat that centralization of power poses to the most

---

[7] Alan Harrington, *Life in the Crystal Palace* (New York: Alfred Knopf, 1959).

[8] Aldous Huxley, *Brave New World Revisited* (New York: Harper & Bros., 1958).

basic components of individual liberty. Again Aldous Huxley: "Democracy can hardly be expected to flourish in societies where political and economic power is being progressively concentrated and centralized." In such societies the individual has no recourse when he is wronged. There is nowhere to turn. James Madison wrote in the *Federalist Papers* that the surest protection against tyranny is the existence of small, competing centers of power. These are lacking today. The bureaucracies operate as one. Often there is no effective recourse from oppressive social policy, and when there is, the process is lengthy and difficult.

Hence, as we examine the quality of national life we observe a strange paradox—a country whose beliefs remain strongly individualistic but where in reality individualism is undermined. There is no question that Americans cling to their belief in the primacy of the individual—politicians speak of it in Fourth of July speeches, business leaders pay homage to it, and that famous American, "the man in the street," expresses his political and social beliefs in terms of individual freedom and opportunity. Indeed, it is our dedication to individualism that lies at the root of much of the current despair in America, for the reality of our lives hardly corresponds to our ideals.

Despite the seemingly grim future faced by the individual in America, there are important counterforces working against manipulation and dehumanization. Together these forces comprise what Arthur Mendel [9] has characterized as the "Great Refusal" to submit to technocratic manipulation. The most obvious source of this refusal has been the young.

Students are attempting to recapture individualism. This spirit was best expressed in the "Port Huron Statement," the founding charter of S.D.S.

> We regard *men* as infinitely precious and possessed of unfulfilled capacities for reason, freedom, and love. In affirming these principles we are aware of countering perhaps the dominant perception of man in the

[9] Arthur P. Mendel, "Robots and Rebels," *The New Republic*, January 11, 1969, pp. 16–19.

twentieth century; that he is a thing to be manipulated; and that he is inherently incapable of directing his own affairs. We oppose the depersonalization that reduced human beings to the status of things. . . . The individualism we affirm is not egoism, the selflessness we affirm is not self-elimination. On the contrary, we believe in generosity of a kind that imprints one's unique individual qualities in the relation to other men, and to all human activity.

This is a philosophical, not a tactical, statement and it enunciates the commitment to individualism and individual dignity which lies at the root of the student unrest and turmoil of recent years. Students are revolting against schools which process them, the manipulation of the draft, the degradation of poverty, the sterility of jobs, and the exaltation of materialism—all of which seem to them to characterize America.

The New Left represents only the top of the iceberg. Many students who do not engage in direct political activity share the activists' concern for individual dignity. A *Fortune* [10] magazine survey found that 15 percent of college students were sympathetic to the radical activists. Even more students share some of the radicals' views. Moreover, the radical analysis has seeped down into the high schools, and there is no rooting it out. Students are questioning the basic values and assumptions of mass society, and graduates are flocking into social service and humanistic careers. Business and law firms, for example, are finding it increasingly difficult to attract first-rate students.

Some argue that the youth rebellion is a passing phenomenon or, at worst, the dying romantic gasp of rebels struggling against the inevitable triumph of technology. The evidence is to the contrary. The conditions which have led to the rebellion are likely to continue. The paradoxes of America—enormous wealth and tragic poverty, democratic values and discrimination, belief in self-determination and conduct around the world—are going to continue. Furthermore, the number of young attending college is increasing, and it is clear that the extended isolation from the work

[10] *Fortune* magazine, January 1969.

world that college entails encourages critical social analysis. Each generation of student critics will educate the next, and only resolution of the paradox in America will bring the "Great Refusal" to an end.

Politics is only one way in which the young have expressed their dissatisfaction with the prevailing lack of individual freedom and opportunity. Many have gone further and begun to create alternative life-styles. The forms vary widely, from drug culture to radical art groups to communes. Yet in all cases the commitment is the same— to create a style of living which encourages individual diversity and freedom and which rejects the constraints and limitations of a bureaucratic society.

The young are not the only source of dissatisfaction. Increasingly, groups are forming to attack and dismantle the large bureaucracies which have come to dominate America. An example is the movement to decentralize big-city school systems. Racial and educational issues play a large part in this effort, but equally important is the attempt to knock the huge school systems down to size and make them more responsive to local communities and to individual needs. Another example is the welfare system, which has in the past often treated welfare recipients impersonally and harshly. The National Welfare Rights Movement represents an attempt to organize welfare recipients into a potent political force capable of forcing the welfare system to respond adequately to individual needs. In the area of urban renewal, bureaucracies are accustomed to making decisions regarding neighborhoods without consulting the residents. Today, in almost all large cities, active neighborhood groups demand a full voice in all decisions affecting local development.

The current turmoil in America—whether its source is young people attacking the impersonality of the university, community groups demanding a voice in their schools or poor people demanding their share of power—is rooted in the issue of individualism. As many writers have noted, America is entering a postindustrial period. Until recently the central problem in our development has been production. Now we have settled the West and built an industrial system capable of providing all Americans with a high standard of living. This is a historically unprecedented situation, and Americans don't quite know what to make of it. Given an economy of abundance, we are faced with two problems: developing a just system of distribution and assuring a meaningful and decent style of living. History has not prepared Americans to meet these twin problems. Individualism has been the central value in our history—yet our interpretation of individualism has most often meant competition and laissez-faire. Hard work, deferred gratification and wide open spaces have been central to our value structure, but in a postindustrial society these values are not meaningful or useful.

Unfortunately, no other system of values has arisen to fill the gap. In a real sense we are at a crossroads in our history. Faced with a historically new situation, we can, on the one hand, follow the path predicted by Seidenberg, by allowing the great bureaucracies to expand and exercise an ever greater control over our lives. Were we to follow this path, men would probably have their material wants satisfied, but would lose a great measure of individual freedom and initiative. The alternative is to seize the opportunity offered by the prospect of material abundance and to reshape society in such a way as to maximize opportunities for individuality.

The latter path would be a daring and uncertain enterprise. It would mean flying in the face of the persuasive arguments of those who say that modern life must be characterized by large-scale organization, centralization and uniformity. It would mean taking on the powerful array of forces which favor centralization, and these elements are well organized and entrenched. And most of all, it would involve formulating an alternative vision of life in America, it would mean creating a new ideal of individualism and selling that new individualism so forcefully that it would become a part of the national ideology.

Yet there are good reasons to believe that such a struggle could be successful. While there is no question that we are entering a new age, its final shape is far from resolved. We still have a measure of control over our destiny, and we still have the ability to determine what direction the postindustrial society will take. The current unrest in America, though inchoate and not always articulately focused, clearly indicates that men will not readily allow their destiny to be determined by others. The idea of a "human nature" is old and much debunked, yet those qualities of man which demand the right to express his individuality and to determine his own fate seem to be at the root of the current dissatisfaction with America. Furthermore, a strong constituency for change has developed which has the potential for capturing power. A "mugwump" middle class would have real opportunity to influence decisively the choices America makes in the next decade. As Arthur P. Mendel [11] wrote:

> There is good reason to think that it is the rebels of the Great Refusal and not the technetronic servitors who speak for the future. I have in mind the increasing number of youth in the universities and their growing role throughout society; the spread among them of all sorts of cults for letting go and their leading involvement in all the movements opposed to [the anti-]utopia; the revival among the social sciences of personalist, subjectivist approaches in opposition to the heretofore dominant behaviorists; the spread of the humanistic psychology movement; the not-so-coincidental upsurge of anthropological studies of primitive societies, religious studies in mythology, and historians' interest in aristocracies; the richly emotional qualities of contemporary art; the leisure and sexual-sensual liberation; the growing influence of the underground church; the ubiquitous sprouting of small groups of all sorts where personal communion is rediscovered. . . . It is mainly a quiet revolution . . . taking place now, gradually changing the face of our society, the quality of our thought and experience, and character of our behavior.

Central to this process is the development of a new individualism. This philosophy would be at once a reaffirmation of the idea of individuality which has played so central a role in American history, and a rejection of the outdated ideas of laissez-faire and the rugged individualist. The individualism of nonconformity would be an element of

[11] Arthur P. Mendel, *op. cit.*

the new pattern, yet it would not be enough. Redistributing power would be crucial to the new individualism, because each individual must have control over his own destiny. Hence the new individualism would seek to remake our social institutions to assure that each man would enjoy control over the institutions affecting him. Opportunity would also be central to the new individualism, and concomitant to this would be the just distribution of our abundance.

Since America's inception as a nation, individualism has been the central concept which helped Americans understand what their country was about. Today a new individualism is central to our efforts to create a decent society. The purpose of this book is to present the views of a wide range of distinguished thinkers on the history and state of individualism in America. Only when we achieve this understanding can we fulfill Thomas Wolfe's American Dream.

> To every man his chance, regardless of his birth: his shining golden opportunity—to every man to live, to work, to be himself, and to become whatever thing his manhood and his vision can make him.

PART I

AN OVERVIEW

THE ROLE OF INDIVIDUALITY

Bertrand Russell

[Bertrand Russell looks at the question of individualism
in historical perspective, comparing present-day opportunities with those of the past. Historically, some societies have been centralized, some diffuse; some have
encouraged individual initiative, others have placed a
premium on obedience. But there have perennially been
ways for the gifted individual to achieve prominence.

[In modern times, however, Russell finds that giant
bureaucracies decrease the chances for exceptional individual achievement. Of course, the author's own extraordinary life testifies to the continued importance
of remarkable individuals in achieving intellectual and
political progress.

[The late Bertrand Russell received the Nobel Prize
for Literature in 1950. His works include, among many
others: *Authority and the Individual, New Hopes for
a Changing World, The Impact of Science on Society*,
and his autobiography.]

I propose to consider the importance, both for good and
evil, of impulses and desires that belong to some members
of a community but not to all. In a very primitive community such impulses and desires play very little part.
Hunting and war are activities in which one man may be
more successful than another, but in which all share a common purpose. So long as a man's spontaneous activities are
such as all the tribe approves of and shares in, his initiative
is very little curbed by others within the tribe, and even his
most spontaneous actions conform to the recognized pattern

of behavior. But as men grow more civilized there comes to
be an increasing difference between one man's activities
and another's, and a community needs, if it is to prosper, a
certain number of individuals who do not wholly conform
to the general type. Practically all progress, artistic, moral,
and intellectual, has depended upon such individuals, who
have been a decisive factor in the transition from barbarism
to civilization. If a community is to make progress, it needs
exceptional individuals whose activities, though useful, are
not of a sort that ought to be general. There is always a
tendency in highly organized society for the activities of
such individuals to be unduly hampered, but on the other
hand, if the community exercises no control, the same kind
of individual initiative which may produce a valuable innovator may also produce a criminal. The problem, like all
those with which we are concerned, is one of balance; too
little liberty brings stagnation, and too much brings chaos.
There are many ways in which an individual may differ
from most of the other members of his herd. He may be
exceptionally anarchic or criminal; he may have rare artistic talent; he may have what comes in time to be recognized as a new wisdom in matters of religion and morals,
and he may have exceptional intellectual powers. It would
seem that from a very early period in human history there
must have been some differentiation of function. The pictures in the caves in the Pyrenees which were made by
Paleolithic men have a very high degree of artistic merit,
and one can hardly suppose that all the men of that time
were capable of such admirable work. It seems far more
probable that those who were found to have artistic talent
were sometimes allowed to stay at home making pictures
while the rest of the tribe hunted. The chief and the priest
must have begun from a very early time to be chosen for
real or supposed peculiar excellences: medicine men could
work magic, and the tribal spirit was in some sense incar-
nate in the chief. But from the earliest time there has been
a tendency for every activity of this kind to become institutionalized. The chieftain became hereditary, the medicine men became a separate caste, and recognized bards
became the prototypes of our Poets Laureate. It has always
been difficult for communities to recognize what is necessary for individuals who are going to make the kind of

exceptional contribution that I have in mind, namely, elements of wildness, of separateness from the herd, of domination by rare impulses of which the utility was not always obvious to everybody.

I wish to consider both in history and in the present day the relation of the exceptional man to the community, and the conditions that make it easy for his unusual merits to be socially fruitful. I shall consider this problem first in art, then in religion and morals, and, finally, in science.

The artist in our day does not play nearly so vital a part in public life as he has done in many former ages. There is a tendency in our days to despise a court poet, and to think that a poet should be a solitary being proclaiming something that Philistines do not wish to hear. Historically the matter was far otherwise; Homer, Virgil, and Shakespeare were court poets, they sang the glories of their tribe and its noble traditions. (Of Shakespeare, I must confess, this is only partially true, but it certainly applies to his historical plays.) Welsh bards kept alive the glories of King Arthur, and these glories came to be celebrated by English and French writers; King Henry II encouraged them for imperialistic reasons. The glories of the Parthenon and of the medieval cathedrals were intimately bound up with public objects. Music, though it could play its part in courtship, existed primarily to promote courage in battle—a purpose to which, according to Plato, it ought to be confined by law. But of these ancient glories of the artist little remains in the modern world except the piper to a Highland regiment. We still honor the artist, but we isolate him; we think of art as something separate, not as an integral part of the life of the community. The architect alone, because his art serves a utilitarian purpose, retains something of the ancient status of the artist.

The decay of art in our time is not only due to the fact that the social function of the artist is not as important as in former days; it is due also to the fact that spontaneous delight is no longer felt as something which it is important to be able to enjoy. Among comparatively unsophisticated populations folk dances and popular music still flourish, and something of the poet exists in very many men. But as men grow more industrialized and regimented, the kind of delight that is common in children becomes impossible to adults, because they are always thinking of the next thing, and cannot let themselves be absorbed in the moment. This habit of thinking of the "next thing" is more fatal to any kind of aesthetic excellence than any other habit of mind that can be imagined, and if art, in any important sense, is to survive, it will not be by the foundation of solemn academies, but by recapturing the capacity for wholehearted joys and sorrows which prudence and foresight have all but destroyed.

The men conventionally recognized as the greatest of mankind have been innovators in religion and morals. In spite of the reverence given to them by subsequent ages, most of them during their lifetime were in a greater or less degree in conflict with their own communities. Moral progress has consisted, in the main, of protest against cruel customs, and of attempts to enlarge the bounds of human sympathy. Human sacrifice among the Greeks died out at the beginning of the fully historical epoch. The Stoics taught that there should be sympathy not only for free Greeks but for barbarians and slaves, and, indeed, for all mankind. Buddhism and Christianity spread a similar doctrine far and wide. Religion, which had originally been part of the apparatus of tribal cohesion, promoting conflict without just as much as cooperation within, took on a more universal character, and endeavored to transcend the narrow limits which primitive morality had set. It is no wonder if the religious innovators were execrated in their own day, for they sought to rob men of the joy of battle and the fierce delights of revenge. Primitive ferocity, which had seemed a virtue, was now said to be a sin, and a deep duality was introduced between morality and the life of impulse—or rather between the morality taught by those in whom the impulse of humanity was strong, and the traditional morality that was preferred by those who had no sympathies outside their own herd.

Religious and moral innovators have had an immense effect upon human life, not always, it must be confessed, the effect that they intended, but nevertheless on the whole profoundly beneficial. It is true that in the present century we have seen in important parts of the world a loss of moral values which we had thought fairly secure, but we may hope that this retrogression will not last. We owe it to the moral innovators who first attempted to make morality a universal and not merely a tribal matter, that there has come to be a disapproval of slavery, a feeling of duty toward prisoners of war, a limitation of the powers of husbands and fathers, and a recognition, however imperfect, that subject races ought not to be merely exploited for the benefit of their conquerors. All these moral gains, it must be admitted, have been jeopardized by a recrudescence of ancient ferocity, but I do not think that in the end the moral advance which they have represented will be lost to mankind.

The prophets and sages who inaugurated this moral advance, although for the most part they were not honored in their own day, were, nevertheless, not prevented from doing their work. In a modern totalitarian state matters are worse than they were in the time of Socrates, or in the time of the Gospels. In a totalitarian state an innovator whose ideas are disliked by the government is not merely put to death, which is a matter to which a brave man may remain indifferent, but is totally prevented from causing his doctrine to be known. Innovations in such a community can come only from the government, and the government now, as in the past, is not likely to approve of anything contrary to its own immediate interests. In a totalitarian state such events as the rise of Buddhism or Christianity are scarcely possible, and not even by the greatest heroism can a moral reformer acquire any influence whatever. This is a new fact in human history, brought about by the much increased control over individuals which the modern technique of government has made possible. It is a very grave fact, and one which shows how fatal a totalitarian regime must be to every kind of moral progress.

In our own day an individual of exceptional powers can hardly hope to have so great a career or so great a social influence as in former times, if he devotes himself to art or to religious and moral reform. There are, however, still four careers which are open to him: he may become a great political leader, like Lenin; he may acquire vast industrial power, like Rockefeller; he may transform the world by scientific discoveries, as is being done by the atomic physicists; or, finally, if he has not the necessary capacities for any of these careers, or if opportunity is lacking, his energy in default of other outlet may drive him into a life of crime. Criminals, in the legal sense, seldom have much influence upon the course of history, and therefore a man of overweening ambition will choose some other career if it is open to him.

The rise of men of science to great eminence in the state is a modern phenomenon. Scientists, like other innovators, had to fight for recognition: some were banished; some were burned; some were kept in dungeons; others merely had their books burned. But gradually it came to be realized that they could put power into the hands of the state. The French revolutionaries, after mistakenly guillotining Lavoisier, employed his surviving colleagues in the manufacture of explosives. In modern war the scientists are recognized by all civilized governments as the most useful citizens, provided they can be tamed and induced to place their services at the disposal of a single government rather than of mankind.

Both for good and evil almost everything that distinguishes our age from its predecessors is due to science. In daily life we have electric light, and the radio, and the cinema. In industry we employ machinery and power which we owe to science. Because of the increased productivity of labor, we are able to devote a far greater proportion of our energies to wars and preparations for wars than was formerly possible, and we are able to keep the young in school very much longer than we formerly could. Owing to science we are able to disseminate information and misinformation through the press and the radio to practically everybody. Owing to science we can make it enormously more difficult than it used to be for people whom the government dislikes to escape. The whole of our daily life and our social organization is what it is because of science. The whole of this vast development is supported nowadays by the state, but it grew up originally in opposition to the state, and where, as in Russia, the state has reverted to an earlier pattern, the old opposition would again appear if the state were not omnipotent to a degree undreamed of by the tyrants of former ages.

The opposition to science in the past was by no means surprising. Men of science affirmed things that were contrary to what everybody had believed; they upset preconceived ideas and were thought to be destitute of reverence. Anaxagoras taught that the sun was a red-hot stone and that the moon was made of earth. For this impiety he was banished from Athens, for was it not well known that the sun was a god and the moon, a goddess? It was only the power over natural forces conferred by science that led bit by bit to a toleration of scientists, and even this was a very slow process, because their powers were at first attributed to magic.

It would not be surprising if, in the present day, a powerful antiscientific movement were to arise as a result of the dangers to human life that are resulting from atom bombs and may result from bacteriological warfare. But whatever people may feel about these horrors, they dare not turn against the men of science so long as war is at all probable, because if one side were equipped with scientists and the other not, the scientific side would almost certainly win.

Science, insofar as it consists of knowledge, must be regarded as having value, but insofar as it consists of technique, the question whether it is to be praised or blamed depends upon the use that is made of the technique. In itself it is neutral, neither good nor bad, and any ultimate views that we may have about what gives value to this or that must come from some other source than science.

The men of science, in spite of their profound influence upon modern life, are in some ways less powerful than the politicians. Politicians in our day are far more influential than they were at any former period in human history. Their relation to the men of science is like that of a magician in the *Arabian Nights* to a djinn who obeys his orders. The djinn does astounding things which the magician, without his help, could not do, but he does them only because he is told to do them, not because of any impulse in himself. So it is with the atomic scientists in our day; some government captures them in their homes or on the high seas, and they are set to work, according to the luck of their capture, to slave for the one side or for the other. The politician, when he is successful, is subject to no such coercion. The most astounding career of our times was that of Lenin. After his brother had been put to death by the Czarist government, he spent years in poverty and exile, and then rose within a few months to command of one of the greatest of states. And this command was not like that of Xerxes or Caesar, merely the power to enjoy luxury and adulation, which but for him some other man would have been enjoying. It was the power to mold a vast country according to a pattern conceived in his own mind, to alter the life of every worker, every peasant, and every middle-class person; to introduce a totally new kind of organization, and to become throughout the world the symbol of a new order, admired by some, execrated by many, but ignored by none. No megalomaniac's dream could have been more terrific. Napoleon had asserted that you can do everything with bayonets except sit upon them; Lenin disproved the exception.

The great men who stand out in history have been partly benefactors of mankind and partly quite the reverse. Some, like the great religious and moral innovators, have done what lay in their power to make men less cruel toward each other, and less limited in their sympathies; some, like the men of science, have given us a knowledge and understanding of natural processes which, however it may be misused, must be regarded as in itself a splendid thing. Some, like the great poets and composers and painters, have put into the world beauties and splendors which, in moments of discouragement, do much to make the spectacle of human destiny endurable. But others, equally able, equally effective in their way, have done quite the opposite. I cannot think of anything that mankind has gained by the existence of Jenghiz Khan. I do not know what good came of Robespierre, and, for my part, I see no reason to be grateful to Lenin. But all these men, good and bad alike, had a quality which I should not wish to see disappear from the world—a quality of energy and personal initiative, of independence of mind, and of imaginative vision. A man who possesses these qualities is capable of doing much good, or of doing great harm, and if mankind is not to sink into dullness, such exceptional men must find scope, though one could wish that the scope they find should be for the benefit of mankind. There may be less difference than is sometimes thought between the temperament of a great criminal and a great statesman. It may be that Captain Kidd and Alexander the Great, if a magician had interchanged them at birth, would have each fulfilled the career which, in fact, was fulfilled by the other. The same thing may be said of some artists; the memoirs of Benvenuto Cellini do not give a picture of a man with that respect for law which every right-minded citizen ought to have. In the modern world, and still more, so far as can be guessed, in the world of the near future, important achievement is and will be almost impossible to an individual if he cannot dominate some vast organization. If he can make himself head of a state like Lenin, or monopolist of a great industry like Rockefeller, or a controller of credit like the elder Pierpont Morgan, he can produce enormous effects in the world. And so he can if, being a man of science, he persuades some government that his work may be useful in war. But the man who works without the help of an organization, like a Hebrew prophet, a poet, or a solitary philosopher such as Spinoza, can no longer hope for the kind of importance which such men had in former days. The change applies to the scientist as well as to other men. The scientists of the past did their work very largely as individuals, but the scientist of our day needs enormously expensive equipment and a laboratory with many assistants. All this he can obtain through the favor of the government, or, in America, of very rich men. He is thus no longer an independent worker, but essentially part and parcel of some large organization. This change is very unfortunate, for the things which a great man could do in solitude were apt to be more beneficial than those which he can only do with the help of the powers that be. A man who wishes to influence human affairs finds it difficult to be successful, except as a slave or a tyrant: as a politician he may make himself the head of a state, or as a scientist he may sell his labor to the government, but in that case he must serve its purposes and not his own.

And this applies not only to men of rare and exceptional greatness, but to a wide range of talent. In the ages in which there were great poets, there were also large numbers of little poets, and when there were great painters, there were large numbers of little painters. The great German composers arose in a milieu where music was valued, and where numbers of lesser men found opportunities. In those days poetry, painting, and music were a vital part of the daily life of ordinary men, as only sport is now. The great prophets were men who stood out from a host of minor prophets. The inferiority of our age in such respects is an inevitable result of the fact that society is centralized and organized to such a degree that individual initiative is reduced to a minimum. Where art has flourished in the past it has flourished as a rule amongst small communities which had rivals among their neighbors, such as the Greek city-states, the little principalities of the Italian Renaissance, and the petty courts of German eighteenth-century rulers. Each of these rulers had to have his musician, and once in a way he was Johann Sebastian Bach, but even if he was not, he was still free to do his best. There is something about local rivalry that is essential in such matters. It played its part even in the building of the cathedrals, because each bishop wished to have a finer cathedral than the neighboring bishop. It would be a good thing if cities could develop an artistic pride leading them to mutual rivalry, and if each had its own school of music and painting, not without a vigorous contempt for the school of the next city. But such local patriotisms do not readily flourish in a world of empires and free mobility. A Manchester man does not readily feel toward a man from Sheffield as an Athenian felt toward a Corinthian, or a Florentine toward a Venetian. But in spite of the difficulties, I think that this problem of giving importance to localities will have to be tackled if human life is not to become increasingly drab and monotonous.

The savage, in spite of his membership of a small community, lived a life in which his initiative was not too much hampered by the community. The things that he wanted to do, usually hunting and war, were also the things that his neighbors wanted to do, and if he felt an inclination to become a medicine man, he only had to ingratiate himself with some individual already eminent in that profession, and so, in due course, to succeed to his powers of magic. If he was a man of exceptional talent, he might invent some improvement in weapons, or a new skill in hunting. These would not put him into any opposition to the community, but, on the contrary, would be welcomed. The modern man lives a very different life. If he sings in the street he will be thought to be drunk, and if he dances, a policeman will reprove him for impeding the traffic. His working day, unless he is exceptionally fortunate, is occupied in a completely monotonous manner in producing something which is valued, not, like the shield of Achilles, as a beautiful piece of work, but mainly for its utility. When his work is over, he cannot, like Milton's Shepherd, "tell his tale under the hawthorn in the dale," because there is often no dale anywhere near where he lives, or, if there is, it is full of tins. And always, in our highly regularized way of life, he is obsessed by thoughts of the morrow. Of all the precepts in the Gospels, the one that Christians have most neglected is the commandment to take no thought for the morrow. If he is prudent, thought for the morrow will lead him to save; if he is imprudent, it will make him apprehensive of being unable to pay his debts. In either case the moment loses its savor. Everything is organized, nothing is spontaneous. The Nazis organized "Strength Through Joy," but joy prescribed by the government is likely to be not very joyful. In those who might otherwise have worthy ambitions, the effect of centralization is to bring them into competition with too large a number of rivals, and into subjection to an unduly uniform standard of taste. If you wish to be a painter you will not be content to pit yourself against the men with similar desires in your own town; you will go to some school of painting in a metropolis where you will probably conclude that you are mediocre, and having come to this conclusion, you may be so discouraged that you are tempted to throw away your paintbrushes and take to moneymaking or to drink, for a certain degree of self-confidence is essential to achievement. In Renaissance Italy you might have hoped to be the best painter in Siena, and this position would have been quite sufficiently honorable. But you would not now be content to acquire all your training in one small town and pit yourself against your neighbors. We know too much and feel too little. At least we feel too little of those creative emotions from which a good life springs. In regard to what is important we are passive; where we are active it is over trivialities. If life is to be saved from boredom relieved only by disaster, means must be found of restoring individual initiative, not only in things that are trivial, but in the things that really matter. I do not mean that we should destroy those parts of modern organization upon which the very existence of large populations depends, but I do mean that organization should be much more flexible, more relieved by local autonomy, and less oppressive to the human spirit through its impersonal vastness, than it has become through its unbearably rapid growth and centralization, with which our ways of thought and feeling have been unable to keep pace.

INDIVIDUALITY AND ITS LIMITS

John W. Gardner

[The conflict between individual rights and the claims of society is an old and vexing problem. John Gardner examines the conflicting claims, and attempts to develop a compromise philosophy which both protects the individual and defines his responsibilities to the society of which he is an integral part.

[John Gardner, former Secretary of the Department of Health, Education and Welfare, is the author of *Excellence, Self-Renewal,* and *No Easy Victories.*]

ESTRANGEMENT FOR ALL

If one had to select a single conception that is central to the consensus in our own society, it would be the idea of the dignity and worth of the individual. The individual is not just so many pounds of assorted chemicals plus a bucket of water. He is not just a link in a genetic chain or an element in a biological-social system. He is not just a "resource" (as in the phrase "human resources") that may be used to strengthen the social group. There is not only something important about him, there is something inviolable. At the most basic level this involves a right to life and to security of person; but it involves much more. There are limits beyond which his privacy should not be invaded, his individuality not threatened, his dignity not impaired.

Yet man is a social being, and to talk about individuality without talking about the social system that makes it possible is to talk nonsense. It will be useful for us to examine more closely the relationship of the individual to the group.

Most human beings who have trod the earth have been rather completely embedded in the culture of their tribe or community. The testimony of historians on earlier periods and of anthropologists on contemporary primitive societies agrees on this point. The man embedded in a traditional society hardly thinks of himself as separate or separable from his group. He is engulfed by his culture. He accepts the traditions, beliefs and way of life of his group so completely that he is not even aware that he is accepting them. He is a culturally defined man.

For such a man, his community is for all practical purposes "the world." Daniel Lerner found that when Turkish villagers were asked, "If you could not live in Turkey, where would you want to live?" they could not answer the question because they could not imagine living anywhere else. They could more easily imagine destroying the self ("I would rather die") than separating that self from its familiar context.[1]

Although such embeddedness places severe limits on individuality and freedom as we think of them, the men and women involved are not conscious of these limits. It is said that the last thing a fish would be conscious of would be water. Embedded man swims just as innocently in the culture of his community.

Such embeddedness cannot exist unless the community enjoys some degree of insulation from other cultures. Even in the ancient world there were relatively cosmopolitan centers in which a good many individuals were by no means embedded in their culture. One need only call to mind Plato, who viewed his society with the cool eye of a physician studying a difficult patient.

In the light of these facts it is not strictly accurate to say—as some writers do—that "the emergence of the individual" came with the Renaissance. What does date from the Renaissance is the appearance of men who made a considerable point about their individuality—who were even, one might say, rather theatrical about it. The men of the Renaissance found that it was exciting not only to be an

[1] Daniel Lerner, *The Passing of Traditional Society* (Free Press, 1958), p. 148.

individual but to talk about it, to preen one's self on it
and to build a life around it.

The premonitions of modern individualism in the Renaissance were amply confirmed in the course of the next three
centuries. The Reformation, the rise of science, the Enlightenment, the Industrial Revolution—each in its way
contributed powerfully to the dissolution of embeddedness
as a social norm. Only as this process gained ground did it
become possible to think of the free society as we conceive
it today—a society in which every man is encouraged and
expected to become a free and morally responsible individual.

By the nineteenth century the stage was set for some of
the more extreme manifestations of the modern cult of the
individual. We encounter on a wide scale the individual
who is intensely conscious of—even preoccupied with—his
individuality. Kierkegaard said, ". . . if I were to desire
an inscription for my tombstone, I should desire none
other than 'That individual.' " [2] We encounter the individual
who harbors an intense and explicit hostility toward his
own society, the individual who is capable of the deepest
feelings of alienation with respect to his community.

The rebellious individualists of the nineteenth century
paved the way for an army of followers. The circumstances of modern life are highly favorable to the achievement of certain kinds of individual detachment and autonomy. Mobility is one such circumstance; traditions are
apt to be strongly linked to family and locality, and cannot maintain their strength among a transient population.
Urbanization and modern communications produce a confrontation of differing traditions. In the resulting confusion of voices, the hold of all traditions is weakened.
Under such conditions the authority of the church
diminishes, as does the authority of parents. In addition, a
powerful literature of rebellion and dissent has accumulated
and is available to all young people.

By the time the nineteenth century was finished, any

[2] Søren Kierkegaard, *"That Individual": Two "Notes" Concerning My Work as an Author*, 1859. (In Søren Kierkegaard, *The Point
of View*, Walter Lowrie (trans.), (Oxford University Press: 1939),
p. 131.

young man intelligent enough and literate enough to know his own tradition could rebel in the grand manner. Today it doesn't even require intelligence or education. The opportunity for estrangement has been fully democratized.

ESCAPE FROM WHAT?

Against this background, any observer at the beginning of the twentieth century might easily have believed that the path was leading on to ever loftier heights of individual autonomy. But he would have been wrong. Two major developments of the twentieth century forced us to reexamine that view. First, it became apparent that modern mass society was placing new restraints on the individual, a subject we have already discussed. Second, new totalitarian forms emerged and enjoyed devastating success. Most contemporary discussions of the individual and the group are attempts to cope with one or the other of these developments.

It is not easy for young people today to comprehend the shocking impact on free men everywhere of the rise of modern totalitarianism. During the eighteenth, nineteenth and early twentieth century, the notion had become more and more widespread that man was indeed progressing toward freedom. It was believed that slowly but surely he was liberating himself from benighted traditions, tyrannical social institutions and power-hungry rulers. Then in the face of twentieth-century totalitarianism the ideology of freedom that had grown into such a sturdy plant over the centuries appeared to wither. The depressing thought occurred to many observers that there might be something in human nature that was not, after all, antagonistic to tyranny; perhaps even something that welcomed it.

That this is not strictly a modern phenomenon is emphasized by E. R. Dodds in describing the rising vogue of astrology in Greece in the second century B.C.:

For a century or more the individual has been face to face with his own intellectual freedom, and now he turned tail and bolted from the horrid prospect—bet-

For two generations now we have seen (but have not always understood) that when modern civilization loosens the ties that bind the individual to his tradition and famil' it may result in greater freedom or it may result in alie tion and loss of a sense of community. Similarly, when individual seeks autonomy he may achieve freedom moral responsibility or he may achieve only aggran ment of the self, with all the accompanying disorde. self-regard: cancerous pride, uncontrolled inflation o self-evaluations, unfulfillable self-expectations.

Most human beings *are* capable of achieving the measure of autonomy and mature individuality required by our conceptions of individual dignity and worth. But certain kinds of separation of *the self from all that is beyond the self* are inherently destructive and intolerable to human beings.

It is important to keep these facts in mind when we use the phrase "escape from freedom." Unless we specify what the individual is running away from and what form the running away takes, we may conceal under one label a wide range of distinctive behavior patterns.

It makes a great deal of difference whether the individual is really running away from freedom—i.e., from the moral responsibility of individual choice—or from the meaningless isolation that modern life so often thrusts on us and the arid egocentrism into which we are so often driven by romantic notions of individualism. If it is the latter, then the flight is justifiable, and the only question is what the individual chooses to run *to*. He may make the catastrophic mistake of submerging his individuality in mindless conformity to a cause or group. Or he may be wise enough to relate himself—as a free and morally responsible individual—to the larger social enterprise and to values that transcend the self. This will be difficult, of course, if the larger social enterprise is so fragmented or decayed that he cannot in fact relate himself to it.

The mature person must achieve a considerable measure of independence if he is to meet the standards implicit in our ideals of individual freedom and dignity; but at the same time he must acknowledge the limitations of the self, come to terms with his membership in the society at large and to the best in his own social, moral and intellectual tradition. If we address ourselves seriously to this task, we shall soon discover that one of the reasons young people do not commit themselves to the larger social enterprise is that they are genuinely baffled as to the nature of that enterprise. They do not really understand their own free society. They do not know their own social and intellectual tradition. They do not understand the requirements and realities of a complex modern society. They do not see where they fit in. If they are to commit themselves to the best in their own society, it is not exhortation they need but instruction.

We must also help the individual to discover how such commitments may be made without surrendering individuality. We must help him to understand and resist any impulse he may have to flee the responsibility of individual choice by mindless submission to a Cause or Movement. In short, he must recognize the hazard of having no commitments beyond the self and the hazard of commitments that imperil the self.

If we succeed in our delicate task, then we shall no longer need to agree with Yeats' grim comment on the modern world:

> The best lack all conviction, while the worst
> Are full of passionate intensity.[9]

[9] W. B. Yeats, "The Second Coming" (1921).

benefactors, obeying the Almighty effort and advancing on Chaos and the Dark.

What pretty oracles nature yields us on this text in the face and behavior of children, babes, and even brutes! That divided and rebel mind, that distrust of a sentiment because our arithmetic has computed the strength and means opposed to our purpose, these have not. Their mind being whole, their eye is as yet unconquered, and when we look in their faces we are disconcerted. Infancy conforms to nobody; all conform to it; so that one babe commonly makes four or five out of the adults who prattle and play to it. So God has armed youth and puberty and manhood no less with its own piquancy and charm, and made it enviable and gracious and its claims not to be put by, if it will stand by itself. Do not think the youth has no force, because he cannot speak to you and me. Hark! in the next room his voice is sufficiently clear and emphatic. It seems he knows how to speak to his contemporaries. Bashful or bold then, he will know how to make us seniors very unnecessary.

The nonchalance of boys who are sure of a dinner, and would disdain as much as a lord to do or say aught to conciliate one, is the healthy attitude of human nature. A boy is in the parlor what the pit is in the playhouse; independent, irresponsible, looking out from his corner on such people and facts as pass by, he tries and sentences them on their merits, in the swift, summary way of boys, as good, bad, interesting, silly, eloquent, troublesome. He cumbers himself never about consequences, about interests; he gives an independent, genuine verdict. You must court him; he does not court you. But the man is as it were clapped into jail by his consciousness. As soon as he has once acted or spoken with *éclat* he is a committed person, watched by the sympathy or the hatred of hundreds, whose affections must now enter into his account. There is no Lethe for this. Ah, that he could pass again into his neutrality! Who can thus avoid all pledges and, having observed, observe again from the same unaffected, unbiased, unbribable, unaffrighted innocence—must always be formidable. He would utter opinions on all passing affairs, which being seen to be not private but necessary, would sink like darts into the ear of men and put them in fear.

These are the voices which we hear in solitude, but they grow faint and inaudible as we enter into the world. Society everywhere is in conspiracy against the manhood of every one of its members. Society is a joint-stock company, in which the members agree, for the better securing of his bread to each shareholder, to surrender the liberty and culture of the eater. The virtue in most request is conformity. Self-reliance is its aversion. It loves not realities and creators, but names and customs.

Whoso would be a man, must be a nonconformist. He who would gather immortal palms must not be hindered by the name of goodness, but must explore if it be goodness. Nothing is at last sacred but the integrity of your own mind. Absolve you to yourself, and you shall have the suffrage of the world. I remember an answer which when quite young I was prompted to make to a valued adviser who was wont to importune me with the dear old doctrines of the church. On my saying, "What have I to do with the sacredness of traditions, if I live wholly from within?" my friend suggested, "But these impulses may be from below, not from above." I replied, "They do not seem to me to be such; but if I am the Devil's child, I will live then from the Devil." No law can be sacred to me but that of my nature. Good and bad are but names very readily transferable to that or this; the only right is what is after my constitution; the only wrong what is against it. A man is to carry himself in the presence of all opposition as if everything were titular and ephemeral but he. I am ashamed to think how easily we capitulate to badges and names, to large societies and dead institutions. Every decent and well-spoken individual affects and sways me more than is right. I ought to go upright and vital, and speak the rude truth in all ways. If malice and vanity wear the coat of philanthropy, shall that pass? If an angry bigot assumes this bountiful cause of Abolition, and comes to me with his last news from Barbadoes, why should I not say to him, "Go love thy infant; love thy wood-chopper; be good-natured and modest; have that grace; and never varnish your hard, uncharitable ambition with this incredible tenderness for black folk a thousand miles off. Thy love afar is spite at home." Rough and graceless would be such greeting, but truth is handsomer than the affectation of love. Your goodness must have some edge to it—else it is none. The doctrine of hatred must be preached, as the counteraction of the doctrine of love, when that pules and whines. I shun father and mother and wife and brother when my genius calls me. I would write on the lintels of the door-post, *Whim.* I hope it is somewhat better than whim at last, but we cannot spend the day in explanation. Expect me not to show cause why I seek or why I exclude company. Then again, do not tell me, as a good man did today, of my obligation to put all poor men in good situations. Are they *my* poor? I tell thee, thou foolish philanthropist, that I grudge the dollar, the dime, the cent I give to such men as do not belong to me and to whom I do not belong. There is a class of persons to whom by all spiritual affinity I am bought and sold; for them I will go to prison if need be; but your miscellaneous popular charities; the education at college of fools; the building of meeting-houses to the vain end to which many now stand; alms to sots, and the thousand-fold Relief Societies—though I confess with shame I sometimes succumb and give the dollar, it is a wicked dollar, which by and by I shall have the manhood to withhold.

Virtues are, in the popular estimate, rather the exception than the rule. There is the man *and* his virtues. Men do what is called a good action, as some piece of courage or charity, much as they would pay a fine in expiation of daily nonappearance on parade. Their works are done as an apology or extenuation of their living in the world—as invalids and the insane pay a high board. Their virtues are penances. I do not wish to expiate, but to live. My life is for itself and not for a spectacle. I much prefer that it should be of a lower strain, so it be genuine and equal, than that it should be glittering and unsteady. I wish it to be sound and sweet, and not to need diet and bleeding. I ask primary evidence that you are a man, and refuse this appeal from the man to his actions. I know that for myself it makes no difference whether I do or forbear those actions which are reckoned excellent. I cannot consent to pay for a privilege where I have intrinsic right. Few and mean as my gifts may be, I actually am, and do not need for my own assurance or the assurance of my fellows any secondary testimony.

What I must do is all that concerns me, not what the people think. This rule, equally arduous in actual and in intellectual life, may serve for the whole distinction between greatness and meanness. It is the harder because you will always find those who think they know what is your duty better than you know it. It is easy in the world to live after the world's opinion; it is easy in solitude to live after our own; but the great man is he who in the midst of the crowd keeps with perfect sweetness the independence of solitude.

The objection to conforming to usages that have become dead to you is that it scatters your force. It loses your time and blurs the impression of your character. If you maintain a dead church, contribute to a dead Bible-society, vote with a great party either for the government or against it, spread your table like base housekeepers—under all these screens I have difficulty to detect the precise man you are: and of course so much force is withdrawn from your proper life. But do your work, and I shall know you. Do your work, and you shall reinforce yourself. A man must consider what a blindman's-buff is this game of conformity. If I know your sect I anticipate your argument. I hear a preacher announce for his text and topic the expediency of one of the institutions of his church. Do I not know beforehand that not possibly can he say a new and spontaneous word? Do I not know that with all this ostentation of examining the grounds of the institution he will do no such thing? Do I not know that he is pledged to himself not to look but at one side, the permitted side, not as a man, but as a parish minister? He is a retained attorney, and these airs of the bench are the emptiest affectation. Well, most men have bound their eyes with one or another handkerchief, and attached themselves to some one of these communities of opinion. This conformity makes them not false in a few particulars, authors of a few lies, but false in all particulars. Their every truth is not quite true. Their two is not the real two, their four not the real four; so that every word they say chagrins us and we know not where to begin to set them right. Meantime nature is not slow to equip us in the prison-uniform of the party to which we adhere. We come to wear one cut of face and figure, and acquire by degrees the gentlest asinine expression. There is a mortifying experience in particular, which does not fail to wreak itself also in the general history; I mean "the foolish face of praise," the forced smile which we put on in company where we do not feel at ease, in answer to conversation which does not interest us. The muscles, not spontaneously moved but moved by a low usurping wilfulness, grow tight about the outline of the face, with the most disagreeable sensation.

For nonconformity the world whips you with its displeasure. And therefore a man must know how to estimate a sour face. The bystanders look askance on him in the public street or in the friend's parlor. If this aversion had its origin in contempt and resistance like his own he might well go home with a sad countenance; but the sour faces of the multitude, like their sweet faces, have no deep cause, but are put on and off as the wind blows and a newspaper directs. Yet is the discontent of the multitude more formidable than that of the senate and the college. It is easy enough for a firm man who knows the world to brook the rage of the cultivated classes. Their rage is decorous and prudent, for they are timid, as being very vulnerable themselves. But when to their feminine rage the indignation of the people is added, when the ignorant and the poor are aroused, when the unintelligent brute force that lies at the bottom of society is made to growl and mow, it needs the habit of magnanimity and religion to treat it godlike as a trifle of no concernment.

The other terror that scares us from self-trust is our consistency; a reverence for our past act or word because the eyes of others have no other data for computing our orbit than our past acts, and we are loth to disappoint them.

But why should you keep your head over your shoulder? Why drag about this corpse of your memory, lest you contradict somewhat you have stated in this or that public place? Suppose you should contradict yourself; what then? It seems to be a rule of wisdom never to rely on your memory alone, scarcely even in acts of pure memory, but to bring the past for judgment into the thousand-eyed present, and live ever in a new day. In your metaphysics you have denied personality to the Deity, yet when the devout motions of the soul come, yield to them heart and life, though they should clothe God with shape and color.

Leave your theory, as Joseph his coat in the hand of the harlot, and flee.

A foolish consistency is the hobgoblin of little minds, adored by little statesmen and philosophers and divines. With consistency a great soul has simply nothing to do. He may as well concern himself with his shadow on the wall. Speak what you think now in hard words and to-morrow speak what tomorrow thinks in hard words again, though it contradict every thing you said today. "Ah, so you shall be sure to be misunderstood." Is it so bad then to be misunderstood? Pythagoras was misunderstood, and Socrates, and Jesus, and Luther, and Copernicus, and Galileo, and Newton, and every pure and wise spirit that ever took flesh. To be great is to be misunderstood.

I suppose no man can violate his nature. All the sallies of his will are rounded in by the law of his being, as the inequalities of Andes and Himmaleh are insignificant in the curve of the sphere. Nor does it matter how you gauge and try him. A character is like an acrostic or Alexandrian stanza—read it forward, backward, or across, it still spells the same thing. In this pleasing contrite wood-life which God allows me, let me record day by day my honest thought without prospect or retrospect, and, I cannot doubt, it will be found symmetrical, though I mean it not and see it not. My book should smell of pines and resound with the hum of insects. The swallow over my window should interweave that thread or straw he carries in his bill into my web also. We pass for what we are. Character teaches above our wills. Men imagine that they communicate their virtue or vice only by overt actions, and do not see that virtue or vice emit a breath every moment.

There will be an agreement in whatever variety of actions, so they be each honest and natural in their hour. For of one will, the actions will be harmonious, however unlike they seem. These varieties are lost sight of at a little distance, at a little height of thought. One tendency unites them all. The voyage of the best ship is a zigzag line of a hundred tacks. See the line from a sufficient distance, and it straightens itself to the average tendency. Your genuine action will explain itself and will explain your other genuine actions. Your conformity explains nothing. Act singly, and what you have already done singly will justify you now. Greatness appeals to the future. If I can be firm enough today to do right and scorn eyes, I must have done so much right before as to defend me now. Be it how it will, do right now. Always scorn appearances and you always may. The force of character is cumulative. All the foregone days of virtue work their health into this. What makes the majesty of the heroes of the senate and the field, which so fills the imagination? The consciousness of a train of great days and victories behind. They shed a united light on the advancing actor. He is attended as by a visible escort of angels. That is it which throws thunder into Chatham's voice, and dignity into Washington's port, and America into Adams's eye. Honor is venerable to us because it is no ephemera. It is always ancient virtue. We worship it today because it is not of today. We love it and pay it homage because it is not a trap for our love and homage, but is self-dependent, self-derived, and therefore of an old immaculate pedigree, even if shown in a young person.

I hope in these days we have heard the last of conformity and consistency. Let the words be gazetted and ridiculous henceforward. Instead of the gong for dinner, let us hear a whistle from the Spartan fife. Let us never bow and apologize more. A great man is coming to eat at my house. I do not wish to please him; I wish that he should wish to please me. I will stand here for humanity, and though I would make it kind, I would make it true. Let us affront and reprimand the smooth mediocrity and squalid contentment of the times, and hurl in the face of custom and trade and office, the fact which is the upshot of all history, that there is a great responsible Thinker and Actor working wherever a man works; that a true man belongs to no other time or place, but is the center of things. Where he is, there is nature. He measures you and all men and all events. Ordinarily, everybody in society reminds us of somewhat else, or of some other person. Character, reality, reminds you of nothing else; it takes place of the whole creation. The man must be so much that he must make all circumstances indifferent. Every true man is a cause, a country, and an age; requires infinite spaces and numbers and time fully to accomplish his design; and posterity seem to follow his steps as a train of clients. A man Caesar is born, and for ages after we have a Roman Empire. Christ is born, and millions of minds so grow and cleave to his genius that he is confounded with virtue and the possible of man. An institution is the lengthened shadow of one man; as, Monachism, of the Hermit Antony; the Reformation, of Luther; Quakerism, of Fox; Methodism, of Wesley; Abolition, of Clarkson. Scipio, Milton called "the height of Rome;" and all history resolves itself very easily into the biography of a few stout and earnest persons.

Let a man then know his worth, and keep things under his feet. Let him not peep or steal, or skulk up and down with the air of a charity-boy, a bastard, or an interloper in the world which exists for him. But the man in the street, finding no worth in himself which corresponds to the force which built a tower or sculptured a marble god, feels poor when he looks on these. To him a palace, a statue, or a costly book have an alien and forbidding air, much like a gay equipage, and seem to say like that, "Who are you, Sir?" Yet they all are his, suitors for his notice, petitioners to his faculties that they will come out and take possession. The picture waits for my verdict; it is not to command me, but I am to settle its claims to praise. That popular fable of the sot who was picked up dead-drunk in the street, carried to the duke's house, washed and dressed and laid in the duke's bed, and, on his waking, treated with all obsequious ceremony like the duke, and assured that he had been insane, owes its popularity to the fact that it symbolizes so well the state of man, who is in the world a sort of sot, but now and then wakes up, exercises his reason and finds himself a true prince.

Our reading is mendicant and sycophantic. In history our imagination plays us false. Kingdom and lordship, power and estate, are a gaudier vocabulary than private John and Edward in a small house and common day's work; but the things of life are the same to both; the sum total of both is the same. Why all this deference to Alfred and Scanderbeg and Gustavus? Suppose they were virtuous; did they wear out virtue? As great a stake depends on your private act today as followed their public and renowned steps. When private men shall act with original views, the luster will be transferred from the actions of kings to those of gentlemen.

The world has been instructed by its kings, who have so magnetized the eyes of nations. It has been taught by this colossal symbol the mutual reverence that is due from man to man. The joyful loyalty with which men have everywhere suffered the king, the noble, or the great proprietor to walk among them by a law of his own, make his own scale of men and things and reverse theirs, pay for benefits not with money but with honor, and represent the law in his person, was the hieroglyphic by which they obscurely signified their consciousness of their own right and comeliness, the right of every man.

The magnetism which all original action exerts is explained when we inquire the reason of self-trust. Who is the Trustee? What is the aboriginal Self, on which a universal reliance may be grounded? What is the nature and power of that science-baffling star, without parallax, without calculable elements, which shoots a ray of beauty even into trivial and impure actions, if the least mark of independence appear? The inquiry leads us to that source, at once the essence of genius, of virtue, and of life, which we call Spontaneity or Instinct. We denote this primary wisdom as Intuition, whilst all later teachings are tuitions. In that deep force, the last fact behind which analysis cannot go, all things find their common origin. For the sense of being which in calm hours rises, we know not how, in the soul, is not diverse from things, from space, from light, from time, from man, but one with them and proceeds obviously from the same source whence their life and being also proceed. We first share the life by which things exist and afterwards see them as appearances in nature and forget that we have shared their cause. Here is the fountain of action and of thought. Here are the lungs of that inspiration which giveth man wisdom and which cannot be denied without impiety and atheism. We lie in the lap of immense intelligence, which makes us receivers of its truth and organs of its activity. When we discern justice, when we discern truth, we do nothing of ourselves, but allow a passage to its beams. If we ask whence this comes, if we seek to pry into the soul that causes, all philosophy is at fault. Its presence or its absence is all we can affirm. Every man discriminates between the voluntary acts of his mind and his involuntary perceptions, and knows that to his involuntary perceptions a perfect faith is due. He may err in the expression of them, but he knows that these things are so, like day and night, not to be disputed. My wilful actions and acquisitions are but roving; the idlest reverie, the faintest native emotion, command my curiosity and respect. Thoughtless people contradict as readily the statement of perceptions as of opinions, or rather much more readily; for they do not distinguish between perception and notion. They fancy that I choose to see this or that thing. But perception is not whimsical, but fatal. If I see a trait, my children will see it after me, and in course of time all mankind—although it may chance that no one has seen it before me. For my perception of it is as much a fact as the sun.

The relations of the soul to the divine spirit are so pure that it is profane to seek to interpose helps. It must be that when God speaketh he should communicate, not one thing, but all things; should fill the world with his voice; should scatter forth light, nature, time, souls, from the center of the present thought; and new date and new create the whole. Whenever a mind is simple and receives a divine wisdom, old things pass away—means, teachers, texts, temples fall; it lives now, and absorbs past and future into the present hour. All things are made sacred by relation to it—one as much as another. All things are dissolved to their center by their cause, and in the universal miracle petty and particular miracles disappear. If therefore a man claims to know and speak of God and carries you backward to the phraseology of some old mouldered nation in another country, in another world, believe him not. Is the acorn better than the oak which is its fulness and completion? Is the parent better than the child into whom he has cast his ripened being? Whence then this worship of the past? The centuries are conspirators against the sanity and authority of the soul. Time and space are but physiological colors which the eye makes, but the soul is light: where it is, is day; where it was, is night; and history is an impertinence and an injury if it be any thing more than a cheerful apologue or parable of my being and becoming.

Man is timid and apologetic; he is no longer upright; he dares not say, "I think," "I am," but quotes some saint or sage. He is ashamed before the blade of grass or the blowing rose. These roses under my window make no reference to former roses or to better ones; they are for what they are; they exist with God today. There is no time to them. There is simply the rose; it is perfect in every moment of its existence. Before a leaf-bud has burst, its whole life acts; in the full-blown flower there is no more; in the leaf-less root there is no less. Its nature is satisfied and it satis-fies nature in all moments alike. But man postpones or re-members; he does not live in the present, but with reverted eye laments the past, or, heedless of the riches that sur-round him, stands on tiptoe to foresee the future. He can-not be happy and strong until he too lives with nature in the present, above time.

This should be plain enough. Yet see what strong intel-lects dare not yet hear God himself unless he speak the phraseology of I know not what David, or Jeremiah, or Paul. We shall not always set so great a price on a few texts, on a few lives. We are like children who repeat by rote the sentences of grandames and tutors, and as they grow older, of the men of talents and character they chance to see—painfully recollecting the exact words they spoke; afterwards, when they come into the point of view which those had who uttered these sayings, they understand them and are willing to let the words go; for at any time they can use words as good when occasion comes. If we live truly, we shall see truly. It is as easy for the strong man to be strong, as it is for the weak to be weak. When we have new perception, we shall gladly disburden the mem-ory of its hoarded treasures as old rubbish. When a man lives with God, his voice shall be as sweet as the murmur of the brook and the rustle of the corn.

And now at last the highest truth on this subject re-mains unsaid; probably cannot be said; for all that we say is the far-off remembering of the intuition. That thought by what I can now nearest approach to say it, is this. When good is near you, when you have life in your-self, it is not by any known or accustomed way; you shall not discern the footprints of any other; you shall not see the face of man; you shall not hear any name—the way, the thought, the good, shall be wholly strange and new. It shall exclude example and experience. You take the way from man, not to man. All persons that ever existed are its forgotten ministers. Fear and hope are alike beneath it. There is somewhat low even in hope. In the hour of vision there is nothing that can be called gratitude, nor properly joy. The soul raised over passion beholds identity and eternal causation, perceives the self-existence of Truth and Right, and calms itself with knowing that all things go well. Vast spaces of nature, the Atlantic Ocean, the South Sea; long intervals of time, years, centuries, are of no account. This which I think and feel underlay every former state of life and circumstances, as it does underlie my present, and what is called life and what is called death.

Life only avails, not the having lived. Power ceases in the instant of repose; it resides in the moment of transition from a past to a new state, in the shooting of the gulf, in the darting to an aim. This one fact the world hates; that the soul *becomes;* for that forever degrades the past, turns all riches to poverty, all reputation to a shame, confounds the saint with the rogue, shoves Jesus and Judas equally aside. Why then do we prate of self-reliance? Inasmuch as the soul is present there will be power not confident but agent. To talk of reliance is a poor external way of speaking. Speak rather of that which relies because it works and is. Who has more obedience than I masters me, though he should not raise his finger. Round him I must revolve by the gravitation of spirits. We fancy it rhetoric when we speak of eminent virtue. We do not yet see that virtue is Height, and that a man or a company of men, plastic and permeable to principles, by the law of nature must overpower and ride all cities, nations, kings, rich men, poets, who are not.

This is the ultimate fact which we so quickly reach on this, as on every topic, the resolution of all into the ever-blessed ONE. Self-existence is the attribute of the Supreme Cause, and it constitutes the measure of good by the degree in which it enters into all lower forms. All things real are so by so much virtue as they contain. Commerce, husbandry, hunting, whaling, war, eloquence, personal weight, are somewhat, and engage my respect as examples of its presence and impure action. I see the same law working in nature for conservation and growth. Power is, in nature, the essential measure of right. Nature suffers nothing to remain in her kingdoms which cannot help itself. The genesis and maturation of a planet, its poise and orbit, the bended tree recovering itself from the strong wind, the vital resources of every animal and vegetable, are demonstrations of the self-sufficing and therefore self-relying soul.

Thus all concentrates: let us not rove; let us sit at home with the cause. Let us stun and astonish the intruding rabble of men and books and institutions by a simple declaration of the divine fact. Bid the invaders take the shoes from off their feet, for God is here within. Let our simplicity judge them, and our docility to our own law demonstrate the poverty of nature and fortune beside our native riches.

But now we are a mob. Man does not stand in awe of man, nor is his genius admonished to stay at home, to put itself in communication with the internal ocean, but it goes abroad to beg a cup of water of the urns of other men. We must go alone. I like the silent church before the service begins, better than any preaching. How far off, how cool, how chaste the persons look, begirt each one with a precinct or sanctuary! So let us always sit. Why should we assume the faults of our friend, or wife, or father, or child, because they sit around our hearth, or are said to have the same blood? All men have my blood and I all men's. Not for that will I adopt their petulance or folly, even to the extent of being ashamed of it. But your isolation must not be mechanical, but spiritual, that is, must be elevation. At times the whole world seems to be in conspiracy to importune you with emphatic trifles. Friend, client, child, sickness, fear, want, charity, all knock at once at thy closet door and say, "Come out unto us." But keep thy state; come not into their confusion. The power men possess to annoy me I give them by a weak curiosity. No man can come near me but through my act. "What we love that we have, but by desire we bereave ourselves of the love."

If we cannot at once rise to the sanctities of obedience and faith, let us at least resist our temptations; let us enter into the state of war and wake Thor and Woden, courage and constancy, in our Saxon breasts. This is to be done in our smooth times by speaking the truth. Check this lying hospitality and lying affection. Live no longer to the expectation of these deceived and deceiving people with whom we converse. Say to them, "O father, O mother, O wife, O brother, O friend, I have lived with you after ap-

pearances hitherto. Henceforward I am the truth's. Be it
known unto you that henceforward I obey no law less than
the eternal law. I will have no covenants but proximities.
I shall endeavor to nourish my parents, to support my family, to be the chaste husband of one wife—but these relations I must fill after a new and unprecedented way. I appeal from your customs. I must be myself. I cannot break
myself any longer for you, or you. If you can love me
for what I am, we shall be the happier. If you cannot, I
will still seek to deserve that you should. I will not hide my
tastes or aversions. I will so trust that what is deep is holy,
that I will do strongly before the sun and moon whatever
inly rejoices me and the heart appoints. If you are noble,
I will love you; if you are not, I will not hurt you and
myself by hypocritical attentions. If you are true, but not
in the same truth with me, cleave to your companions; I
will seek my own. I do this not selfishly but humbly and
truly. It is alike your interest, and mine, and all men's,
however long we have dwelt in lies, to live in truth. Does
this sound harsh today? You will soon love what is dictated by your nature as well as mine, and if we follow the
truth it will bring us out safe at last." But so may you give
these friends pain. Yes, but I cannot sell my liberty and
my power, to save their sensibility. Besides, all persons
have their moments of reason, when they look out into the
region of absolute truth; then will they justify me and do
the same thing.

The populace think that your rejection of popular standards is a rejection of all standards, and mere antinomian-
ism; and the bold sensualist will use the name of philosophy to gild his crimes. But the law of consciousness abides.
There are two confessionals, in one or the other of which
we must be shriven. You may fulfil your round of duties
by clearing yourself in the *direct,* or in the *reflex* way. Consider whether you have satisfied your relations to father,
mother, cousin, neighbor, town, cat and dog—whether any
of these can upbraid you. But I may also neglect this reflex
standard and absolve me to myself. I have my own stern
claims and perfect circle. It denies the name of duty to
many offices that are called duties. But if I can discharge
its debts it enables me to dispense with the popular code.

If any one imagines that this law is lax, let him keep its commandment one day.

And truly it demands something godlike in him who has cast off the common motives of humanity and has ventured to trust himself for a taskmaster. High be his heart, faithful his will, clear his sight, that he may in good earnest be doctrine, society, law, to himself, that a simple purpose may be to him as strong as iron necessity is to others!

If any man consider the present aspects of what is called by distinction *society,* he will see the need of these ethics. The sinew and heart of man seem to be drawn out, and we are become timorous, desponding whimperers. We are afraid of truth, afraid of fortune, afraid of death, and afraid of each other. Our age yields no great and perfect persons. We want men and women who shall renovate life and our social state, but we see that most natures are insolvent, cannot satisfy their own wants, have an ambition out of all proportion to their practical force and do lean and beg day and night continually. Our housekeeping is mendicant, our arts, our occupations, our marriages, our religion we have not chosen, but society has chosen for us. We are parlor soldiers. We shun the rugged battle of fate, where strength is born.

If our young men miscarry in their first enterprises they lose all heart. If the young merchant fails, men say he is *ruined.* If the finest genius studies at one of our colleges and is not installed in an office within one year afterwards in the cities or suburbs of Boston or New York, it seems to his friends and to himself that he is right in being disheartened and in complaining the rest of his life. A sturdy lad from New Hampshire or Vermont, who in turn tries all the professions, who *teams it, farms it, peddles,* keeps a school, preaches, edits a newspaper, goes to Congress, buys a township, and so forth, in successive years, and always like a cat falls on his feet, is worth a hundred of these city dolls. He walks abreast with his days and feels no shame in not "studying a profession," for he does not postpone his life, but lives already. He has not one chance, but a hundred chances. Let a Stoic open the resources of man and tell men they are not leaning willows, but can and must detach themselves; that with the exercise of self-trust, new powers shall appear; that a man is the word made flesh, born to shed healing to the nations; that he should be ashamed of our compassion, and that the moment he acts from himself, tossing the laws, the books, idolatries and customs out of the window, we pity him no more but thank and revere him—and that teacher shall restore the life of man to splendor and make his name dear to all history.

It is easy to see that a greater self-reliance must work a revolution in all the offices and relations of men; in their religion; in their education; in their pursuits; their modes of living; their association; in their property; in their speculative views.

1. In what prayers do men allow themselves! That which they call a holy office is not so much as brave and manly. Prayer looks abroad and asks for some foreign addition to come through some foreign virtue, and loses itself in endless mazes of natural and supernatural, and mediatorial and miraculous. Prayer that craves a particular commodity, anything less than all good, is vicious. Prayer is the contemplation of the facts of life from the highest point of view. It is the soliloquy of a beholding and jubilant soul. It is the spirit of God pronouncing his works good. But prayer as a means to effect a private end is meanness and theft. It supposes dualism and not unity in nature and consciousness. As soon as the man is at one with God, he will not beg. He will then see prayer in all action. The prayer of the farmer kneeling in his field to weed it, the prayer of the rower kneeling with the stroke of his oar, are true prayers heard throughout nature, though for cheap ends. Caratach, in Fletcher's "Bonduca," when admonished to inquire the mind of the god Audate, replies,

> His hidden meaning lies in our endeavors;
> Our valors are our best gods.

Another sort of false prayers are our regrets. Discontent is the want of self-reliance: it is infirmity of will. Regret calamities if you can thereby help the sufferer; if not, attend your own work and already the evil begins to be repaired. Our sympathy is just as base. We come to them who weep foolishly and sit down and cry for company, instead of imparting to them truth and health in rough electric shocks, putting them once more in communication with their own reason. The secret of fortune is joy in our hands. Welcome evermore to gods and men is the self-helping man. For him all doors are flung wide; him all tongues greet, all honors crown, all eyes follow with desire. Our love goes out to him and embraces him because he did not need it. We solicitously and apologetically caress and celebrate him because he held on his way and scorned our disapprobation. The gods love him because men hated him. "To the persevering mortal," said Zoroaster, "the blessed Immortals are swift."

As men's prayers are a disease of the will, so are their creeds a disease of the intellect. They say with those foolish Israelites, "Let not God speak to us, lest we die. Speak thou, speak any man with us, and we will obey." Everywhere I am hindered of meeting God in my brother, because he has shut his own temple doors and recites fables merely of his brother's, or his brother's brother's God. Every new mind is a new classification. If it prove a mind of uncommon activity and power, a Locke, a Lavoisier, a Hutton, a Bentham, a Fourier, it imposes its classification on other men, and lo! a new system. In proportion to the depth of the thought, and so to the number of the objects it touches and brings within reach of the pupil, is his complacency. But chiefly is this apparent in creeds and churches, which are also classifications of some powerful mind acting on the elemental thought of duty and man's relation to the Highest. Such is Calvinism, Quakerism, Swedenborgism. The pupil takes the same delight in subordinating every thing to the new terminology as a girl who has just learned botany in seeing a new earth and new seasons thereby. It will happen for a time that the pupil will find his intellectual power has grown by the study of his master's mind. But in all unbalanced minds the classification is idolized, passes for the end and not for a speedily exhaustible means, so that the walls of the system blend to their eye in the remote horizon with the walls of the universe; the luminaries of heaven seem to them hung on the arch their master built. They cannot imagine how you aliens have any right to see—how you can see; "It must be somehow that you stole the light from us." They do not yet perceive that light, unsystematic, indomitable, will break into any cabin, even into theirs. Let them chirp awhile and call it their own. If they are honest and do well, presently their neat new pinfold will be too strait and low, will crack, will lean, will rot and vanish, and the immortal light, all young and joyful, million-orbed, million-colored, will beam over the universe as on the first morning.

2. It is for want of self-culture that the superstition of Travelling, whose idols are Italy, England, Egypt, retains its fascination for all educated Americans. They who made England, Italy, or Greece venerable in the imagination, did so by sticking fast where they were, like an axis of the earth. In manly hours we feel that duty is our place. The soul is no traveller; the wise man stays at home, and when his necessities, his duties, on any occasion call him from his house, or into foreign lands, he is at home still and shall make men sensible by the expression of his countenance that he goes, the missionary of wisdom and virtue, and visits cities and men like a sovereign and not like an interloper or a valet.

I have no churlish objection to the circumnavigation of the globe for the purposes of art, of study, and benevolence, so that the man is first domesticated, or does not go abroad with the hope of finding somewhat greater than he knows. He who travels to be amused, or to get somewhat which he does not carry, travels away from himself, and grows old even in youth among old things. In Thebes, in Palmyra, his will and mind have become old and dilapidated as they. He carries ruins to ruins.

Travelling is a fool's paradise. Our first journeys discover to us the indifference of places. At home I dream that at Naples, at Rome, I can be intoxicated with beauty and lose my sadness. I pack my trunk, embrace my friends, embark on the sea and at last wake up in Naples, and there beside me is the stern fact, the sad self, unrelenting, identical, that I fled from. I seek the Vatican and the palaces. I affect to be intoxicated with sights and suggestions, but I am not intoxicated. My giant goes with me wherever I go.

3. But the rage of travelling is a symptom of a deeper unsoundness affecting the whole intellectual action. The intellect is vagabond, and our system of education fosters

restlessness. Our minds travel when our bodies are forced to stay at home. We imitate; and what is imitation but the travelling of the mind? Our houses are built with foreign taste; our shelves are garnished with foreign ornaments; our opinions, our tastes, our faculties, lean, and follow the Past and the Distant. The soul created the arts wherever they have flourished. It was in his own mind that the artist sought his model. It was an application of his own thought to the thing to be done and the conditions to be observed. And why need we copy the Doric or the Gothic model? Beauty, convenience, grandeur of thought and quaint expression are as near to us as to any, and if the American artist will study with hope and love the precise thing to be done by him, considering the climate, the soil, the length of the day, the wants of the people, the habit and form of the government, he will create a house in which all these will find themselves fitted, and taste and sentiment will be satisfied also.

Insist on yourself; never imitate. Your own gift you can present every moment with the cumulative force of a whole life's cultivation; but of the adopted talent of another you have only an extemporaneous half possession. That which each can do best, none but his Maker can teach him. No man yet knows what it is, nor can, till that person has exhibited it. Where is the master who could have taught Shakspeare? Where is the master who could have instructed Franklin, or Washington, or Bacon, or Newton? Every great man is a unique. The Scipionism of Scipio is precisely that part he could not borrow. Shakspeare will never be made by the study of Shakspeare. Do that which is assigned you, and you cannot hope too much or dare too much. There is at this moment for you an utterance brave and grand as that of the colossal chisel of Phidias, or trowel of the Egyptians, or the pen of Moses or Dante, but different from all these. Not possibly will the soul, all rich, all eloquent, with thousand-cloven tongue, deign to repeat itself; but if you can hear what these patriarchs say, surely you can reply to them in the same pitch of voice; for the ear and the tongue are two organs of one nature. Abide in the simple and noble regions of thy life, obey thy heart, and thou shalt reproduce the Foreworld again.

4. As our Religion, our Education, our Art look abroad,

so does our spirit of society. All men plume themselves on the improvement of society, and no man improves.

Society never advances. It recedes as fast on one side as it gains on the other. It undergoes continual changes; it is barbarous, it is civilized, it is christianized, it is rich, it is scientific; but this change is not amelioration. For every thing that is given something is taken. Society acquires new arts and loses old instincts. What a contrast between the well-clad, reading, writing, thinking American, with a watch, a pencil and a bill of exchange in his pocket, and the naked New Zealander, whose property is a club, a spear, a mat and an undivided twentieth of a shed to sleep under! But compare the health of the two men and you shall see that the white man has lost his aboriginal strength. If the traveller tell us truly, strike the savage with a broadaxe and in a day or two the flesh shall unite and heal as if you struck the blow into soft pitch, and the same blow shall send the white to his grave.

The civilized man has built a coach, but has lost the use of his feet. He is supported on crutches, but lacks so much support of muscle. He has a fine Geneva watch, but he fails of the skill to tell the hour by the sun. A Greenwich nautical almanac he has, and so being sure of the information when he wants it, the man in the street does not know a star in the sky. The solstice he does not observe; the equinox he knows as little; and the whole bright calendar of the year is without a dial in his mind. His notebooks impair his memory; his libraries overload his wit; the insurance-office increases the number of accidents; and it may be a question whether machinery does not encumber; whether we have not lost by refinement some energy, by a Christianity, entrenched in establishments and forms, some vigor of wild virtue. For every Stoic was a Stoic; but in Christendom where is the Christian?

There is no more deviation in the moral standard than in the standard of height or bulk. No greater men are now than ever were. A singular equality may be observed between the great men of the first and of the last ages; nor can all the science, art, religion, and philosophy of the nineteenth century avail to educate greater men than Plutarch's heroes, three or four and twenty centuries ago. Not in time is the race progressive. Phocion, Socrates, Anaxagoras, Diogenes, are great men, but they leave no class. He who is really of their class will not be called by their name, but will be his own man, and in his turn the founder of a sect. The arts and inventions of each period are only its costume and do not invigorate men. The harm of the improved machinery may compensate its good. Hudson and Behring accomplished so much in their fishing-boats as to astonish Parry and Franklin, whose equipment exhausted the resources of science and art. Galileo, with an opera-glass, discovered a more splendid series of celestial phenomena than any one since. Columbus found the New World in an undecked boat. It is curious to see the periodical disuse and perishing of means and machinery which were introduced with loud laudation a few years or centuries before. The great genius returns to essential man. We reckoned the improvements of the art of war among the triumphs of science, and yet Napoleon conquered Europe by the bivouac, which consisted of falling back on naked valor and disencumbering it of all aids. The Emperor held it impossible to make a perfect army, says Las Cases, "without abolishing our arms, magazines, commissaries and carriages, until, in imitation of the Roman custom, the soldier should receive his supply of corn, grind it in his hand-mill and bake his bread himself."

Society is a wave. The wave moves onward, but the water of which it is composed does not. The same particle does not rise from the valley to the ridge. Its unity is only phenomenal. The persons who make up a nation today, next year die, and their experience dies with them.

And so the reliance on Property, including the reliance on governments which protect it, is the want of self-reliance. Men have looked away from themselves and at things so long that they have come to esteem the religious, learned and civil institutions as guards of property, and they deprecate assaults on these, because they feel them to be assaults on property. They measure their esteem of each other by what each has, and not by what each is. But a cultivated man becomes ashamed of his property, out of new respect for his nature. Especially he hates what he has if he sees that it is accidental—came to him by inheritance, or gift, or crime; then he feels that it is not having; it does not belong to him, has no root in him and merely lies there because no revolution or no robber takes it away. But that which a man is, does always by necessity acquire; and what the man acquires, is living property, which does not wait the beck of rulers, or mobs, or revolutions, or fire, or storm, or bankruptcies, but perpetually renews itself wherever the man breathes. "Thy lot or portion of life," said the Caliph Ali, "is seeking after thee; therefore be at rest from seeking after it." Our dependence on these foreign goods leads us to our slavish respect for numbers. The political parties meet in numerous conventions; the greater the concourse and with each new uproar of announcement, The delegation from Essex! The Democrats from New Hampshire! The Whigs of Maine! The young patriot feels himself stronger than before by a new thousand of eyes and arms. In like manner the reformers summon conventions and vote and resolve in multitude. Not so, O friends! will the God deign to enter and inhabit you, but by a method precisely the reverse. It is only as a man puts off all foreign support and stands alone that I see him to be strong and to prevail. He is weaker by every recruit to his banner. Is not a man better than a town? Ask nothing of men, and, in the endless mutation, thou only firm column must presently appear the upholder of all that surrounds thee. He who knows that power is inborn, that he is weak because he has looked for good out of him and elsewhere, and, so perceiving, throws himself unhesitatingly on his thought, instantly rights himself, stands in the erect position, commands his limbs, works miracles; just as a man who stands on his feet is stronger than a man who stands on his head.

So use all that is called Fortune. Most men gamble with her, and gain all, and lose all, as her wheel rolls. But do thou leave as unlawful these winnings, and deal with Cause and Effect, the chancellors of God. In the Will work and acquire, and thou hast chained the wheel of Chance, and shall sit hereafter out of fear from her rotations. A political victory, a rise of rents, the recovery of your sick or the return of your absent friend, or some other favorable event raises your spirits, and you think good days are preparing for you. Do not believe it. Nothing can bring you peace but yourself. Nothing can bring you peace but the triumph of principles.

AMERICAN INDIVIDUALISM
IN THE TWENTIETH CENTURY

David M. Potter

["Self-reliance" is the classic statement of one variety
of American individualism. But the idea keeps reap-
pearing, sometimes quite transformed, throughout our
history. David M. Potter succinctly surveys this progress. He disarms two key meanings—laissez-faire and
nonconformity. But both concepts set sharp limits, to
protect other people from the individual's excesses.

[David M. Potter is professor of American History at
Stanford University, and the author of *Economic Abun-
dance and the American Character* and *Nationalism and
Sectionalism in America*.]

At the beginning of his essay "Individualism Reconsidered," David Riesman remarks, "Such terms as 'society'
and 'individual' tend to pose a false as well as a shifting
dichotomy." [1] We might take Riesman's remark and extend it by observing that, in general, we tend to discuss
questions too much in terms of antitheses, and frequently
in terms of antitheses which are deceptive. Thus, we speak
in polarities about liberty versus authority, dissent versus
conformity, and, of course, individualism versus collectivism. But in fact we know all the while that no one intends
to choose starkly between these alternatives. Liberty would
be intolerable to the most independent-minded person without some measure of authority, or dissent without some
conformity. In fact, human life presents us with a whole

[1] David Riesman, *Individualism Reconsidered, and Other Essays*
(Glencoe, Illinois: Free Press, 1954), p. 26.

series of situations in which diverse and, to some extent, conflicting values must be kept in some kind of working relationship with one another. Two junior officers both bucking for promotion will presumably work together for the improvement of their unit while they work in rivalry with one another for advancement. Indeed, the principle of "antagonistic cooperation" probably goes much deeper than this, for even nature seems to abound in situations where two elements are linked in a relationship of tension and at the same time of interdependence. The basic case is the relationship of men and women, eternally needing one another and eternally engaged in a "battle of the sexes"; but there is also the case of youth and age, with youth forever restive under its dependence upon the elders, and the elders forever vexed by the brashness of a youth which they have lost, and with each unwillingly drawing upon the other for qualities which it, itself, lacks. Along with these classic dualisms, there is also the relationship between man alone and man in society—man constantly straining against the compulsion imposed by the group and man continuously driven by need for identity with the group. These conflicting needs must forever be mediated and accommodated, and the ultimate choice of either one to the complete exclusion of the other would be equally unthinkable. In our literature, any story of the complete isolation, either physical or psychological, of a man from his fellowman, such as the story of Robinson Crusoe before he found a human footprint on the beach, is regarded as essentially a horror story. But the tale of any man having his identity completely swallowed up by total absorption into the group, as happened for the members of the Party in Oceania in George Orwell's *1984*, is also regarded as a kind of nightmare.

If this principle of balance or beneficent tension between conflicting values has any validity in the cases which I have mentioned, it might be argued that it has even more in the case of individualism, especially in the United States. For is it not notoriously true that historically American individualism has always been sanctioned only within very sharply defined limits? The word "individualism," of course, has been included in our litany of sacred terms, and in many respects, America has placed an immense premium upon the individualistic values of independence, self-reliance, and rejection of authority. But American society has never, I believe, sanctioned the attempt of a person to practice the kind of individualism which one would find in a society with a recognized élite. An élite or aristocratic individualist is likely to regard the principles of individualism as conferring a franchise for self-indulgence as well as for self-expression. This was the kind of individualism which Lord Byron practiced—the kind which he defended in his epic of Don Juan. It lends itself to the idea that the talented man may become a superman and that he is quite justified in sacrificing less talented men and in riding roughshod over them. Nietzsche is unfavorably remembered for exalting this superman version of individualism, and of course one finds the ideal set forth also in Shaw's *Man and Superman*.

Individualism in this form seems profoundly alien to the American tradition—so alien that we who are in the American tradition do not usually even recognize it as a form of individualism. Yet occasionally we will find a traveller from overseas who regards individualism as involving the right of the individualist to indulge his own impulses at the expense of others, to attain self-expression regardless of its effect on other people. Such a person is astonished that American individualism carries no such franchise. The writings of Tocqueville abound in observations on the lack of real variety in American life, despite all its claims to individualism. But the most vivid statement of the point that I think I have ever seen was made by Tocqueville's compatriot Michael de Chevalier, also in the 1830s:

As for us [the French], who resemble each other in nothing except in differing from everybody else, for us, to whom variety is as necessary as the air, to whom a life of rules would be a subject of horror, the Yankee system would be torture. Their liberty is not the liberty to outrage all that is sacred on earth, to set religion at defiance, to laugh morals to scorn, to undermine the foundations of social order, to mock at all traditions and received opinions. It is neither the liberty of being a monarchist in a republican country, nor that of sacrificing the honor of the poor man's

wife or daughter to one's base passions; it is not even
the liberty to enjoy one's wealth by a public display,
for public opinion has its sumptuary laws, to which
all must conform under pain of moral outlawry; nor
even that of living in private differently from the rest
of the world.[2]

Just how serious Chevalier was in asserting the right to
seduce a poor man's wife as one of the prerequisites of individualism in its Gallic form, I do not know. But his mere
voicing of this assertion gives us, I believe, a kind of
benchmark which may help to define the limits of individualism in its Yankee form. This assertion of individualism
would not do at all for Americans; and why, we may ask,
would it not? Why are Chevalier's suggestions more or less
offensive to us, and why, particularly, does the suggestion
about the poor man's wife grate on us more than the proposal to "outrage all that is sacred"? I would suggest that
it is because Chevalier is implicitly denying the American
proposition that men are intrinsically equal, even though
their physical circumstances may vary immensely. For a
rich man to seduce the wife of another rich man might be
accepted in a spirit of joviality, under the axiom that all
is fair in love and war, but for him to seduce the wife of
a poor man is to treat a fellowman as less than an equal
simply because he is poor. In the American creed this is,
perhaps, the sin against the Holy Ghost.

It may seem that I am dwelling too much here upon
what may have been a random phrase in the writing of one
Frenchman now dead for more than a century, but I have
lingered over it because I believe it may illustrate, in a
particularly vivid way, the fact that American individualism
has always been limited and held in balance by other cher-
ished principles which were not entirely consistent with it.
It could never be asserted in a way which would violate
the principle of equality, and we will do well to look
twice before we even assume that it placed the values of

[2] John William Ward (ed.), *Society, Manners, and Politics in the
United States: Letters on North America by Michael Chevalier*
(Garden City, New York: Doubleday & Company, Inc. [Anchor
Books], 1961), pp. 327–328.

man in isolation ahead of the values of man in a group, or man in society.

Thus far I have avoided attempting a definition of individualism, but at this point it may be necessary for me to pause and declare myself as to what I understand individualism to have meant in American life. If so, I must venture an assertion that American individualism in the nineteenth century and American individualism in the twentieth century have had two fundamentally different emphases, but that both of them have placed great weight upon the belief that individualism should serve as a means to group welfare rather than as a way of exalting man in isolation. This assertion may be difficult to prove, but let us examine it. To specify more fully, let me suggest that the individualism of the nineteenth century stressed the element of self-reliance while that of the twentieth century has stressed the element of nonconformity or dissent, but that in each case there was a strong emphasis upon the value of the quality in question for society as a whole and not simply for the individual apart from society.

Theoretically, perhaps, it might be supposed that these two emphases are not very different: that self-reliance and nonconformity would go together and would tend to converge. It is logical to argue that a man who does not depend on other people for his physical welfare will certainly not be very quick to borrow his ideas from them. If he has the habit of fending for himself, will he not also have the habit of thinking for himself? If he shows initiative in his endeavors to attain success, will he not also show initiative in forming his social ideas? If individualism equals independence and independence equals freedom and freedom equals dissent, then doesn't it follow that individualism equals dissent? Perhaps the plausibility of this kind of equation has led us to the fallacy of using one term, "individualism," to express the ideas of both self-reliance and nonconformity.

But history often mocks logic, and in our historical experience, the believers in self-reliance, in the sense of taking care of oneself, and the believers in nonconformity, in the sense of encouraging dissent, have often been far, far apart. In fact, these two types of individualists seem to be almost natural antagonists, for the "rugged individualist" of laissez-faire economics is likely to be what we call a conservative, as orthodox in his ideas of success as he is enterprising in his efforts to succeed, while the nonconforming individualist is likely to treasure unconventional forms of self-expression and to regard the orthodoxy of the laissez-faire individualist as a threat to such self-expresssion and to novel ideas in general.

As these two types of individualists feud with one another, it is ironical that the ultimate accusation which each makes is that the other is betraying the community. Thus, while each in his own way places the individual before the group, each at the same time pays inverted tribute to the importance of the group by making the betrayal of the group the basis of his rejection of the other. To the nonconforming individualist the sin of the laissez-faire individualist is that he sacrifices the weak to the strong and that he values the opportunity for private advantage more than he values the general welfare. To the self-reliant individualist, the sin of the nonconforming individualist is that he denies the community the means of protecting its values and the morale of its members against injury by hostile or irresponsible persons or groups. His concept of the right of dissent is so absolute that he extends it not only to responsible critics who want to improve the society, but also to enemies who want to destroy it and to exploiters who are alert to every chance for arousing and playing upon the anxieties, the lusts, and the sadistic impulses which society, from the beginning of time, has struggled to control.

But before looking further at the relationship of these two modes of individualism to one another, let us first look at the historical context of the two. The individualism of self-reliance was essentially the response or adaptation of a people who had an undeveloped continent in front of them and who lacked institutional or technological devices for conquering it. Society needed persons who are what we call self-starters, persons who would go ahead and tackle the wilderness without waiting for signals to be given or for arrangements that would make it easy. It needed qualities of initiative and of ruggedness. It needed the attitude of Stonewall Jackson when he said that he would care for his own wounded and bury his own dead.

In the conditions of pioneer America, where the services of the police and the church and the school and the hospital and the specialized economic occupations were often not available, it needed a man who could tote his own gun, pray his own prayers, and learn to read, write, and cipher by the light of a pine-knot fire. Andrew Jackson's mother is said to have admonished him at the parental knee, "Andy, never sue nobody. Always settle them matters yourself."

America needed a breed of men who would swarm over a wilderness which was a continent wide, and it produced the adaptation that was needed—the frontier American, famous in song and story as well as in the classic formulations of Frederick Jackson Turner. He was, it appears, rugged; he was self-reliant; he seems to have been magnificently successful; and he did tame the continent in record time—with the important aid, it must be added, of a tremendously effective new technology of power and machines. But was his self-reliance individualism? And, insofar as it was individualism, what were the social costs of developing this kind of individualism to such a pronounced degree? These questions are somewhat harder to answer.

Turner himself suggested that the frontier experience stimulated innovation, which of course means a break with conformity, a break with the past. He offered the hypothesis, which research has failed to vindicate, that the frontiersmen showed great fertility in working out new and untraditional political devices for the governments of their new states. But in fact, the tendency to imitate and copy the older political models was high. Professor Walter P. Webb has made a considerably more tenable argument that the men of the Great Plains seized upon certain technological innovations: the six-shooter, barbed wire, and the windmill. But this seems more a matter of physical adaptation than of a capacity for independent or deviant thought. The status of the frontiersman as an independent thinker is questionable indeed. Perhaps, one might add, it is unfair even to expect of him that he should have been an independent thinker. The physical demands upon him were very rigid, and rigid demands necessarily require one specific response, thus limiting the range or spectrum or variety of response. Nonconformity and diversity in attitude will flourish where the demands of the physical environment are not so harshly rigorous, and where they leave more latitude for variation from man to man. Nonconformity implies the possibility of varied reactions to the same situation; but the frontier, with its rigorous conditions of life, was too exacting in its demands to allow much choice for the frontiersman in the mode of his reaction.

In the past generation we have come to see, with increasing clarity, that the individualism of the American frontier was an individualism of personal self-reliance and of hardihood and stamina rather than an individualism of intellectual independence and personal self-expression. Arthur Schlesinger, Jr., for instance, has argued, I think convincingly, that the frontier was slow to perceive the problems arising in connection with the application of democracy to an industrial society and slow to develop social ideas of reform, so that these ideas, in fact, developed predominantly in the cities. At the same time when we were recognizing this, we were also beginning to count the social costs of the individualism of self-reliance, so that there has grown up a tendency to doubt whether the frontier influence was altogether a beneficial one in American life. As far back as Alexis de Tocqueville, we were warned in the clearest possible terms that American equality, which is peculiarly identified with the frontier, was conducive to conformity rather than to freedom, since it places the stigma of arrogance upon any man who ventures to set his personal judgment against the judgment of a majority of his equals. Arthur K. Moore, in his study of the frontier mind as exemplified in the backwoodsmen of Kentucky, has shown how readily the practicality of the frontier took the form of a blighting anti-intellectualism.[3] Many writers have begun to say that the frontiersman was spiritually and culturally impoverished by his isolation and by his predilection for a society in which the ties of community life were so weakened that he ceased to be, in any adequate sense, a social being. One who has stated this most strikingly, and perhaps in the most controversial way, is Leslie Fiedler with his famous (or, as some citizens of

[3] Arthur K. Moore, *The Frontier Mind* (Lexington: University of Kentucky Press, 1957).

Montana would say, infamous) comments on his earliest impressions of the people of that frontier state. Upon his arrival in Montana, says Fiedler:

> I was met unexpectedly by the Montana Face. What I had been expecting, I do not clearly know; zest, I suppose, naïveté, a ruddy and straightforward kind of vigor—perhaps even honest brutality. What I found seemed, at first glance, reticent, sullen, weary—full of self-sufficient stupidity; a little later it appeared simply inarticulate, with all the dumb pathos of what cannot declare itself; a face developed not for sociability or feeling, but for facing into the weather. It said friendly things to be sure, and meant them; but it had no adequate physical expressions even for friendliness, and the muscles around the mouth and eyes were obviously unprepared to cope with the demands of any more complicated emotion. I felt a kind of innocence behind it, but an innocence difficult to distinguish from simple ignorance. In a way there was something heartening in dealing with people who had never seen, for instance, a Negro or a Jew or a servant, and were immune to all their bitter meanings; but the same people, I knew, had never seen an art museum or a ballet or even a movie in any language but their own, and the poverty of experience had left the possibilities of the human face in them completely unrealized.[4]

Here, in effect, is the assertion that society had to pay too high a price for frontier individualism—that men as a group were penalized for the freedom of men as separate beings, and, in short, that individualism is not justified if it serves only individuals. It must serve society. Our conviction that it must is why we have never had any élite individualism that amounted to anything, and is also a striking commentary upon the paradoxical elements in the fact that we are committed to individualism at all.

Along with frontier individualism, the nineteenth cen-

[4] Leslie A. Fiedler, *An End of Innocence* (Boston: The Beacon Press, 1955), pp. 134–135. Courtesy also of the *Kenyon Review*.

tury also subscribed to the economic individualism of lais-sez-faire. The two shared a great deal in common. Both exalted strength and stamina and scorned weakness or lack of practicality. Both enjoined the individual to fight for his own aspirations first and to subordinate consideration for the group to consideration for the enterpriser acting alone. Both made a virtue of independence but their inde-pendence meant a self-propelled drive toward the goals which society had prescribed rather than any real inde-pendence of mind in setting the goals for which to strive. Both were individualistic in a sense—certainly in the sense of "rugged individualism"—but it was an individualism that was more conservative than liberal, more hostile to dissent than favorable toward it.

It is a notable fact about laissez-faire individualism, how-ever, that while it exalted the virtues of unregimented, un-controlled, independent action by man acting alone, it never for a moment contended that the success of the unusual individual was more important than the welfare of the community. Instead, it constantly stressed the idea that the bold enterpriser served the community by daring to undertake projects which the community needed but which the rank and file were too unimaginative to initiate. The argument was much like that of the modern noncon-forming individualist who defends dissenters not on the ground that the dissenter matters and that the conventional thinkers from whom he dissents do not, but that the com-munity needs ideas which the conventional or orthodox thinkers cannot supply.

There is no need for me to recite here the elaborate arguments which Adam Smith stated so ingeniously, and which nineteenth-century publicists so dearly loved to re-peat, that a providentially designed economic system (the unseen hand of God at work) took the selfish impulses and selfish actions of individuals and translated them into results which served the welfare of the community. This concept that the antagonistic rivalries of selfish and com-peting producers would create an optimum relationship be-tween the social need for goods and the economic supply of goods is not only a subtle and by no means preposterous economic theory. It is also a renewed testimony that even the ardent individualists of the nineteenth century were not willing to base their faith in individualism upon any concept of the primacy of the interests of the individual over the interests of the group. Instead, they made the interests of the group—that is, the society—the ground for their insistence that society must not be deprived of the contribution which the independent-minded individual can make.

During the Great Depression, a great many Americans grew to doubt that laissez-faire individualism really did serve the interests of the whole society. Our government under the New Deal abandoned it, and though we have had a span of a quarter of a century since that time, with two Republican administrations in the interim, there is no indication that we will return to the old faith in self-reliance and private action. Richard Hofstadter has subtitled his essay on Herbert Hoover "The Last Stand of Rugged Individualism," and there are probably not many, even among the conservatives, who would quarrel very much with this verdict.

In saying that the individualism of self-reliance has passed its high tide, I don't mean to suggest by any means that it has disappeared, or even that it does not remain, in some forms, a very dominant American attitude. Anyone who thinks that it is becoming extinct might well ponder over an analysis which Martha Wolfenstein and Nathan Leites made only a few years ago of the plots of a year's crop of American motion pictures of the A grade.

> The major plot configuration in American films [they wrote] contrasts with both the British and the French. Winning is terrifically important and always possible though it may be a tough fight. The conflict is not an internal one [as in *Hamlet*]; it is not our own impulses which endanger us nor our own scruples that stand in our way. The hazards are all external, but they are not rooted in the nature of life itself. They are the hazards of a particular situation with which we find ourselves confronted. The hero is typically in a strange town where there are apt to be dangerous men and women of ambiguous character and where the forces of law and order are not to be

relied on. If he sizes up the situation correctly, if he does not go off half-cocked but is still able to beat the other fellow to the punch once he is sure who the enemy is, if he relies on no one but himself, if he demands sufficient evidence of virtue from the girl, he will emerge triumphant. He will defeat the dangerous men, get the right girl, and show the authorities what's what.[5]

We all know that American boys, from the early years of childhood, are taught to stand up and fight back. Margaret Mead, incidentally, has commented cogently on this point.[6] So long as this is true, and so long as the self-reliant protagonist in the movie gets the desirable girl, it would be premature indeed to suggest that all the bark has been rubbed off the tradition of individualism in its rugged form. But certainly the tradition has come under attack and certainly it is, as we might say, selling at a discount.

Now what is the basis of our discontent with the tradition of self-reliance? This is certainly a complex and difficult question, to which it may be brash to venture a simple answer, but in many respects it appears that the point of the criticism is that stress on self-reliance was carried to a point where it emphasized private goals and private values too much at the cost of community goals and community values. The coherence of the community was impaired, the vitality of the community was lowered. Leslie Fiedler's men with the Montana face are essentially men who have been starved of the psychological nourishment which community life could offer.

This criticism can be detected, I think, in quite a number of different forms. For instance, Stanley Elkins, in his comparison of slavery in North America and in South America, comments on the fact that in South America certain community institutions such as the church and the government were strong enough to assert a concern for the slave, and to stand, as it were, in certain respects, between

[5] Martha Wolfenstein and Nathan Leites, *Movies: A Psychological Study* (Glencoe, Illinois: Free Press, 1950), p. 298.

[6] Margaret Mead, *And Keep Your Powder Dry: An Anthropologist Looks at America* (New York: William Morrow & Company, Inc., 1942), p. 141.

the slave and his master.[7] But in North America, the naked authority of the master was tempered in hardly any way by the institutional force of the community. This amounts to saying that private values had eclipsed public values in the United States. Many other writers have expressed concern about the lack of corporate *esprit* among Americans, and some of the concern about the lack of reciprocal support for one another among American prisoners of war in Korea, as contrasted, for instance, with that among Turkish prisoners of war, was also addressed to the fear that we have emphasized private values, or what may be called privatism, too much and community values not enough. The old Yankee prayer:

> God save me and my wife,
> My son John and his wife,
> Us four and no more

may have expressed an attitude that was rooted too deep for comfort.

Many of the comments that we have had on privatism as an unfortunate dimension of American individualism have been expressed in strong and somewhat controversial terms, but Gabriel Almond, in his *The American People and Foreign Policy*, gave us what might be regarded as a sober and measured statement of this point.

> The American, [said Almond,] is primarily concerned with "private values," as distinguished from social-group, political, or religious-moral values. His concern with private, worldly success is his most absorbing aim. In this regard it may be suggested by way of hypothesis that in other cultures there is a greater stress on corporate loyalties and values and a greater personal involvement with political issues or with other-worldly religious values.[8]

[7] Stanley M. Elkins, *Slavery: A Problem in American Institutional and Intellectual Life* (Chicago: University of Chicago Press, 1959), pp. 27–80.

[8] Gabriel A. Almond, *The American People and Foreign Policy* (New York: Harcourt, Brace and Company, Inc., 1950), p. 48.

With the twentieth century, as I have already tried to suggest, American individualism took on a new emphasis. The frontier was disappearing, and laissez-faire was having its wings clipped. According to a well-known phrase which is perhaps a trifle too pat, human rights were replacing property rights. The new expounders of the American tradition reexamined the sacred documents and concluded that the priceless feature of our heritage was the principle of nonconformity, or dissent. Of course, they had perfectly sound historical grounds for tracing the principle of dissent far back in American history. Puritanism itself was a fairly radical form of dissent, as well as a harsh system for enforcing conformity. Ralph W. Emerson, that great apostle of individualism, had not only exalted self-reliance; he had exalted dissent also. "Whoso would be a man," Emerson said, "must be a nonconformist." In our own day, the sanction which we give to dissent is suggested quite clearly in the antithesis which we constantly set up of liberty versus authority and of self-expression versus conformity.

The exponents of this new kind of individualism went forward rejoicing, for quite some time, that individualism was now purged of the taints of privatism and of conformity. For the spokesmen of the individualism of nonconformity were very often men who could in no sense be accused of indifference to the interests of the group, of society. Most of them are what we call liberals—using the term with a fairly clear understanding of what kind of people we mean, even if we cannot quite define their exact quality—and the liberals were so concerned with the welfare of the group that they often gave it a priority over the rights of the individual. Their opponents offered an implicit recognition to this fact by angrily denouncing them as "collectivists." How could a man whose fault, if he has one, is that he is too collectivist—too group-minded —legitimately be accused of privatism? How could a man who supports the American Civil Liberties Union and consistently *épaters* the bourgeoise be suspected of conformity? The new individualism, then, was an emancipated individualism, cleansed of its old, middle-class sins of privatism and of conformity.

Yet before we accept the conclusion that the nineteenth-century doctrine of Progress has been vindicated again, and that individualism has reached a new and perfected condition, it may be worthwhile to apply one of the weapons of dissent, the weapon of skepticism, and to ask in a truly searching way whether conformity and privatism are really dead, whether true self-expression has come into its own at last, or whether, to some extent, conformity and privatism have merely found new modes of expression.

To pursue this question, as it relates to conformity, one would have to ask whether we have ceased to follow the crowd, or whether we have to some extent merely changed the crowd which we follow? Have we ceased to be cultists, or have we primarily changed our cults? Does the liberal who makes a fetish of his nonconformity actually show much more readiness to get out of step with his fellow liberals than does the avowedly conformist conservative with his fellow conservatives?

Stated a little differently and a little more abstractly conformity is the faithful, unquestioning compliance with the standards imposed by a group. But to say this is to say that whether you call a man a conformist or a dissenter is very often not a question of his intrinsic independence, but a question of what group you measure him by. A Communist, for instance, measured by the reference group of the American public, is a dissenter and a nonconformist, but measured by the reference group of his own adoption, the Communist group, he is the supreme conformist—more so than a Baptist or a Rotarian, for he has completely abdicated his capacity to judge questions on their own merits and has embraced, *verbatim ac litteratim*, a whole body of doctrine which, like medieval theology, has answered all questions before they arise.

David Riesman has dealt with this point with sharp perception in his essay "The Saving Remnant," where he says, "The Bohemians and rebels are not usually autonomous; on the contrary, they are zealously tuned in to the signals of a defiant group that finds the meaning of life in a compulsive nonconformity to the majority group." [9] In an extraordinarily acute article called "The Bored and the Violent," Arthur Miller has discussed this point in con-

[9] Riesman, *op. cit.*, p. 117.

nection with extreme manifestations of sadistic violence among juvenile delinquents. Miller makes the striking point that, among these youths, who are responding to society by defiance in its most extreme form, the real pattern is not one of deviation but of conformity—a blind, abject conformity to the expectations of their peers. As Miller says, "The delinquent, far from being the rebel, is the conformist *par excellence*. He is actually incapable of doing anything alone." [10] His reliance upon his gang is, of course, the measure of this lack of capability. Here, one is reminded of a cartoon in the *New Yorker* some time ago showing a young woman, attractive and appearing very much an average American girl, speaking somewhat crossly to her husband, who was dressed in the prescribed uniform of a beatnik. Her question to him was, "Why do you have to be a nonconformist like everyone else?"

If there is any group in our society which makes a truly earnest effort to cultivate real intellectual freedom and fearless inquiry, it is no doubt the academic and intellectual community. Yet even here, do we not have a certain incidence of what might be called academic conformity? Would not an academic who in 1960 spoke out loud and clear for Richard Nixon have shocked the sense of propriety of a gathering of academics as much as an overt glorification of the New Frontier would shock a group of investment bankers? Do not even the academics have their orthodoxies and their conventions? Do not these conventions require that in the case of a novelist, for example, he make a conforming obeisance to nonconformity by following the practice of employing as frequently as possible the monosyllabic words for the functions of sex and bodily elimination which have now become almost trite but which still have a gratifying capacity to startle a good many readers and to attract a good many buyers who hope to be startled? And do not the conventions also require that the book reviewer also conform and prove that he too is an emancipated spirit by dutifully praising the fearless realism of the author without reference to whether his work has merit?

[10] Arthur Miller, "The Bored and the Violent," *Harper's Magazine* (November, 1962) pp. 51–52.

One more illustration may be in order here—the case of an academic of irreproachable standing. When Hannah Arendt published an article questioning whether the integration of public schools ought to be attempted by the exercise of public authority, the result was not, as one might have hoped, a rough-and-tumble scrimmage between her and persons who disagreed with her. It was rather a shocked silence, a polite looking in the other direction as if no one had noticed. It was, indeed, the same reaction as if she had belched in church. Miss Arendt had questioned a point on which liberals have established a dogma to which they require conformity, and they were shocked in a prudish way to hear this dogma questioned.

If there is some question about the completeness of the triumph of nonconformity, there is perhaps also a question concerning the finality of the victory over privatism. Surely the shaggy, long-haired, or rugged breed of individualism is gone for good, and we will no longer sacrifice the interests of society to the individualism of laissez-faire. But can any generation, even our own, completely reconcile the social needs of the group with other personal needs of the individual? And must we not expect that even the new style of defense of individual right will sometimes be conducted at the expense of what might best serve society as a whole? The new individualism firmly repudiates all the nineteenth-century freebooters who used to exploit the public economically, but it still thinks, and perhaps ought to think, in terms of man as separate rather than of man in the group. Thus, when it is confronted with what we call crime—the large-scale incidence of violence in our society—it seems more concerned with the rehabilitation of the deviant individual who has committed the violence than with safeguarding those anonymous persons upon whom the violence is committed. When confronted with the sale in every drugstore of magazines which exploit sex, it does not really ask whether it would be better for society if the drugstores did not purvey this material. It does not ask whether the publisher who makes a fast buck by this shoddy commercial enterprise is different from a patent-medicine manufacturer who also makes a fast buck by selling nostrums but is regulated, hopefully, by the Pure Food and Drug Act. It asks instead who will dare to violate freedom of the press in maintaining an informed public opinion.

Perhaps this is the right question to ask. I would hesitate to say that it is clearly wrong. But what I do venture to suggest is that the freedom of the individual, in relation to his society, cannot be absolute, basically because the individual and the society are not really separate. The individual acquires his full identity only as a member of society, and society itself is, in the last analysis, a multiplicity of individuals. The American tradition, which rejected élite individualism from the beginning, has always shown enough concern for the social values to seek to justify its individualism—whether self-reliant or nonconformist—in social terms. Thus the competitive system in economics was defended not on the ground of the great profits which it would bring to some individuals, but with the claim that it would assure economic vigor for the society. Similarly, the sanctions which have surrounded dissent were based less upon approval of the dissenter than upon the need of society for an unrestricted "free trade in ideas." Moreover, each school of individualism cared enough for social values to attack the other for betraying them. Thus the dissentients accused the self-reliants of sacrificing the weak to the strong and the community to its predatory members, while the self-reliants accused the dissentients of sacrificing the strong to the weak and the community to its aberrant members. Perhaps both accusations have been justified, for both groups have remained primarily committed to a strong individualistic emphasis, and in the long struggle between two schools of individualism, the values of the community have often lacked effective defenders on either side. Neither form of individualism has had enough genuine concern for real group values, shared community values, to hold a proper balance between the centrifugal and the centripetal forces.

Neither one has been willing to recognize that the tension between the individual and the group can never be treated as a simple antithesis, involving a simple choice. For each, in its logically pure form, contains implications which are unacceptable to most of us. The emphasis on the individual essentially implies a component of privatism which would sacrifice the interests of the group to the interests of a limited number of its members, and this implication is not acceptable in the long run to a democratic society; the emphasis on the group implies the subordination of the qualities of the mind and spirit of man, standing by himself, to the pressures of men in a herd, and this implication, too, is unacceptable to a people who believe that society exists for man and not man for society. Therefore, we can never make a clear-cut, exclusive choice in favor of either individualism, as it is called, or collectivism, as it is called. While philosophers are engaged in pursuing one or the other of these two to their logical extremes and even their logical absurdities, people in everyday life will go on, trying in the future, as they have tried in the past, to accommodate these two and imperfectly to reconcile the indispensable values which are inherent in them both. As Riesman stated it, "Such terms as 'society' and 'individual' tend to pose a false, as well as a shifting dichotomy."

INDIVIDUALISM RECONSIDERED

David Riesman

[Can the competition between the individual's needs and society's claims on him be accommodated? David Riesman confronts this issue of individualism versus groupism, and comes to some conclusions about its implications. Though written in the 1950s, this piece, based as it is on his wide-ranging empirical knowledge of our developing national character, has been a touchstone of recent debate about the individual in America.

[David Riesman is Professor of Social Relations at Harvard University. His many books include *The Lonely Crowd, Individualism Reconsidered,* and *The Academic Revolution.*]

Since such terms as "society" and "individual" tend to pose a false as well as a shifting dichotomy, I must anticipate misunderstanding; if I succeed in being suggestive to at least a few, I shall be satisfied. We live in a social climate in which, in many parts of the world and of the United States, the older brands of ruthless individualism are still a social danger, while in other parts of the world and of the United States, the newer varieties of what we may term "groupism" become increasingly menacing. Actually, we can distinguish conceptually between the needs of society (as a system of social organization) and those of the environing groups (as a system of psychological ties and expectations). As so defined, society, the larger territorial organization, often provides the mechanisms by which the individual can be protected against the group, both by such formal legal procedures as bills of rights, and by the fact that large-scale organization may permit the social mobility by which individuals can escape from any particular group. Prior to the rise of passports and totalitarianism, the modern Western city provided such an asylum and opportunity for many, while the existence of this safety valve helped alleviate the pressure of "groupism" everywhere.

I

Just as a self-proclaimed "realist" is a different fellow in the Middle Ages, in the Enlightenment, and in modern America, so also the meaning of "individualism" depends on the historical setting. And it is worth tracing here the paradoxical development which, in the course of the modern era, freed Western men progressively from many previous restraints while at the same time developing a seemingly individualistic character-type enclosed within new psychological restraints. Men of the emerging middle classes, after the Renaissance, were turned loose in an economic order freed from the supervision of mercantilism, in a political order freed from the supervision of a hereditary aristocracy, in a religious order freed from the supervision of ecclesiastical hierarchy. To many observers of this process, whether radical or reactionary, these men who were freed of external restraints under the slogans of laissez-faire economics, utilitarian philosophy, and so on, appeared fiercely and viciously individualistic and competitive.[1] But if we look at these new men from the inside, so to speak, we can see that it was precisely their internalization of a great deal of restraint that allowed them to become free of the group sanctions that might have been arrayed against their "individualism." They could disregard the religious anti-moneymaking attitudes that had survived from the medieval and early Reformation period only because (as Max Weber pointed out) their Puritan reli-

---

[1] To Werner Sombart, these men appeared free of "scruples"—that is, free from such traditional obligations as those of guild morality. The fighting slogans were, of course, often blatantly individualistic.

gious ethics provided them with stern justification and
with a shell of protection against the shocked attitudes of
their contemporaries.

Today, with some old evils behind us, we can admit
that the hardy men who pioneered on the frontiers of production, exploration, and colonization in the last three hundred years were usually men who acted according to a code
and who, though of course there were many pirates like
Daniel Drew and the slave traders among them, were more
likely to subscribe to high moral principles (e.g., the elder
Rockefeller). These men were bound by a character orientation I have termed "inner-direction": they were guided
by internalized goals and ideals which made them appear
to be more individualistic than they actually were. Often,
they were men who walked in the imagined footsteps of
idealized parents—and this gave them their seven-league
boots and their feeling of having a personal destiny. And
since the ideals that were internalized included many vestiges of older traditions, they were frequently paternalistic
men, who, despite nominal belief in free enterprise, helped
ameliorate the worst abuses brought about by their innovations. They shared, then, more than appears of the ethics
of their anti-individualistic critics, from Owen and Marx
to Karl Mannheim and Tawney. Evidence of this may be
found in comparing these Western enterprisers with their
counterparts in other countries, such as South America or
China or the Soviet Union, where when traditional restraints on ruthlessness broke down, fewer internalized restraints were available to take their place. In sum, it
proved possible in the West in early modern times to carry
individualism to its limits of usefulness—and, in some
cases, far beyond these limits—because a fair amount of
social cohesiveness was taken for granted. . . .

Moreover, the same sort of moral compulsions which
many of these "freedmen" carried within themselves, as the
result of their socialization in a patriarchal family, were
also turned loose upon the society at large. Individualistic
"promoters" turned up not only in business and colonization, but in the many zealous reform movements of the last
several hundred years. These movements fastened new restraints on a society that was shaking loose from old ones—
how effectively, we can see by contrasting the attitudes

toward law and society in India today, as the legacy of British rule, with the attitudes in neighboring countries which were not compelled to internalize the "white man's burden." In the West, the nineteenth century witnessed the triumph of the Victorian way: a triumph of legal and orderly justice, of honesty in business and government, of greater concern for women and children, and so on. (Inclined as we are today to patronize the Victorians, we generally see the seamy side of their attainments and emphasize their hypocrisy, failing to observe that this hypocrisy was itself some evidence of their success in driving corruption, vice, and social sadism underground.) In the eighteenth century it was impossible to walk unarmed in many English cities, let alone in the country; public and private violence abounded; corruption was taken for granted; the slave trade was thriving. By the middle of the nineteenth century, the lower orders had been freed, the lower impulses (as well as some higher ones) subdued. The development in America ran parallel, but was never, of course, as complete or as spectacular; as we all know, lawlessness reigns in many areas of American life today.

Nevertheless, anti-individualist writers such as Tawney, while they may have neglected the dangers of collectivism out of their disgust with their acquisitive society (and their failure to appreciate that medieval society was in some ways more acquisitive still), do express a very common mood of dislike for the cash nexus—a mood which appears in more astringent form in Veblen. It is hard for people to find satisfaction in a society whose best defense is that it is a lesser evil than some other social form. People can become greatly attached only to a society which takes account of their longings for connection with each other, and they may even opt for totalitarianism because it pretends to satisfy these longings and to get rid of the felt indecency of the cash nexus. To the degree that capitalist individualism has fostered an ethic of callousness, the result has been to undermine all forms of individualism, good and bad.

II

In the perspective of hindsight, we can see how Darwin's *Origin of Species* came to be so completely misinterpreted when it first appeared, as a brief for struggle to death *among individuals*. We can see, as the pendulum has swung toward groupism, that Darwin's book might just as well be interpreted as demonstrating the need for social solidarity or symbiosis within and among given species in order to achieve survival; thus (as Kropotkin pointed out) the book has much to say about cooperation as a technique of competition.

But the hardy Victorians, who had freed themselves from external restraints on economic competition and who were at the same time still sensitive, as I have indicated, to anti-moneymaking ethics, welcomed their interpretation of Darwin as a support in their continuing polemic against restraints—a polemic carried out also within themselves. One can, for instance, almost watch William Graham Sumner trying to stamp out, with the aid of Darwin, any softness and tenderness toward those who were pushed aside in the competitive struggle; he would have been less violent toward "do-gooders" if he had not feared their echo inside himself.

Today the argument against Sumner, and against this nineteenth-century variety of individualism, seems very dated. We have come to realize that men who compete primarily for wealth are relatively harmless as compared with men who compete primarily for power (though, to be sure, there are violent, even totalitarian, implications in the treatment of labor, at home and abroad, as a commodity). Nevertheless, we are still inclined to use the word "bourgeois" as an epithet; we are well aware of the vices of the money-grubber, and perhaps less sensitive to the meannesses of spirit that develop in a monastery or a university where wealth as a goal is minimized. Even so, the centuries-old campaign against the middle class should not have hidden from us the advantages of a social system in which some men seek wealth (including wealth through power), pretty much for its own sake, and others seek power (including power through wealth), pretty much for its own sake, thus establishing a dichotomy of drives in which protective separation of specifically political powers can take its stand.

I recall Walter Duranty talking some twenty years ago about the Soviet abandonment of the "New Economic Policy," the policy by which, in the early twenties, a moderate capitalism had been encouraged in Russia. He spoke of the horror with which the ascetic Communists had reacted to the champagne parties and lovely ladies of the burgeoning NEP-men who were speculating in commodities and making fortunes overnight by methods hard to distinguish from black-marketing. I felt then, and still feel, that if these Communists had been more historically minded and less morally indignant, they might have seen that the NEP policy offered the only chance of curbing the totalitarianism which sets in when only power, and not money, talks. (The Communists were like those farmers who, in their hatred of varmints, get rid of the very creatures on whom the whole ecological balance depends.) At the same time, we can see that if the Russian capitalists had not allowed moral restraint to be monopolized by the Communists, they might have aroused less of this sort of antagonism. (Today, it is the top Party functionaries—and occupation troops—who have access to champagne and ladies!) And we also see that economic control through the "impersonal" market mechanism (Adam Smith's "invisible hand"), where this is at all possible, is decidedly preferable to the all too visible and personal hand of the state or private monopolist.

III

In the epoch when "money talked," the conception of human nature underwent a series of changes quite as ironical as the social developments themselves. The view of man as naturally cooperative runs through the writings of a number of otherwise quite diverse nineteenth-century thinkers: St. Simon and Comte, Kingsley and Marx, Durkheim and Bellamy, Kropotkin and Ruskin. All these writers, more or less explicitly, reject competitive capitalism in favor of a medieval type of guild harmony and order, while differing in their attitudes toward the machine and in their remedies for the diseases of industrialization.

Likewise, the view of man as naturally antagonistic has given rise to a number of diverse solutions to the problem of the social order thus presented. Freud, for example, deeming men innately aggressive, thought that a strong élite, with a monopoly on the capacity for being reasonable, would have to compel the majority to cooperate in the tasks of civilization, at once demanding submission from the masses and providing them with consolation. In Elton Mayo and in other recent writers, one can find a similar élitism and a similar concern with the formation of group consensus through strong leadership.

All these writers thus arrive at positions in which they become advocates of what I have labelled "groupism," whether they start from reactionary or revolutionary political positions, or from Rousseauistic or Freudian and even Hobbesian views of human nature. That is, whether one begins with the assumption that cooperation is man's natural state, which he is prevented from attaining by a reactionary social order, or with the assumption that the "state of nature" is one of war of all against all, one can readily end by focussing on forcing or allowing men to define themselves entirely as social animals. (To be sure, in the early Marx, and even in Bellamy, one finds more anarchistic strains; and some thinkers of the last century and of this one, such as John Stuart Mill and Bertrand Russell, have worried less about order than about liberty.)

Obviously, the preoccupation with the desires and needs of men for group affiliation testifies, often enough, to the actual presence of disorder in the society. But it often testifies also to the obsessive feeling on the part of some intellectuals that disorder in itself is a terrible thing. Furthermore, one of the themes that unifies many of these writers is their attitude toward the disorderly trait of "selfishness"; in true medieval fashion, they denounce it and welcome, if not always altruism as such, then at least a class or national consciousness that submerges individual self-interest. The confidence in self-interest that ran from Mandeville through Smith to Sumner, seems to have been almost utterly defeated among influential thinkers by the end of World War I; it is still assumed that self-interest is natural—and sometimes, indeed, that an "enlightened" self-interest is called for—but on the whole, reliance is placed on concern for the needs of the group.

This altruism might have worked during the 1900–1950 shift toward emphasis on the group, if those group needs had themselves been clear. In that case, people might have developed a pattern of obedience to the group in certain limited spheres (regarding the group demands as a kind of tax collection), while retaining individuality in other spheres. If this had happened, the shift from the preceding attitudes of subtly socialized individualism would hardly have been noticeable. But in fact, the group needs have not been clear; moreover, they have been constantly changing. There has developed today a great preoccupation, less with specific needs, than with group mood—a feeling on the part of individuals that they wanted or felt they had to spend their energies, first in making a group, and second, in attending to and improving its morale.

This groupism, which rests not on obvious group emergencies but on the vague disquietude of lonely individuals, is probably strongest in America, where people appear to be most vocally concerned about the problems of group participation and belongingness. Americans have devoted less scientific attention to the measurement of group needs and potential wants through market-research techniques (save in the most obvious commercial forms) than to what we might term "mood engineering" in work, play, and politics. Mood engineering leads not so much to specific "altruistic" behavior as to a general readiness to participate in the given group activities of the moment, even if their only purpose is to help other people pass the evening. As Margaret Mead has pointed out, Americans feel selfish if they stay at home when they might be amusing people who are "underprivileged" in the skills of self-amusement.

It would take us too far afield even to begin to try to explain the reasons for the psychological changes which have occurred at least as rapidly as those in social and political organization. For example, shifting patterns of child socialization are important: among other things, parents today face the responsibility of "making a group" with their children—are on the defensive vis-à-vis their children's moods—in a way quite different from the attitude of parents in an earlier day. Not all the developments toward groupism are to be deplored. Groupism rests in part on an increasing sensitivity to subtle states of feeling, and this is an advance. Only, as always, such advances bring with them a dialectical train of new perplexities and limitations. We must skeptically question the demands for greater social participation and belongingness among the group-minded while, on another front, opposing the claims of those who for outworn reasons cling to individualism as a (largely economic) shibboleth.

IV

It is not easy, for obvious reasons, to discover the actual state of this conflict in Soviet Russia today. We do not know, for instance, to what extent people have become cynical and apathetic as a way of resisting an enforced group belongingness. However, occasional arguments appear in the press which, by claiming that the issue is settled, show that it is not settled. Thus, in 1940 there was a discussion of a psychology textbook which was attacked, not only for its "objectivity," but for its failure to realize that the whole science had undergone a profound change in the Soviet Union. "The tragedy of the loneliness of the individual," it was asserted, "which characterizes a society founded on classes, has been liquidated. The conflict between the individual and the community has disappeared. The interests of the Soviet people are harmoniously identified with the interests of Soviet society." Furthermore, theories about "unchanging human nature" are damned as bourgeois (an issue not absent from American social-science polemics)—it would seem that Lysenko-ism operates in the field of psychology, too.[2]

---

[2] A poignant newspaper story from Warsaw indicates that the Poles may be maintaining some resistance to the Stalinist extremes of groupism. A young Polish girl loosed a flood of abuse and correction on herself by writing a letter to the newspaper *Standard of Youth* declaring that "my private life does not concern anyone." She continued that the ideal member of the Union of Polish Youth was a "creature with wings . . . wearing a long and clean cloak

To be sure, it is no adequate answer to Western advocates of groupism to show how the idea has fitted so well into the totalitarian pattern (which eventually serves to destroy all local groupings). In fact, the advocates of an anti-individualist position use the seeming success of the dictatorships to buttress their views (not seeing to what extent the dictatorships, beneath their ideology, are seeking to imitate *us*), pointing out that men welcome social solidarity even if they must pay, in the loss of freedom, a high and terrible price for it; and that actually they want demands made on them—a point to which war experience also testifies—rather than to be left alone and forced to direct their own efforts. Still other voices argue that, in order to defeat the USSR, we must evoke our own spirit of sacrifice and devotion to the group: our alleged anarchy will be our undoing in the war of the two worlds. And still other, though few, voices would like to see international anarchy put down by an all-powerful world state.

What strikes me in many of these proposals is an ascetic uninventiveness reminiscent of the discussions which bored the Polish letter writer quoted in the footnote. We assume that all possible forms of human relatedness have already been experienced, so that if present forms are unsatisfying, then better ones must be looked for in our own past, in wartime comradeship, or in the grisly present of the Soviet Union. Ironically, the very people who extol groupism, whether as an inexorable necessity or as desirable in its own right, usually do not themselves lead parochial and "groupy" lives; they draw sustenance from all the continents and all of history; they have friends everywhere, just as

---

of sackcloth. When it meets a pal it discusses only Marxism. It does not push in tramways nor spit on the floor and walks only on the right side of the street. . . . According to you we should wear only a spotless uniform of our organization, straight hair and, of course, no trace of makeup . . . —all, in order to discuss the development of education in the New China! . . . I am young and lucky enough to have survived the war and have a right to live as I like. Z.M.P. meetings, discussions and some artistic shows are not enough for me." For this display of "selfishness," the writer was termed demoralized by war and occupation, said to "almost sanction(s) debauchery," and informed that "exceeding the production target . . . is happiness. Work in the organization provides happiness certainly greater than that gotten out of dancing or making up."

their material needs, through the modern division of labor, are met from everywhere. But like Plato and many other unhappy intellectuals since, they believe that those others, the masses (obviously, the very term "masses" is heavily value-loaded), can be saved from a Durkheimian anomie only by an enforced groupism and its concomitant ideology.

We can see, moreover, other forces than a simple nostalgia, or even simple élitism, at work. Anti-urbanites, for example, argue among themselves, in the guise of instructing the "masses." Unable to stand alone, lacking the "nerve of failure," they tend to project onto others their own uneasiness and frequently their own contempt for intellectuality. I do not mean, of course, that there is no malaise in our great middle and working classes in urban life; but rather, on the one hand, that the intellectuals greatly underestimate the terror, misery, and disorder of the "status society" of the past which they so much admire, while underestimating, on the other hand, the tremendous achievements of modern men in making themselves comfortable in the face of the novelty of a fluid industrial society.

Americans of the more mobile classes have not only adapted themselves to a fluid society, but have also begun to adapt the society to their own needs. They have achieved an extraordinary ability to make judgments about, and friends with, a great variety of humankind. Whereas more traditional societies have an etiquette to govern the relation between people of different age, class, and sex groups, these Americans have abandoned etiquette for a more individualized and personalized approach. And while we are familiar with the negative aspects of this development—its enforced joviality of the "greeter" and glad-hander, its enforced politeness of the Helen Hokinson type—we may in our self-contempt be less ready to see its great adventurousness: the liberation of people and their movements from the chain mail of etiquette.

In the arts of consumption as well as in the arts of production, Americans have moved so fast that, in architecture and design, in moving pictures and in poetry and criticism, we are living in what I believe to be one of the great cultures of history. It is not fashionable to say this. Yet we may ask, as Crane Brinton does in *Ideas and Men:* What is there in Pericles' famous praise of Athens that does not apply to us, in some or even in extended measure?

Sensitive Americans—and they are more in number than each individually is apt to think—have become exceedingly allergic to anything that smacks of chauvinism. . . . Vis-à-vis Europe, we have lost the defensive aggression of Mark Twain, though his was a needed corrective; vis-à-vis Asia, we were until recently taken in by the image of the peaceable, unaggressive, technologically-unseduced Chinese. It now seems likely that we shall fall for the idea that the Russians have more to offer the Far East than we; and that they have unequivocally convinced the peasants that this is so. While this attitude stems in part from our disenchantment with machine civilization and our failure to use machinery as a means to greater, more creative leisure, it would appear ludicrous to that part of the world which needs machines before it can realize the possibility of becoming disenchanted with them!

One of the interesting semantic expressions of our own disenchantment is that of bewailing our society as "impersonal." What would the member of the village group or small town not give at times for an impersonal setting where he was not constantly part of a web of gossip and surveillance? Furthermore, this use of the term "impersonal" is a way of deprecating our great human achievement of turning over productive routines to machinery and to formal organization. One result of this attitude is clear enough: the sphere of work tends to come increasingly under the supervision of the engineers whose concern is less to reduce the time and strain of the worker, than to render the workaday world "meaningful" in terms of shared emotions reminiscent of the guilds, or perhaps of our nostalgic image of the guilds.

A contrary attitude would assume that we should be grateful to find, in our work, areas of freedom from people, where the necessary minimum of productive activity could be accomplished without the strain and waste of time involved in continuous concern for the morale of the working group. If men were not compelled to be sociable at work, they could enjoy sociability in their leisure much more than they often do now. In fact, while men in the nineteenth century may have underestimated their satisfactions from solitary occupations, hobbies and other pursuits, we tend today to reverse these extremes and to forget that men can enjoy, let us say, the physical rhythms of work or the private fantasies of leisure even when they are for long periods deprived of social comradeship at work and play. What is necessary is some sort of balance which will find room for quite idiosyncratic individual desires to be, variously, alone and with others. The flexibility of modern industrial organization, no longer bound geographically to rail lines and power sites, the steady decrease of hours of compulsory work which our abundance allows, and our increasing sensitivity to the psychic as well as physical hazards of the different occupations—these developments permit us to move toward the reorganization of work so that it can offer a greater variety of physical and social challenges and stimulations. But work should never be allowed to become an end in itself simply out of a need to keep ourselves busy.

V

Apart from the ever-present threat of war—not seldom used as a rationalization to sop up our "excessive" comforts, leisures, and painfully-attained easygoingnesses— most of our social critics cannot imagine a society being held together without putting organized work in the forefront of its goals and agendas. Their efforts to restore the participative significance of work, allegedly enjoyed in earlier social stages, show the same poverty of imagination as their belief in the inevitable need for the parochial group as the only conceivable building block of society. When we turn to formal politics, we see that the same fundamentally reactionary ideology leads to a demand for national unity and a distrust of the chaos of democratic politics and of the war among the so-called "special interests."

The notion that there must be "agreement on fundamentals" in order that democratic politics may go on is an illusion. Carl J. Friedrich, in *The New Image of the Common Man*, provides a discriminatory critique. While it is true that people must be prepared to accept the fact of a vote or election going against them, and to accept certain legal and juridical minima of the same sort, this is not what is meant when agreement on fundamentals is asked as the price of national unity and survival. What is meant is actually a surrender of special-interest claims, whether these grow out of ethnic loyalties, church affiliation, regional, occupational, or other ties. What is meant is agreement that democracy itself (defined to mean more, much more, than the legal minimum) is a good thing; agreement on equality of races; agreement to put American needs ahead of any foreign loyalty. Yet the fact is that our democracy, like that of Switzerland, has survived without securing such agreements. In our country, this has been attained by a party system that serves as broker among the special-interest groups: the parties do not ask for agreement on fundamentals—certainly, not on ideological fundamentals—but for much more mundane and workable concessions. At the same time, our expanding economy (and concomitantly expanding state services) has made these concessions possible without bankruptcy and, on the whole, with a steady reduction in hardship and injustice.

Those who would like to see the parties "stand for something," and those who have framed their own image of the future in terms of some Armaggedon of proletarian revolution or overthrow of the "interests," feel unhappy and misgoverned under such a system. To them it seems simply a lack of system. Thus, we are in part the victims of ideals of polity which turn our virtues into vices and which have confused the Western world since Plato's *Republic,* if not before. What we need are new ideals, framed with the future rather than the past in mind—ideals closer to the potentialities actually realizable under the impetus of industrialization.

One of the elements in such a new ideal would seem to be a relaxation of the demand for political dutifulness now made by many citizens who are worried about apathy. Apathy has many meanings. Its expression today may be one of the ways the individual—in the Soviet zone or Franco's Spain, no less than here—hides from ideological pressures, hides from "groupism." Lacking an active counterfaith in individualism, or any way of meeting up with others who share his resentments, he falls back on apathy as a mask behind which he can protect the remnants of his privacy. If it were widely recognized that not all people in a democracy need concern themselves continuously with public affairs (or with the union, or with the PTA, or what not), but that all should have a "right of veto" of which to make sparing, residual exercise, they might more readily agree to comply with the minimal demands for information and participation that such a veto would need for its effectiveness. And with politics no longer regarded as a continuous duty, people might feel less resistance to participation.

VI

If the international (and hence domestic) outlook continues to be as grim as during recent months [written in early 1950], readers may wonder whether this advocacy of "irresponsible" individualism is not sheer escapism. It would be insufficient to answer that "escape," like "compromise" or "appeasement," has become a bad word to the crusaders for political and group commitment. It would perhaps be a better answer to observe that if America is to be saved from destruction or self-destruction, it will be by preserving, as part of our armory of significant escapes, our humor and creativity and sense of perspective.

I recognize, of course, that many Americans feel guilty about their "luxuries" if others are forced to fight and suffer, and so would welcome a kind of edited hardship as an alleviation of their guilt. But though this is understandable and, in many ways, desirable, it provides the privileged countries and groups with much too limited and hence too easy a morality. The present international dangers menacing America (real enough in the view I hold of Stalinism) can obviously be used by many people in America to rationalize their partiality for the shared hardships of war against the solitary hardships of developing their individuality in time of peace.

Again, it should be obvious to the reader that I speak in a social context in which anarchy and "unbridled" individuality are much less likely prospects (except on the international scene) than the all too evident danger of the "garrison state." This danger must make us particularly sensitive to the fact that we depend for advance, in morals no less than in physical science, on individuals who have developed their individuality to a notable degree. We must give every encouragement to people to develop their private selves—to escape from groupism—while realizing that, in many cases, they will use their freedom in unattractive or "idle" ways. Our very abundance makes it possible for us, even in the midst of war, to take the minor risks and losses involved in such encouragement as against the absolutely certain risks involved in a total mobilization of intellect and imagination.

Yet in these remarks I find myself, as a final irony, addressing the defense of individualism to some presumed director of unselective service: I am using, Adam Smith style, group-survival arguments to justify the "selfish" living of an individual life. (Much of the same irony overtakes many devout people who "sell" religion as a variety of group therapy—because it is good for morale rather than for morals.) Possibly I am thereby revealing my own arguments against my own guilts. But I think more is involved. I am trying to answer Dostoevsky's Grand Inquisitor in terms that he would understand, as well as in the transcendent terms that his interlocutor, Jesus, understands. I am insisting that no ideology, however noble, can justify the sacrifice of an individual to the needs of the group. Whenever this occurs, it is the starkest tragedy, hardly less so if the individual consents (because he accepts the ideology) to the instrumental use of himself. . . .

Social science has helped us become more aware of the extent to which individuals, great and little, are the creatures of their cultural conditioning; and so we neither blame the little nor exalt the great. But the same wisdom has sometimes led us to the fallacy that, since all men have their being in culture and as the result of the culture, they owe a debt to that culture which even a lifetime of altruism could not repay. (One might as well argue, and in fact many societies in effect do, that since we are born of parents, we must feel guilt whenever we transcend their limitations!) Sometimes the point is pushed to the virtual denial of individuality: since we arise in society, it is assumed with a ferocious determinism that we can never transcend it. All such concepts are useful correctives of an earlier solipsism. But if they are extended to hold that conformity with society is not only a necessity but also a duty, they destroy that margin of freedom which gives life its savor and its endless possibility for advance.

PART III
THE INDIVIDUAL TODAY

ONE-DIMENSIONAL MAN

Herbert Marcuse

[Amidst the intellectual underpinnings of the New Left in America, the work of Herbert Marcuse figures prominently. During much of his scholarly career, he has tried, through a synthesis of Marx and Freud, to forge a radical theory of society. Here he analyzes, in materialistic and psychological terms, the impact of modern technology and apparent affluence on the individual. Marcuse concludes that modern society suppresses the real needs of individuals, supplanting them with false needs, and at the same time, manipulates the individual so that he can't tell the difference.

[Herbert Marcuse is professor of philosophy at the University of California at San Diego. He is the author of *Reason and Revolution, Eros and Civilization, Soviet Marxism, One-Dimensional Man,* and *An Essay on Liberation.*]

THE NEW FORMS OF CONTROL

A comfortable, smooth, reasonable, democratic unfreedom prevails in advanced industrial civilization, a token of technical progress. Indeed, what could be more rational than the suppression of individuality in the mechanization of socially necessary but painful performances; the concentration of individual enterprises in more effective, more productive corporations; the regulation of free competition among unequally equipped economic subjects; the curtailment of prerogatives and national sovereignties which impede the international organization of resources. That this technological order also involves a political and intellectual coordination may be a regrettable and yet promising development.

The rights and liberties which were such vital factors in the origins and earlier stages of industrial society yield to a higher stage of this society: they are losing their traditional rationale and content. Freedom of thought, speech, and conscience were—just as free enterprise, which they served to promote and protect—essentially *critical* ideas, designed to replace an obsolescent material and intellectual culture by a more productive and rational one. Once institutionalized, these rights and liberties shared the fate of the society of which they had become an integral part. The achievement cancels the premises.

To the degree to which freedom from want, the concrete substance of all freedom, is becoming a real possibility, the liberties which pertain to a state of lower productivity are losing their former content. Independence of thought, autonomy, and the right to political opposition are being deprived of their basic critical function in a society which seems increasingly capable of satisfying the needs of the individuals through the way in which it is organized. Such a society may justly demand acceptance of its principles and institutions, and reduce the opposition to the discussion and promotion of alternative policies *within* the status quo. In this respect, it seems to make little difference whether the increasing satisfaction of needs is accomplished by an authoritarian or a nonauthoritarian system. Under the conditions of a rising standard of living, nonconformity with the system itself appears to be socially useless, and the more so when it entails tangible economic and political disadvantages and threatens the smooth operation of the whole. Indeed, at least insofar as the necessities of life are involved, there seems to be no reason why the production and distribution of goods and services should proceed through the competitive concurrence of individual liberties.

Freedom of enterprise was from the beginning not altogether a blessing. As the liberty to work or to starve, it spelled toil, insecurity, and fear for the vast majority of the population. If the individual were no longer compelled to prove himself on the market, as a free economic subject, the disappearance of this kind of freedom would be one of the greatest achievements of civilization. The technological processes of mechanization and standardization might release individual energy into a yet uncharted realm of freedom beyond necessity. The very structure of human existence would be altered; the individual would be liberated from the work world's imposing upon him alien needs and alien possibilities. The individual would be free to exert autonomy over a life that would be his own. If the productive apparatus could be organized and directed toward the satisfaction of the vital needs, its control might well be centralized; such control would not prevent individual autonomy, but render it possible.

This is a goal within the capabilities of advanced industrial civilization, the "end" of technological rationality. In actual fact, however, the contrary trend operates: the apparatus imposes its economic and political requirements for defense and expansion on labor time and free time, on the material and intellectual culture. By virtue of the way it has organized its technological base, contemporary industrial society tends to be totalitarian. For "totalitarian" is not only a terroristic political coordination of society, but also a nonterroristic economic-technical coordination which operates through the manipulation of needs by vested interests. It thus precludes the emergence of an effective opposition against the whole. Not only a specific form of government or party rule makes for totalitarianism, but also a specific system of production and distribution which may well be compatible with a "pluralism" of parties, newspapers, "countervailing powers," etc.

Today political power asserts itself through its power over the machine process and over the technical organization of the apparatus. The government of advanced and advancing industrial societies can maintain and secure itself only when it succeeds in mobilizing, organizing, and exploiting the technical, scientific, and mechanical productivity available to industrial civilization. And this productivity mobilizes society as a whole, above and beyond any particular individual or group interests. The brute fact that the machine's physical (only physical?) power surpasses that of the individual, and of any particular group of individuals, makes the machine the most effective political instrument in any society whose basic organization is that of the machine process. But the political trend may be reversed; essentially the power of the machine is only the stored-up and projected power of man. To the extent to which the work world is conceived of as a machine and mechanized accordingly, it becomes the *potential* basis of a new freedom for man.

Contemporary industrial civilization demonstrates that it has reached the stage at which "the free society" can no longer be adequately defined in the traditional terms of economic, political, and intellectual liberties, not because these liberties have become insignificant, but because they are too significant to be confined within the traditional forms. New modes of realization are needed, corresponding to the new capabilities of society.

Such new modes can be indicated only in negative terms because they would amount to the negation of the prevailing modes. Thus economic freedom would mean freedom *from* the economy—from being controlled by economic forces and relationships; freedom from the daily struggle for existence, from earning a living. Political freedom would mean liberation of the individuals *from* politics over which they have no effective control. Similarly, intellectual freedom would mean the restoration of individual thought now absorbed by mass communication and indoctrination, abolition of "public opinion" together with its makers. The unrealistic sound of these propositions is indicative, not of their utopian character, but of the strength of the forces which prevent their realization. The most effective and enduring form of warfare against liberation is the implanting of material and intellectual needs that perpetuate obsolete forms of the struggle for existence.

The intensity, the satisfaction and even the character of human needs, beyond the biological level, have always been preconditioned. Whether or not the possibility of doing or leaving, enjoying or destroying, possessing or rejecting something is seized as a *need* depends on whether or not it can be seen as desirable and necessary for the prevailing societal institutions and interests. In this sense, human needs are historical needs and, to the extent to which the society demands the repressive development of the individual, his needs themselves and their claim for satisfaction are subject to overriding critical standards.

We may distinguish both true and false needs. "False" are those which are superimposed upon the individual by particular social interests in his repression: the needs which perpetuate toil, aggressiveness, misery, and injustice. Their satisfaction might be most gratifying to the individual, but this happiness is not a condition which has to be maintained and protected if it serves to arrest the development of the ability (his own and others) to recognize the disease of the whole and grasp the chances of curing the disease. The result then is euphoria in unhappiness. Most of the prevailing needs to relax, to have fun, to behave and consume in accordance with the advertisements, to love and hate what others love and hate, belong to this category of false needs.

Such needs have a societal content and function which are determined by external powers over which the individual has no control; the development and satisfaction of these needs is heteronomous. No matter how much such needs may have become the individual's own, reproduced and fortified by the conditions of his existence; no matter how much he identifies himself with them and finds himself in their satisfaction, they continue to be what they were from the beginning—products of a society whose dominant interest demands repression.

The prevalence of repressive needs is an accomplished fact, accepted in ignorance and defeat, but a fact that must be undone in the interest of the happy individual as well as all those whose misery is the price of his satisfaction. The only needs that have an unqualified claim for satisfaction are the vital ones—nourishment, clothing, lodging at the attainable level of culture. The satisfaction of these needs is the prerequisite for the realization of *all* needs, of the unsublimated as well as the sublimated ones.

For any consciousness and conscience, for any experience which does not accept the prevailing societal interest as the supreme law of thought and behavior, the established universe of needs and satisfactions is a fact to be questioned —questioned in terms of truth and falsehood. These terms are historical throughout, and their objectivity is historical.

The judgment of needs and their satisfaction, under the given conditions, involves standards of *priority*—standards which refer to the optimal development of the individual, of all individuals, under the optimal utilization of the material and intellectual resources available to man. The resources are calculable. "Truth" and "falsehood" of needs designate objective conditions to the extent to which the universal satisfaction of vital needs and, beyond it, the progressive alleviation of toil and poverty, are universally valid standards. But as historical standards, they do not only vary according to area and stage of development, they also can be defined only in (greater or lesser) *contradiction* to the prevailing ones. What tribunal can possibly claim the authority of decision?

In the last analysis, the question of what are true and false needs must be answered by the individuals themselves, but only in the last analysis; that is, if and when they are free to give their own answer. As long as they are kept incapable of being autonomous, as long as they are indoctrinated and manipulated (down to their very instincts), their answer to this question cannot be taken as their own. By the same token, however, no tribunal can justly arrogate to itself the right to decide which needs should be developed and satisfied. Any such tribunal is reprehensible, although our revulsion does not do away with the question: how can the people who have been the object of effective and productive domination by themselves create the conditions of freedom?

The more rational, productive, technical, and total the repressive administration of society becomes, the more unimaginable the means and ways by which the administered individuals might break their servitude and seize their own liberation. To be sure, to impose Reason upon an entire society is a paradoxical and scandalous idea—although one might dispute the righteousness of a society which ridicules this idea while making its own population into objects of total administration. All liberation depends on the consciousness of servitude, and the emergence of this consciousness is always hampered by the predominance of needs and satisfactions which, to a great extent, have become the individual's own. The process always replaces one system of preconditioning by another; the optimal goal is the replacement of false needs by true ones, the abandonment of repressive satisfaction.

The distinguishing feature of advanced industrial society is its effective suffocation of those needs which demand liberation—liberation also from that which is tolerable and rewarding and comfortable—while it sustains and absolves the destructive power and repressive function of the affluent society. Here, the social controls exact the overwhelming need for the production and consumption of waste; the need for stupefying work where it is no longer a real necessity; the need for modes of relaxation which soothe and prolong this stupefaction; the need for maintaining such deceptive liberties as free competition at administered prices, a free press which censors itself, free choice between brands and gadgets.

Under the rule of a repressive whole, liberty can be made into a powerful instrument of domination. The range of choice open to the individual is not the decisive factor in determining the degree of human freedom, but *what* can be chosen and what *is* chosen by the individual. The criterion for free choice can never be an absolute one, but neither is it entirely relative. Free election of masters does not abolish the masters or the slaves. Free choice among a wide variety of goods and services does not signify freedom if these goods and services sustain social controls over a life of toil and fear—that is, if they sustain alienation. And the spontaneous reproduction of superimposed needs by the individual does not establish autonomy; it only testifies to the efficacy of the controls.

Our insistence on the depth and efficacy of these controls is open to the objection that we overrate greatly the indoctrinating power of the "media," and that by themselves the people would feel and satisfy the needs which are now imposed upon them. The objection misses the point. The preconditioning does not start with the mass production of radio and television and with the centralization of their control. The people enter this stage as preconditioned receptacles of long standing; the decisive difference is in the flattening out of the contrast (or conflict) between the given and the possible, between the satisfied and the unsatisfied needs. Here, the so-called equalization of class distinctions reveals its ideological function. If the worker and his boss enjoy the same television program and visit the same resort places, if the typist is as attractively made up as the daughter of her employer, if the Negro owns a Cadillac, if they all read the same newspaper, then this assimilation indicates not the disappearance of classes, but the extent to which the needs and satisfactions that serve the preservation of the Establishment are shared by the underlying population.

Indeed, in the most highly developed areas of contemporary society, the transplantation of social into individual needs is so effective that the difference between them seems to be purely theoretical. Can one really distinguish between the mass media as instruments of information and entertainment, and as agents of manipulation and indoctrination? Between the automobile as nuisance and as convenience? Between the horrors and the comforts of functional architecture? Between the work for national defense and the work for corporate gain? Between the private pleasure and the commercial and political utility involved in increasing the birthrate?

We are again confronted with one of the most vexing aspects of advanced industrial civilization: the rational character of its irrationality. Its productivity and efficiency, its capacity to increase and spread comforts, to turn waste into need, and destruction into construction, the extent to which this civilization transforms the object world into an extension of man's mind and body makes the very notion of alienation questionable. The people recognize themselves in their commodities; they find their soul in their automobile, hi-fi set, split-level home, kitchen equipment. The very mechanism which ties the individual to his society has changed, and social control is anchored in the new needs which it has produced.

The prevailing forms of social control are technological in a new sense. To be sure, the technical structure and efficacy of the productive and destructive apparatus has been a major instrumentality for subjecting the population to the established social division of labor throughout the modern period. Moreover, such integration has always been accompanied by more obvious forms of compulsion: loss of livelihood, the administration of justice, the police, the armed forces. It still is. But in the contemporary period, the technological controls appear to be the very embodiment of Reason for the benefit of all social groups and interests—to such an extent that all contradiction seems irrational and all counteraction impossible.

No wonder then that, in the most advanced areas of this civilization, the social controls have been introjected to the point where even individual protest is affected at its roots. The intellectual and emotional refusal "to go along" appears neurotic and impotent. This is the sociopsychological aspect of the political event that marks the contemporary period: the passing of the historical forces which, at the preceding stage of industrial society, seemed to represent the possibility of new forms of existence.

But the term "introjection" perhaps no longer describes the way in which the individual by himself reproduces and perpetuates the external controls exercised by his society. Introjection suggests a variety of relatively spontaneous processes by which a Self (Ego) transposes the "outer" into the "inner." Thus introjection implies the existence of an inner dimension distinguished from and even antagonistic to the external exigencies—an individual consciousness and an individual unconscious *apart from* public opinion and behavior.[1] The idea of "inner freedom" here has its reality: it designates the private space in which man may become and remain "himself."

Today this private space has been invaded and whittled down by technological reality. Mass production and mass distribution claim the *entire* individual, and industrial psychology has long since ceased to be confined to the factory. The manifold processes of introjection seem to be ossified in almost mechanical reactions. The result is, not adjustment but *mimesis:* an immediate identification of the individual with *his* society and, through it, with the society as a whole.

[1] The change in the function of the family here plays a decisive role: its "socializing" functions are increasingly taken over by outside groups and media. See my *Eros and Civilization* (Boston: Beacon Press, 1955), pp. 96ff.

This immediate, automatic identification (which may have been characteristic of primitive forms of association) reappears in high industrial civilization; its new "immediacy," however, is the product of a sophisticated, scientific management and organization. In this process, the "inner" dimension of the mind in which opposition to the status quo can take root is whittled down. The loss of this dimension, in which the power of negative thinking—the critical power of Reason—is at home, is the ideological counterpart to the very material process in which advanced industrial society silences and reconciles the opposition. The impact of progress turns Reason into submission to the facts of life, and to the dynamic capability of producing more and bigger facts of the same sort of life. The efficiency of the system blunts the individuals' recognition that it contains no facts which do not communicate the repressive power of the whole. If the individuals find themselves in the things which shape their life, they do so, not by giving, but by accepting the law of things—not the law of physics but the law of their society.

I have just suggested that the concept of alienation seems to become questionable when the individuals identify themselves with the existence which is imposed upon them and have in it their own development and satisfaction. This identification is not illusion but reality. However, the reality constitutes a more progressive stage of alienation. The latter has become entirely objective; the subject which is alienated is swallowed up by its alienated existence. There is only one dimension, and it is everywhere and in all forms. The achievements of progress defy ideological indictment as well as justification; before their tribunal, the "false consciousness" of their rationality becomes the true consciousness.

This absorption of ideology into reality does not, however, signify the "end of ideology." On the contrary, in a specific sense advanced industrial culture is *more* ideological than its predecessor, inasmuch as today the ideology is in the process of production itself.[2] In a provocative form,

---

[2] Theodor W. Adorno, *Prismen. Kulturkritik und Gesellschaft.* (Frankfurt: Suhrkamp, 1955), pp. 24ff.

this proposition reveals the political aspects of the prevailing technological rationality. The productive apparatus and the goods and services which it produces "sell" or impose the social system as a whole. The means of mass transportation and communication, the commodities of lodging, food, and clothing, the irresistible output of the entertainment and information industry carry with them prescribed attitudes and habits, certain intellectual and emotional reactions which bind the consumers more or less pleasantly to the producers and, through the latter, to the whole. The products indoctrinate and manipulate; they promote a false consciousness which is immune against its falsehood. And as these beneficial products become available to more individuals in more social classes, the indoctrination they carry ceases to be publicity; it becomes a way of life. It is a good way of life—much better than before—and as a good way of life, it militates against qualitative change. Thus emerges a pattern of *one-dimensional thought and behavior* in which ideas, aspirations, and objectives that, by their content, transcend the established universe of discourse and action are either repelled or reduced to terms of this universe. They are redefined by the rationality of the given system and of its quantitative extension.

The trend may be related to a development in scientific method: operationalism in the physical, behaviorism in the social sciences. The common feature is a total empiricism in the treatment of concepts; their meaning is restricted to the representation of particular operations and behavior. The operational point of view is well illustrated by P. W. Bridgman's analysis of the concept of length [3]:

[3] P. W. Bridgman, *The Logic of Modern Physics* (New York: Macmillan, 1928), p. 5. The operational doctrine has since been refined and qualified. Bridgman himself has extended the concept of "operation" to include the "paper-and-pencil" operations of the theorist (in Philipp J. Frank, *The Validation of Scientific Theories* [Boston: Beacon Press, 1954], Chap. II). The main impetus remains the same: it is "desirable" that the paper-and-pencil operations "be capable of eventual contact, although perhaps indirectly, with instrumental operations."

We evidently know what we mean by length if we can tell what the length of any and every object is, and for the physicist nothing more is required. To find the length of an object, we have to perform certain physical operations. The concept of length is therefore fixed when the operations by which length is measured are fixed: that is, the concept of length involves as much and nothing more than the set of operations by which length is determined. In general, we mean by any concept nothing more than a set of operations; *the concept is synonymous with the corresponding set of operations.*

Bridgman has seen the wide implications of this mode of thought for the society at large [4]:

To adopt the operational point of view involves much more than a mere restriction of the sense in which we understand "concept," but means a far-reaching change in all our habits of thought, in that we shall no longer permit ourselves to use as tools in our thinking concepts of which we cannot give an adequate account in terms of operations.

Bridgman's prediction has come true. The new mode of thought is today the predominant tendency in philosophy, psychology, sociology, and other fields. Many of the most seriously troublesome concepts are being "eliminated" by showing that no adequate account of them in terms of operations or behavior can be given. The radical empiricist onslaught thus provides the methodological justification for the debunking of the mind by the intellectuals—a positivism which, in its denial of the transcending elements of Reason, forms the academic counterpart of the socially required behavior.

Outside the academic establishment, the "far-reaching change in all our habits of thought" is more serious. It serves to coordinate ideas and goals with those exacted by the prevailing system, to enclose them in the system, and

4 P. W. Bridgman, *op. cit.*, p. 31.

to repel those which are irreconcilable with the system. The reign of such a one-dimensional reality does not mean that materialism rules, and that the spiritual, metaphysical, and bohemian occupations are petering out. On the contrary, there is a great deal of "Worship together this week," "Why not try God," Zen, existentialism, and beat ways of life, etc. But such modes of protest and transcendence are no longer contradictory to the status quo and no longer negative. They are rather the ceremonial part of practical behaviorism, its harmless negation, and are quickly digested by the status quo as part of its healthy diet.

One-dimensional thought is systematically promoted by the makers of politics and their purveyors of mass information. Their universe of discourse is populated by self-validating hypotheses which, incessantly and monopolistically repeated, become hypnotic definitions or dictations. For example, "free" are the institutions which operate (and are operated on) in the countries of the Free World; other transcending modes of freedom are by definition either anarchism, communism, or propaganda. "Socialistic" are all encroachments on private enterprises not undertaken by private enterprise itself (or by government contracts), such as universal and comprehensive health insurance, or the protection of nature from all too sweeping commercialization, or the establishment of public services which may hurt private profit. This totalitarian logic of accomplished facts has its Eastern counterpart. There, freedom is the way of life instituted by a communist regime, and all other transcending modes of freedom are either capitalistic, or revisionist, or leftist sectarianism. In both camps, nonoperational ideas are nonbehavioral and subversive. The movement of thought is stopped at barriers which appear as the limits of Reason itself.

Such limitation of thought is certainly not new. Ascending modern rationalism, in its speculative as well as empirical form, shows a striking contrast between extreme critical radicalism in scientific and philosophic method on the one hand, and an uncritical quietism in the attitude toward established and functioning social institutions. Thus Descartes' *ego cogitans* was to leave the "great public bodies" untouched, and Hobbes held that "the present ought always to be preferred, maintained, and accounted best." Kant agreed with Locke in justifying revolution *if and when* it has succeeded in organizing the whole and in preventing subversion.

However, these accommodating concepts of Reason were always contradicted by the evident misery and injustice of the "great public bodies" and the effective, more or less conscious rebellion against them. Societal conditions existed which provoked and permitted real dissociation from the established state of affairs; a private as well as political dimension was present in which dissociation could develop into effective opposition, testing its strength and the validity of its objectives.

With the gradual closing of this dimension by the society, the self-limitation of thought assumes a larger significance. The interrelation between scientific-philosophical and societal processes, between theoretical and practical Reason, asserts itself "behind the back" of the scientists and philosophers. The society bars a whole type of oppositional operations and behavior; consequently, the concepts pertaining to them are rendered illusory or meaningless. Historical transcendence appears as metaphysical transcendence, not acceptable to science and scientific thought. The operational and behavioral point of view, practiced as a "habit of thought" at large, becomes the view of the established universe of discourse and action, needs and aspirations. The "cunning of Reason" works, as it so often did, in the interest of the powers that be. The insistence on operational and behavioral concepts turns against the efforts to free thought and behavior *from* the given reality and *for* the suppressed alternatives. Theoretical and practical Reason, academic and social behaviorism meet on common ground: that of an advanced society which makes scientific and technical progress into an instrument of domination.

"Progress" is not a neutral term; it moves toward specific ends, and these ends are defined by the possibilities of ameliorating the human condition. Advanced industrial society is approaching the stage where continued progress would demand the radical subversion of the prevailing direction and organization of progress. This stage would be reached when material production (including the necessary services) becomes automated to the extent that all vital needs can be satisfied while necessary labor time is reduced to marginal time. From this point on, technical progress would transcend the realm of necessity, where it served as the instrument of domination and exploitation which thereby limited its rationality; technology would become subject to the free play of faculties in the struggle for the pacification of nature and of society.

Such a state is envisioned in Marx's notion of the "abolition of labor." The term "pacification of existence" seems better suited to designate the historical alternative of a world which—through an international conflict which transforms and suspends the contradictions within the established societies—advances on the brink of a global war. "Pacification of existence" means the development of man's struggle with man and with nature, under conditions where the competing needs, desires, and aspirations are no longer organized by vested interests in domination and scarcity— an organization which perpetuates the destructive forms of this struggle.

Today's fight against this historical alternative finds a firm mass basis in the underlying population, and finds its ideology in the rigid orientation of thought and behavior to the given universe of facts. Validated by the accomplishments of science and technology, justified by its growing productivity, the status quo defies all transcendence. Faced with the possibility of pacification on the grounds of its technical and intellectual achievements, the mature industrial society closes itself against this alternative. Operationalism, in theory and practice, becomes the theory and practice of *containment*. Underneath its obvious dynamics, this society is a thoroughly static system of life: self-propelling in its oppressive productivity and in its beneficial coordination. Containment of technical progress goes hand in hand with its growth in the established direction. In spite of the political fetters imposed by the status quo, the more technology appears capable of creating the conditions for pacification, the more are the minds and bodies of man organized against this alternative.

The most advanced areas of industrial society exhibit throughout these two features: a trend toward consummation of technological rationality, and intensive efforts to contain this trend within the established institutions. Here is the internal contradiction of this civilization: the irrational element in its rationality. It is the token of its achievements. The industrial society which makes technology and science its own is organized for the ever-more effective domination of man and nature, for the ever-more effective utilization of its resources. It becomes irrational when the success of these efforts opens new dimensions of human realization. Organization for peace is different from organization for war; the institutions which served the struggle for existence cannot serve the pacification of existence. Life as an end is qualitatively different from life as a means.

Such a qualitatively new mode of existence can never be envisaged as the mere by-product of economic and political changes, as the more or less spontaneous effect of the new institutions which constitute the necessary prerequisite. Qualitative change also involves a change in the *technical* basis on which this society rests—one which sustains the economic and political institutions through which the "second nature" of man as an aggressive object of administration is stabilized. The techniques of industrialization are political techniques; as such, they prejudge the possibilities of Reason and Freedom.

To be sure, labor must precede the reduction of labor, and industrialization must precede the development of human needs and satisfactions. But as all freedom depends on the conquest of alien necessity, the realization of freedom depends on the *techniques* of this conquest. The highest productivity of labor can be used for the perpetuation of labor, and the most efficient industrialization can serve the restriction and manipulation of needs.

When this point is reached, domination—in the guise of affluence and liberty—extends to all spheres of private and public existence, integrates all authentic opposition, absorbs all alternatives. Technological rationality reveals its political character as it becomes the great vehicle of better domination, creating a truly totalitarian universe in which society and nature, mind and body are kept in a state of permanent mobilization for the defense of this universe.

BLACK MANHOOD

William H. Grier and Price M. Cobbs

[The most serious and long-standing challenge to the
American ideal of individualism is the nation's treatment of its black minority. Continued segregation and
discrimination, as well as the long heritage of racism,
still make it exceedingly difficult for a black man to
grow up in this country and retain his manhood. Two
psychiatrists analyze the damage to individuality caused
by a racist society.

[William Grier and Price Cobbs are assistant professors of psychiatry at the University of California Medical Center at San Francisco. They are the authors of
Black Rage.]

. . . The black boy in growing up in America encounters some strange impediments. Schools discourage
his ambitions, training for valued skills is not available
to him, and when he does triumph in some youthful competition, he receives compromised praise, not the glory he
might expect. In time he comes to see that society has
locked arms *against* him, that rather than help he can expect opposition to his development, and that he lives not
in a benign community but in a society that views his
growth with hostility.

For the black man in this country, it is not so much a
matter of acquiring manhood as it is a struggle to feel it
his own. Whereas the white man regards his manhood as
an ordained right, the black man is engaged in a never-
ending battle for its possession. For the black man, attaining any portion of manhood is an active process. He

must penetrate barriers and overcome opposition in order to assume a masculine posture. For the inner psychological obstacles to manhood are never so formidable as the impediments woven into American society. By contrast, for a white man in this country, the rudiments of manhood are settled at birth by the possession of a penis and a white skin. This biological affirmation of masculinity and identity as master is enough to insure that, whatever his individual limitations, this society will not systematically erect obstructions to his achievement.

Throughout his life, at each critical point of development the black boy is told to hold back, to constrict, to subvert and camouflage his normal masculinity. Male assertiveness becomes a forbidden fruit, and if it is attained, it must be savored privately.

Manhood must always be defined for the setting in which it occurs. A man in a Siberian village may be very different from a man in a Chicago suburb. Biologically they share the same drives and limitations, but their societies may decree totally different roles. Manhood in this country has many meanings, but a central theme is clear. Men are very early taught that they have certain prerogatives and privileges. They are encouraged to pursue, to engage life, to attack, rather than to shrink back. They learn early that to express a certain amount of aggression and assertion is manly. Every playground, every schoolyard is filled with boys fighting and attacking, playing at being grown up. The popular heroes in this country are men who express themselves aggressively and assertively.

As boys approach adulthood, masculinity becomes more and more bound up with moneymaking. In a capitalistic society economic wealth is inextricably interwoven with manhood. Closely allied is power—power to control and direct other men, power to influence the course of one's own and other lives. The more lives one can influence, the greater the power. The ultimate power is the freedom to understand and alter one's life. It is this power, both individually and collectively, which has been denied the black man.

Under slavery, the black man was a psychologically emasculated and totally dependent human being. Times and conditions have changed, but black men continue to exhibit the inhibitions and psychopathology that had their genesis in the slave experience. It would seem that for masculine growth and development the psychological conditions have not changed very much. Better jobs are available, housing is improving, and all the external signs of progress can be seen, but the American heritage of racism will still not allow the black man to feel himself master in his own land. The black man in this society, more than other men, is shaped by currents more powerful than the course of his own life. There are rules which regulate black lives far more than the lives of white men.

The simplistic view of the black family as a matriarchy is an unfortunate theme repeated too often by scholars who should know better. If a man is stripped of his authority in the home by forces outside that home, the woman naturally must assume the status of head of household. This is the safety factor inherent in a household which includes two adults and it by no means suggests that the woman prefers it that way. If a woman is widowed, she may assume many masculine functions, but the household may be a patriarchy without a patriarch.

In the black household the man faces greater than usual odds in making his way. The care and rearing of children falls even more heavily on the wife; she is the culture bearer. She interprets the society to the children and takes as her task the shaping of their character to meet the world as she knows it. This is every mother's task. But the black mother has a more ominous message for her child and feels more urgently the need to get the message across. The child must know that the white world is dangerous and that if he does not understand its rules, it may kill him.

When black men recall their early life, consistent themes emerge. For example, the mother is generally perceived as having been sharply contradictory. She may have been permissive in some areas and punitive and rigid in others. There are remembrances of stimulation and gratification coexisting with memories of deprivation and rejection. There is always a feeling that the behavior of the mother was purposeful and deliberate.

The black man remembers that his mother underwent frequent and rapid shifts of mood. He remembers the cruelty. The mother who sang spirituals gently at church was capable of inflicting senseless pain at home. These themes of gratification and cruelty are consistent enough to suggest that they played a critical role in preparing the boy for adulthood. It would seem that the boy had to experience the polarities of ambivalence so that he could understand his later role in a white society. He must be adequately prepared.

The black mother shares a burden with her soul sisters of three centuries ago. She must produce and shape and mold a unique type of man. She must intuitively cut off and blunt his masculine assertiveness and aggression lest these put the boy's life in jeopardy.

During slavery the danger was real. A slave boy could not show too much aggression. The feelings of anger and frustration which channeled themselves into aggression had to be thwarted. If they were not, the boy would have little or no use as a slave and would be slain. If any feelings, especially those of assertive manhood, were expressed too strongly, then that slave was a threat, not only to himself and his master but to the entire system as well. For that, he would have to be killed.

The black mother continues this heritage from slavery and simultaneously reflects the world she now knows. Even today, the black man cannot become too aggressive without hazard to himself. To do so is to challenge the delicate balance of a complex social system. Every mother, of whatever color and degree of proficiency, knows what the society in which she lives will require of her children. Her basic job is to prepare the child for this. Because of the institutionalization of barriers, the black mother knows even more surely what society requires of *her* children. What at first seemed a random pattern of mothering has gradually assumed a definite and deliberate, if unconscious, method of preparing a black boy for his subordinate place in the world.

As a result, black men develop considerable hostility toward black women as the inhibiting instruments of an oppressive system. The woman has more power, more accessibility into the system, and therefore she is more feared, while at the same time envied. And it is her lot in life to suppress masculine assertiveness in her sons.

Mr. R. was a writer who presented himself for treatment in his mid-fifties. In his younger days he had enjoyed success and a certain amount of adulation in white society. Throughout the course of treatment he presented a picture of culture and refinement. His trouble was that several years earlier he had lost the spark of creativity and his writing ceased. He made frequent resolutions to resume writing, but this motivation never matched his ambition.

It developed that he was afraid to compete with white men as a writer. Whatever he wrote, his obsessional fears dictated that somewhere someone who was white had written something better. He was a defeated and despairing man when he entered treatment. He had, however, a delicious secret which he used as comfort when he was most depressed.

His face would crease with a smile when he recounted his numerous affairs as a young man. In all his life he never doubted his ability to outperform a white man sexually. He told how he had "banged many white women." He sometimes spoke of himself as a deformed man or as a cripple, but sex was the one area in which he felt completely adequate.

The mythology and folklore of black people is filled with tales of sexually prodigious men. Most boys grow up on a steady diet of folk heroes who have distinguished themselves by sexual feats. It is significant that few, if any, of these folk heroes are directing armies or commanding empires. Dreams must in some way reflect reality, and in this country the black man, until quite recently, had not been in positions of power. His wielding of power had been in the privacy of the boudoir.

To be sure, black men have sexual problems. They may have impotence, premature ejaculation, and the entire range of pathology which limits and distorts sexual life. Such ailments have the same dynamic origins in men of all races. But where sex is employed as armament and used as a conscious and deliberate means of defense, it is the black man who chooses this weapon. If he cannot fight the white man openly, he can and does battle him secretly. Recurrently, the pattern evolves of black men using sex as a dagger to be symbolically thrust into the white man.

A black man who was an orderly in a hospital had an eighth-grade education and felt himself inadequate in most endeavors. If called upon to perform a new duty, he would reflect for a moment and feel dumbstruck. One evening an attractive young nurse made seductive overtures to him. At first he was not convinced that she was serious but thought she was playing a game. When he discovered that she meant it, he took her to bed with a vengeance. During the weekly therapy hour he would elaborate and expand on his feats. One central fact became more and more clear. He was able to state very directly that every time he possessed the girl sexually, he was making up for having sat on the back of the bus and having endured numberless humiliations. He was getting revenge for generations of slavery and degradation.

One of the constant themes in black folklore is the "bad nigger." It seems that every community has had one or was afraid of having one. They were feared as much by blacks as by whites. In the slave legends there are tales of docile fieldhands suddenly going berserk. It was a common enough phenomenon to appear in writings of the times and to stimulate the erection of defenses against this violent kind of man.

Today black boys are admonished not to be a "bad nigger." No description need be offered; every black child knows what is meant. They are angry and hostile. They strike fear into everyone with their uncompromising rejection of restraint or inhibition. They may seem at one moment meek and compromised—and in the next a terrifying killer. Because of his experience in this country, every black man harbors a potential bad nigger inside him. He must ignore this inner man. The bad nigger is bad because he has been required to renounce his manhood to save his life. The more one approaches the American ideal of respectability, the more this hostility must be repressed. The bad nigger is a defiant nigger, a reminder of what manhood could be.

Cultural stereotypes of the savage rapist-Negro express the fear that the black man will turn on his tormentors. Negro organizations dread the presence of the bad nigger. White merchants who have contact with black people have uneasy feelings when they see a tight mouth, a hard look, and an angry black face. The bad nigger in black men no doubt accounts for more worry in both races than any other single factor.

Granting the limitations of stereotypes, we should nevertheless like to sketch a paradigmatic black man. His characteristics seem so connected to employment that we call it "the postal-clerk syndrome." This man is always described as "nice" by white people. In whatever integrated setting he works, he is the standard against whom other blacks are measured. "If they were all only like him, everything would be so much better." He is passive, nonassertive, and non-aggressive. He has made a virtue of identification with the aggressor, and he has adopted an ingratiating and compliant manner. In public his thoughts and feelings are consciously shaped in the direction he thinks white people want them to be. The pattern begins in childhood when the mother may actually say: "You must be this way because this is the only way you will get along with Mr. Charlie."

This man renounces gratifications that are available to others. He assumes a deferential mask. He is always submissive. He must figure out "the man" but keep "the man" from deciphering him. He is prevalent in the middle and upper-middle classes, but is found throughout the social structure. The more closely allied to the white man, the more complete the picture becomes. He is a direct lineal descendant of the "house nigger" who was designed to identify totally with the white master. The danger he poses to himself and others is great, but only the surface of passivity and compliance is visible. The storm below is hidden.

A leading Negro citizen came to a therapy session with his wife, who was suffering from a severe and intractable melancholia. She had several times seriously attempted suicide. The last attempt was particularly serious. She was angry with her husband and berated him for never opening up and exposing his feelings. For his part, the husband remained "nice." He never raised his voice above a murmur. His wife could goad him, but he was the epitome of understanding. He was amenable to all suggestions. His manner and gestures were deliberate, studied, and noninflammatory. Everything was understated. During the course of treatment he was involved in several civil-rights crises. His public life was an extension of his private one, and he used such words as "moderation" and "responsibility." His entire life was a study in passivity, in how to play at being a man without really being one.

It would be easy to write off this man as an isolated passive individual, but his whole community looks upon his career as a success story. He made it in the system to a position of influence and means. And it took an aggressive, driving, determined man to make it against the odds he faced. We must ask how much energy is required for him to conceal his drive so thoroughly. And we wonder what would happen if his controls ever failed.

Starting with slavery, black people, and more particularly black men, have had to devise ways of expressing themselves uniquely and individually and in a manner that was not threatening to the white man. Some methods of giving voice to aggressive masculinity have become institutionalized. The most stylized is the posture of "playing it cool."

The playing-it-cool style repeats itself over and over again in all aspects of black life. It is an important means of expression and is widely copied in the larger white culture. A man may be overwhelmed with conflict, threatened with an eruption of feelings, and barely maintaining his composure, but he will present a serene exterior. He may fear the eruption of repressed feelings if they bring a loss of control, but an important aspect of his containment is the fear that his aggression will be directed against the white world and will bring swift punishment. The intrapsychic dynamics may be similar in a white man, but for the black man it is socially far more important that the facade be maintained.

Patients have come for treatment who have had one or two visits with a variety of psychiatrists, psychologists, and social workers. In many cases they were written off as having no significant pathology or as being "poor patients." The importance of the cool style is apparent when one realizes the cost and suffering required to maintain it. Those who practice it have raised to a high art a life-style which seems a peculiarly black contribution to adaptation in this society.

Several decades ago, observers were impressed by the black community's adulation of Joe Louis. They were a starved and deprived group, but, even so, their deification of him seemed all out of proportion. In retrospect, there is an explanation. In the ring he was the picture of fury. As he demolished foe after foe, every black man could vicariously taste his victory. If his victims were white, the pleasure was even greater. He symbolized assertiveness and unbridled aggression for the black man. In watching him or reading about him, an entire community could find expression through him of inhibited masculine drives. As others have entered professional sports in later years, the heroes have served a similar purpose. Educated and sophisticated Negroes also participate in this hero worship, since all black men swim in the same sea.

A black man in treatment kept reaching for a memory. He finally recalled watching a fight on television, at a time when a black coed, Authurine Lucey, was integrating the University of Alabama. The contest was between a black and white fighter. During the bout he kept hearing someone shout: "Hit him one for Authurine." Even after he had forgotten the fight, the phrase kept returning to his mind, "Hit him one for Authurine." It became his battle cry. Whenever he was pressed, the thought would come again and again in an obsessional fashion. He then began to talk of his own repressed aggression and the pieces of the puzzle began to fit, and the obsession receded.

When all the repressive forces fail and aggression erupts,

it is vital that we ask the right questions. The issue is not what caused the riots of the past few years—that is clear to any man who has eyes. Rather, we must ask: What held this aggression in check for so long and what is the nature of this breached barrier. Dare anyone try to reconstruct it?

During the riots there was a wry saying in the ghetto: "Chuck can't tell where it's going to hit next because we don't know ourselves." And it was a fact. The most baffling aspect to rioting in Newark, Detroit, and Watts was the complete spontaneity of the violence. Authorities turned to "responsible" Negro leaders to calm the black rebels and the Negro leaders did not know where to start. They were confronted with a leaderless mob which needed no leader. Every man was a leader—they were of one mind.

The goods of America, piled high in the neighborhood stores, had been offered to them with a price tag that made work slavery and made balancing a budget a farce. The pressure was ever on parents to buy a television set, to buy kitchen appliances and new cars. The available jobs paid so poorly and the prices (plus interest) of goods were so high that if one made a purchase, he was entering upon years of indebtedness.

The carrot held in front of the ghetto laborer is the consumer item—the auto, the TV, and the hi-fi set. If the poor black man falls into place in America, he takes whatever job is offered, receives minimal pay, purchases hard goods at harder prices, and teeters from insolvency to bankruptcy in the ghetto.

Exhausted, he was offered a stimulant in the form of the civil-rights laws. When it became clear that they were nothing more than words from Washington, he kicked over the traces. He took a shortcut. Instead of working for a lifetime to buy a piece of slum property which might fall at any moment and which he would likely never own anyway—instead of this treadmill, he burned it down. Instead of working for years to pay three times the usual cost of a television set, he broke a window and stole it. Instead of the desperate, frustrating search to find out which white man was friendly and which was hostile, he simply labeled them all the enemy. There never seemed to be a great deal of difference between friends and enemies anyway. So in a spontaneous blast he burned up the ghetto. And the wrong question continued to be asked: Why a riot in Detroit, where conditions were so good?

The worst slum and the best slum are very close together compared with the distance separating the world of black men and the world of whites. At bottom, America remains a slave country which happens to have removed the slave laws from the books. The question we must ask is: What held the slave rebellion in check for so long?

The racist tradition is pervasive and envelops every American. For black men it constitutes a heavy psychological burden. From the unemployed, illiterate ghetto dweller to the urbanized man living in an integrated setting, careful examination shows psychological scars. Black men fight one another, do violence to property, do hurtful things to themselves while nursing growing hatred for the system which oppresses and humiliates them. Their manhood is tested daily. As one patient expressed it: "The black man in this country fights the main event in Madison Square Garden every day."

THE INDIVIDUAL
AND THE TECHNOCRACY

John Kenneth Galbraith

[American business was, at one time, the preeminent domain of "rugged individualism." The independent entrepreneur or swashbuckling corporation president occupies an honored place in our national mythology: John D. Rockefeiier, Andrew Carnegie, J. P. Morgan. Today, however, business is dominated by a "faceless" managerial class. John Kenneth Galbraith sharply sketches these changes and analyzes the implications of the new technocracy for individualism.

[John Kenneth Galbraith is professor of economics at Harvard University. He is the author of *The Affluent Society, The Liberal Hour, Economic Development,* and *The New Industrial State*.]

THE TECHNOSTRUCTURE

. . . The prevalence of group, instead of individual, action is a striking characteristic of management organization in the large corporations.

> —R. A. GORDON, *Business Leadership in the Large Corporation*

1

The individual has far more standing in our culture than the group. An individual has a presumption of accomplishment; a committee has a presumption of inaction.[1]

---

[1] "Of the various mechanisms of management, none is more controversial than committees. . . . Despite their alleged shortcomings, committees are an important device of administration." Paul E.

We react sympathetically to the individual who seeks to safeguard his personality from engulfment by the mass. We call for proof, at least in principle, before curbing his aggressions against society. Individuals have souls; corporations are notably soulless. The entrepreneur—individualistic, restless, with vision, guile and courage—has been the economists' only hero. The great business organization arouses no similar admiration. Admission to heaven is individually and by families; the top management even of an enterprise with an excellent corporate image cannot yet go in as a group. To have, in pursuit of truth, to assert the superiority of the organization over the individual for important social tasks is a taxing prospect.

Yet it is a necessary task. It is not to individuals but to organizations that power in the business enterprise and power in the society has passed. And modern economic society can only be understood as an effort, wholly successful, to synthesize by organization a group personality far superior *for its purposes* to a natural person and with the added advantage of immortality.

The need for such a group personality begins with the circumstance that in modern industry a large number of decisions, and *all* that are important, draw on information possessed by more than one man. Typically they draw on the specialized scientific and technical knowledge, the accumulated information or experience and the artistic or intuitive sense of many persons. And this is guided by further information which is assembled, analyzed and interpreted by professionals using highly technical equipment. The final decision will be informed only as it draws systematically on all those whose information is relevant. Nor, human beings what they are, can it take all of the information that is offered at face value. There must, additionally, be a mechanism for testing each person's contribution for its relevance and reliability as it is brought to bear on the decision.

Holden, Lounsbury S. Fish and Hubert L. Smith, *Top Management Organization and Control* (New York: McGraw, 1951), p. 59.

2

The need to draw on, and appraise, the information of numerous individuals in modern industrial decision-making has three principal points of origin. It derives, first, from the technological requirements of modern industry. It is not that these are always inordinately sophisticated; a man of moderate genius could, quite conceivably, provide himself with the knowledge of the various branches of metallurgy and chemistry, and of engineering, procurement, production management, quality control, labor relations, styling and merchandising which are involved in the development of a modern motorcar. But even moderate genius is in unpredictable supply, and to keep abreast of all these branches of science, engineering and art would be time-consuming even for a genius. The elementary solution, which allows of the use of far more common talent and with far greater predictability of result, is to have men who are appropriately qualified or experienced in each limited area of specialized knowledge or art. Their information is then combined for carrying out the design and production of the vehicle. It is a common public impression, not discouraged by scientists, engineers and industrialists, that modern scientific, engineering and industrial achievements are the work of a new and quite remarkable race of men. This is pure vanity; were it so, there would be few such achievements. The real accomplishment of modern science and technology consists in taking ordinary men, informing them narrowly and deeply and then, through appropriate organization, arranging to have their knowledge combined with that of other specialized but equally ordinary men. This dispenses with the need for genius. The resulting performance, though less inspiring, is far more predictable.

The second factor requiring the combination of specialized talent derives from advanced technology, the associated use of capital, and the resulting need for planning with its accompanying control of environment. The market is, in remarkable degree, an intellectually undemanding institution. The Wisconsin farmer need not anticipate his requirements for fertilizers, pesticides or even machine parts; the market stocks and supplies them. The cost of these is substantially the same for the man of intelligence and for his neighbor who, under medical examination, shows daylight in either ear. And the farmer need have no price or selling strategy; the market takes all his milk at the ruling price. Much of the appeal of the market, to economists at least, has been from the way it seems to simplify life. Better orderly error than complex truth.

For complexity enters with planning and is endemic thereto. The manufacturer of missiles, space vehicles or modern aircraft must foresee the requirements for specialized plant, specialized manpower, exotic materials and intricate components and take steps to insure their availability when they are needed. For procuring such things, the market is either unreliable or unavailable. And there is no open market for the finished product. Everything here depends on the care and skill with which contracts are sought and nurtured in Washington or in Whitehall or Paris.

The same foresight and responding action are required, in lesser degree, from manufacturers of automobiles, processed foods and detergents. They too must foresee requirements and manage markets. Planning, in short, requires a great variety of information. It requires variously informed men and women who are suitably specialized in obtaining the requisite information. There must be men whose knowledge allows them to foresee need and to insure a supply of labor, materials and other production requirements; those who have knowledge to plan price strategies and see that customers are suitably persuaded to buy at these prices; those who, at higher levels of technology, are so informed that they can work effectively with the state to see that it is suitably guided; and those who can organize the flow of information that the above tasks and many others require. Thus, to the requirements of technology for specialized technical and scientific talent are added the very large further requirements of the planning that technology makes necessary.

Finally, following from the need for this variety of specialized talent, is the need for its coordination. Talent must be brought to bear on the common purpose. More specifically, on large and small matters, information must be extracted from the various specialists, tested for its reliability and relevance, and made to yield a decision. This process, which is much misunderstood, requires a special word.

3

The modern business organization, or that part which has to do with guidance and direction, consists of numerous individuals who are engaged, at any given time, in obtaining, digesting or exchanging and testing information. A very large part of the exchange and testing of information is by word of mouth—a discussion in an office, at lunch or over the telephone. But the most typical procedure is through the committee and the committee meeting. One can do worse than think of a business organization as a hierarchy of committees. Coordination, in turn, consists in assigning the appropriate talent to committees, intervening on occasion to force a decision, and, as the case may be, announcing the decision or carrying it as information for a yet further decision by a yet higher committee.

Nor should it be supposed that this is an inefficient procedure. On the contrary it is, normally, the only efficient procedure. Association in a committee enables each member to come to know the intellectual resources and the reliability of his colleagues. Committee discussion enables members to pool information under circumstances which allow also of immediate probing to assess the relevance and reliability of the information offered. Uncertainty about one's information or error is revealed as in no other way. There is also, no doubt, considerable stimulus to mental effort from such association. One may enjoy the luxury of torpor in private but not so comfortably in public at least during working hours. Men who believe themselves deeply engaged in private thought are usually doing nothing. Committees are condemned by the cliché that individual effort is somehow superior to group effort; by those who guiltily suspect that since group effort is more congenial, it must be less productive; and by those who do not see that the process of extracting, and especially of testing, information has necessarily a somewhat undirected quality—briskly conducted meetings invariably decide matters previously decided; and by those who fail to realize that highly paid men, when sitting around a table as a committee, are not necessarily wasting more time than, in the aggregate, they would each waste in private by themselves.[2] Forthright and determined administrators frequently react to belief in the superior capacity of individuals for decision by abolishing all committees. They then constitute working parties, task forces, assault teams or executive groups in order to avoid the one truly disastrous consequence of their action which would be that they should make the decisions themselves.

Thus decision in the modern business enterprise is the product not of individuals but of groups. The groups are numerous, as often informal as formal, and subject to constant change in composition. Each contains the men possessed of the information, or with access to the information, that bears on the particular decision together with those whose skill consists in extracting and testing this information and obtaining a conclusion. This is how men act successfully on matters where no single one, however exalted or intelligent, has more than a fraction of the necessary knowledge. It is what makes modern business possible, and in other contexts it is what makes modern government possible. It is fortunate that men of limited knowledge are so constituted that they can work together in this way. Were it otherwise, business and government, at any given moment, would be at a standstill awaiting the appearance of a man with the requisite breadth of knowledge to resolve the problem presently at hand.

. . . .

[2] Also committees are not, as commonly supposed, alike. Some are constituted not to pool and test information and offer a decision but to accord representation to diverse bureaucratic, pecuniary, political, ideological or other interests. And a particular committee may have some of both purposes. A committee with representational functions will proceed much less expeditiously, for its ability to reach a conclusion depends on the susceptibility of participants to compromise, attrition and cupidity. The representational committee, in its present form, is engaged in a zero sum game, which is to say what some win others lose. Pooling and testing information is nonzero sum—all participants end with a larger score.

7

In the past, leadership in business organization was identified with the entrepreneur—the individual who united ownership of control of capital with capacity for organizing the other factors of production and, in most contexts, with a further capacity for innovation.[3] With the rise of the modern corporation, the emergence of the organization required by modern technology and planning and the divorce of the owner of the capital from control of the enterprise, the entrepreneur no longer exists as an individual person in the mature industrial enterprise.[4] Everyday discourse, except in the economics textbooks, recognizes this change. It replaces the entrepreneur, as the directing force of the enterprise, with management. This is a collective and imperfectly defined entity; in the large corporation it embraces chairman, president, those vice-presidents with important staff or departmental responsibility, occupants of other major staff positions and, perhaps, division or department heads not included above. It includes, however, only a small proportion of those who, as participants, contribute information to group decisions. This latter group is very large; it extends from the most senior officials of the corporation to where it meets, at the outer perimeter, the white- and blue-collar workers whose function is to conform more or less mechanically to instruction or routine. It embraces all who bring specialized knowledge, talent or experience to group decision-making. This, not the management, is the guiding intelligence—the brain—of the enterprise. There is no name for all who participate in group decision-making or the organization which they form. I propose to call this organization the Technostructure.

---

[3] "To act with confidence beyond the range of familiar beacons and to overcome that resistance requires aptitudes that are present in only a small fraction of the population and [they] define the entrepreneurial type as well as the entrepreneurial function." Joseph A. Schumpeter, *Capitalism, Socialism and Democracy,* Second Edition (New York: Harper, 1947), p. 132.

[4] He is still, of course, to be found in smaller firms and in larger ones that have yet to reach full maturity of organization.

THE ENTREPRENEUR
AND THE TECHNOSTRUCTURE

•   •   •   •   •   •   •   •   •   •   •   •   •   •   •   •   •   •   •   •

3

Until recent times, senior officials of the mature corporation were inclined to assume the public mantle of the entrepreneur. They pictured themselves as self-reliant men, individualistic with a trace of justifiable arrogance, fiercely competitive and with a desire to live dangerously. Individualism is the note that "sounds through the business creed like the pitch in a Byzantine Choir." [5] "They're bred to race. It's the same with people. It's something that's born into you." [6] "Business is tough—it's no kissing game." [7] These characteristics are not readily reconciled with the requirements of the technostructure. Not indifference but sensitivity to others, not individualism but accommodation to organization, not competition but intimate and continuing cooperation are the prime requirements for group action.

Nor is any reconciliation possible. The assertion of the competitive individualism of the corporate executive, to the extent that it continues, is ceremonial, traditional and, on occasion, a manifestation of personal vanity. In World War II, commanders of armored units, functioning from well to the rear and worrying about gasoline, spare parts, reinforcements and their influence with Eisenhower, identified themselves, nonetheless, with Lord Cardigan and the Light Brigade.

In romance the past greatly improves on the present. In

---

[5] Francis X. Sutton, Seymour E. Harris, Carl Kaysen and James Tobin, *The American Business Creed* (Cambridge: Harvard University Press, 1956), p. 251.
[6] Charles "Tex" Thornton, President of Litton Industries, describing the qualities of a senior executive. Osborn Elliott, *Men at the Top* (New York: Harper, 1959), p. 21.
[7] J. Peter Grace, President of W. R. Grace and Co. *Ibid.*, p. 69.

the history of almost every industry, there has been a famous and sometimes flamboyant entrepreneur. Like the tank commander, the head of the modern enterprise, in which all important actions are studiously considered by committees, all contingencies carefully anticipated and all adverse ones either prevented or negated, seeks to see himself in the earlier and more heroic image. Doubtless this does no harm. Additionally his function is to lend dignity and an aspect of power to stockholders' and directors' meetings, and other business ceremonials; to salute customers and clients of equal or greater dignity; to give the equivalent of the royal assent to agreements, contracts and indentures; to represent the enterprise in its more honorific relations with government; to act as an emissary to liberal learning; and to affirm, on appropriate public occasions, faith in free enterprise, the social responsibility of business and the continuing relevance of ancestral virtues. For all these rites the mantle of Carnegie, Rockefeller or Henry Ford is more than a little helpful.[8]

And this reaching for the mantle of the classical entrepreneur is, almost certainly, a passing phase. A younger generation of executives accepts the fact of organization and its bearing on behavior. "To a surprising degree, American businessmen and writers about business have [stopped] interpreting our cooperative society as individualist and [have stopped] concealing our quest for security in phrases like competition. . . ."[9] Interdependence is recognized. As in all organization, there is protective compassion for the man who, because of misfortune, temperament, personal inadequacy, or alcohol, falls by the wayside.[10] Executive life, so far from being competitive and dangerous, is highly secure. Of some eight hundred senior executives— the recipients of the highest salaries in each of approxi-

---

[8] We have here the reason generals, admirals and diplomats, after a lifetime in public service, frequently spend their last years as heads of business corporations, and serve with success in a role for which they are manifestly unqualified. It is because they are well qualified for ceremonial functions, and this (including honorific appearance in Washington) is what the position almost exclusively requires.

[9] Earl F. Cheit in *The Business Establishment,* Earl F. Cheit, ed. (New York: Wiley, 1964), p. 155.

[10] Cf. "The Alcoholic Executive," *Fortune,* January 1960, pp. 99ff.

mately three hundred industrial, railroad and utility corporations—who were in office in 1952, three-quarters had been with their particular company for more than twenty years.[11] A few years ago the subsequent careers of 308 senior executives—board chairmen and presidents of the largest corporations—who were in office in 1925 were traced to their end. Of these, 265 continued with the same firm until death or retirement. Only 13 resigned before retirement and this included those who resigned to take better jobs. Sixteen lost their jobs because of changes in the control of the company but this included some who left because they had sold their own interest. Only five lost their jobs because the company failed or because they were fired. These men enjoyed a marked increase in their security of tenure as compared with 313 executives in office in 1900 of whom only 157 eventually achieved death or honorable retirement.[12] A study of more recent classes would almost certainly show, along with some increased mobility between corporations, a yet further increase in security of executive employment in general.

4

It is noteworthy that the financial markets have long since accepted the reality of the technostructure as distinct from the entrepreneur. Were the latter in command of the large corporation—if he exercised important power—anything affecting his tenure in office would have an important effect on its prospective earnings, growth and capital gains. The stock market would then be vitally concerned. Were he taken ill, financial reporters would seek hard news at the hospital. The ticker would carry electrocardiograms. Holders of stock on margin would have doctor's bulletins relayed to them in Nassau. The market would rise and fall with his temperature, blood pressure and cholesterol count.

Similarly, the months preceding his scheduled retirement would be a nervous time. News would be sought on whether a successor had been trained or a replacement

---

[11] *The Executive Life*, p. 30. The responses being not quite complete, the number works out to fewer than three to a company.
[12] Mabel Newcomer, *The Big Business Executive* (New York: Columbia University Press, 1955), pp. 93ff.

found. The new man would be handicapped like a horse
—his special talents would be appraised and his experience, temperament, family situation, working hours and
drinking habits assessed. Stock in firms headed by an able
man who was a heavy cigarette smoker would sell at a
slight discount.

None of this happens for it is known that retirement,
death and replacement, however important for the individual involved, have not the slightest effect on General Motors or Continental Can.[13] Power, it is implicitly recognized,
has passed to the technostructure. So its exercise is unaffected by the age or morbidity of any man. Though men
accord the head of the great corporation the deference his
position calls for, no one allows this to affect his financial
judgment.

5

Because individuals have more standing in the culture than
organizations, they regularly get credit for achievement
that belongs, in fact, to organization. It is not Procter and
Gamble that has been winning new worlds in detergents;
it is Procter and Gamble under the inspired leadership of
Neil H. McElroy. To this tendency, principals, on occasion, contribute. "At every turn the chief executive must
be prepared to persuade people that this point of view must
prevail." [14]

Clearly some individuals do add luster to organization.
The accomplishments of the great physician are his own,
not those of the hospital where he serves. The achievements of the poet are his own, not those of the institution
where he is currently the artist in residence. Similarly the
opera singer or actor and, though not always, the great
scientist.

Men are, in fact, either sustained by organization or they
sustain organization. They are either esteemed because of
organization or the organization is esteemed because of

[13] The stock of a smaller or newer company dominated by one man,
in contrast, does move on news of personnel changes.
[14] John T. Connor, then President of Merck & Company, in *Men
at the Top, op. cit.,* p. 10.

them. The individual is himself rarely a sound judge of these matters. Those who are esteemed because of organization almost invariably attribute the acclaim to their own personality.

But there is an infallible test. That is to observe what happens to the individual when he leaves the organization or retires. The great physician is not greatly diminished by being separated from his hospital. Nor, except as regards regular salary, is the poet when he leaves the university. Nor is the competent newspaperman when he moves on. Nor the great scientist nor the entertainer. They sustained, and were not sustained by, the organization to which they belonged.

By contrast the politician when he is defeated, the ambassador when he retires, the university president when he becomes emeritus and the peacetime general who fails to become a corporation president face total obscurity. They were sustained by organization; on losing its support they pass permanently into the shadows. To some who have naturally assumed that their eminence was their own the shock is very severe. Others sense their situation. Nothing so explains the primordial vigor with which politicians fight for office and seek to retain it to senility and beyond. Between being in and out of political office the difference is not slight. It is total.

But for none is the transition more drastic than for the great business executive. Even the scrupulously inadequate governor or the tediously time-serving senator can count, after well-merited retirement, on some of the graces of public position. He will be a delegate to national conventions, be introduced at fund-raising dinners as "that great statesman" and always be addressed by his former title. For the corporation president, by contrast, there is only Stygian darkness. Following the final flight in the company jet, there will be only an honorific association with the Board of Directors and sometimes not that. His memoirs will not be in demand; the United Fund will want a man more affirmatively identified with affairs; his only continuing public responsibilities will be in his own church; his name will not again appear in the papers until the day following his death. The great entrepreneur lived out his last days disposing of his wealth or resisting those who sought to have him do so. The modern executive does not have enough money so to occupy himself. Such is his recessional. The conclusion requires no undue emphasis: Preeminently the organization man is sustained by organization.

SCHOOLING AND THE INDIVIDUAL

Edgar Z. Friedenberg

[Schools teach far more than subject matter—they teach each youngster what society is like, how he is expected to behave and think, and how he is supposed to regard himself. Because schooling has such enormous impact and because it is the creation and reflection of its society, these effects largely shape what is happening to the individual in America. Edgar Friedenberg examines this issue and argues that today's schools manipulate students and suppress individual development.

[Edgar Friedenberg is professor of sociology and education at the State University of New York at Buffalo. He is the author of *The Vanishing Adolescent, The Dignity of Youth and Other Atavisms,* and *Coming of Age in America.*]

Not far from Los Angeles, though rather nearer to Boston, may be located the town of Milgrim, in which Milgrim High School is clearly the most costly and impressive structure. Milgrim is not a suburb though it is only fifty miles from a large and dishonorable city and a part of its conurbation. Comparatively few Milgrimites commute to the city for work. Milgrim is an agricultural village which has outgrown its nervous system; its accustomed modes of social integration have never even begun to relate its present, recently acquired inhabitants to one another. So, though it is not a suburb, Milgrim is not a community either.

• • • • • • • • • • • • • • • • • • •

Estimates of the proportion of the student body at Milgrim who are, in the ethnocentric language of demography, non-White, vary enormously. Some students who are clearly middle-class and of pinkish-gray color speak as if they were besieged. But responsible staff members estimate from 12 to 30 percent. Observations in the corridors and lunchrooms favor the lower figure. They also establish that the non-Whites are orderly and well behaved, though somewhat more forceful in their movements and manner of speech than their light-skinned colleagues.

What is Milgrim High like? It is a big, expensive building, on spacious but barren grounds. Every door is at the end of a corridor; there is no reception area, no public space in which one can adjust to the transition from the outside world. Between class periods the corridors are tumultuously crowded; during them they are empty; but they are always guarded with teachers and students on patrol duty. Patrol duty does not consist primarily in the policing of congested throngs of moving students, though it includes this, or the guarding of property from damage. Its principal function is the checking of corridor passes. Between classes, no student may walk down the corridor without a form, signed by a teacher, telling where he is coming from, where he is going, and the time, to the minute, at which the pass is valid. A student caught in the corridor without such a pass is taken to the office, where a detention slip is made out against him, and he is required to remain at school for two or three hours after the close of the school day. He may do his homework during this time, but he may not leave his seat or talk.

There is no physical freedom whatever at Milgrim. That is, there is no time at which, or place in which, a student may simply go about his business. Privacy is strictly forbidden. Except during class breaks, the toilets are kept locked, so that a student must not only obtain a pass but find the custodian and induce him to unlock the facility. My mother, who had a certain humor about these matters unusual in her generation, had a favorite story about a golfer who, in a moment of extreme need, asked his caddy to direct him to the nearest convenience. The poor boy, unfortunately, stuttered; and the desperate golfer finally interrupted him, sadly, saying, "Never mind, now, son; I've made other arrangements." How often this occurs at

Milgrim I do not know, but when it does, the victim is undoubtedly sent for detention.

Milgrim High's most memorable arrangements are its corridor passes and its johns; they dominate social interaction. "Good morning, Mr. Smith," an attractive girl will say pleasantly to one of her teachers in the corridor. "Linda, do you have a pass to be in your locker after the bell rings?" is his greeting in reply. There are more different kinds of washrooms than there must have been in the Confederate Navy. The common sort, marked just "Boys" and "Girls," are generally locked. Then, there are some marked "Teachers, Men" and "Teachers, Women," unlocked. Near the auditorium are two others marked simply "Men" and "Women," intended primarily for the public when the auditorium is being used for some function. During the school day a cardboard sign saying "Adults only" is added to the legend on these washrooms; this is removed at the close of the school day. Girding up my maturity, I used this men's room during my stay at Milgrim. Usually it was empty; but once, as soon as the door clicked behind me, a teacher who had been concealed in the cubicle began jumping up and down to peer over his partition and verify my adulthood.

He was not a voyeur; he was checking on smoking. At most public high schools students are forbidden to smoke, and this is probably the most common source of friction with authority. It focuses, naturally, on the washrooms, which are the only places students can go where teachers are not supposed to be. Milgrim, last year, was more liberal than most; its administration designated an area behind the school where seniors might smoke during their lunch period. Since, as a number of students explained to me during interviews, some of these students had "abused the privilege" by lighting up before they got into the area, the privilege had been withdrawn. No student, however, questioned that smoking *was* a privilege rather than a right.

The concept of privilege is important at Milgrim. Teachers go to the head of the chow line at lunch; whenever I would attempt quietly to stand in line the teacher on hall duty would remonstrate with me. He was right, probably; I was fouling up an entire informal social system by my ostentation. Students on hall patrol also, when relieved from duty, were privileged to come bouncing up to the head of the line; so did seniors. Much of the behavior Milgrim depends on to keep it going is motivated by the reward of getting a government-surplus peanut butter or tuna fish sandwich without standing in line for it.

The lunchroom itself is a major learning experience which must make quite an impression over four years' time. There are two large cafeterias which are used as study halls during the periods before and after the middle of the day—the middle three or four are lunch shifts. The food, by and large, is more tempting than the menu; it tastes better than it sounds. The atmosphere is not quite that of a prison, because the students are permitted to talk quietly, under the frowning scrutiny of teachers standing around on duty, during their meal—they are not supposed to talk while standing in line, though this rule is only sporadically enforced. Standing in line takes about a third of their lunch period, and leaves plenty of time for them to eat what is provided them. They may not, in any case, leave the room when they have finished, any more than they may leave class in the middle. Toward the end of the period a steel gate is swung down across the corridor, dividing the wing holding the cafeterias, guidance offices, administrative offices, and auditorium from the rest of the building where the library and classrooms are. Then the first buzzer sounds, and the students sweep out of the cafeteria and press silently forward to the gate. A few minutes later a second buzzer sounds, the gate is opened, and the students file on to their classrooms.

During the meal itself the atmosphere varies in response to chance events and the personality of the teachers assigned supervisory duty, especially in the corridor where the next sitting is standing in line. The norm is a not unpleasant chatter; but about one teacher in four is an embittered martinet, snarling, whining, continually ordering the students to stand closer to the wall and threatening them with detention or suspension for real or fancied insolence. On other occasions, verbal altercations break out between students in the cafeteria or in line and the *student* hall patrolmen. In one of these that I witnessed, the accused student, a handsome, aggressive-looking young man, defended himself in the informal but explicit language of working-class hostility. This roused the teacher on duty, who walked over toward the boy and, silently but with a glare of contempt, beckoned him from the room with a crooked and waggling finger and led him along the corridor to the administrative office: the tall boy rigid in silent protest; the teacher, balding and duck-bottomed in a wrinkled suit, shambling ahead of him. The youth, I later learned, was suspended for a day. At some lunch periods all this is drowned out by Mantovani-type pop records played over the public-address system.

What adults generally, I think, fail to grasp even though they may actually know it, is that there is no refuge or respite from this: no coffee break, no taking ten for a smoke, no room like the teachers' room, however poor, where the youngsters can get away from adults. High schools don't have club rooms; they have organized gym and recreation. A student cannot go to the library when he wants a book; on certain days his schedule provides a forty-five-minute library period. "Don't let anybody leave early," a guidance counselor urged during a group testing session at Hartsburgh, an apparently more permissive school in our sample. "There really isn't any place for them to go." Most of us are as nervous by the age of five as we will ever be; and adolescence adds to the strain; but one thing a high-school student learns is that he can expect no provision for his need to give in to his feelings, or to swing out in his own style, or to creep off and pull himself together.

The little things shock most. High-school students—and not just, or even particularly, at Milgrim—have a prisoner's sense of time. They don't know what time it is outside. The research which occasioned my presence at Milgrim, Hartsburgh, and the other schools in the study required me to interview each of twenty-five to thirty students at each school three times. Just before each interview, the student was given a longish description of an episode at a fictitious high school to read as a basis for our subsequent discussion, and I tried to arrange to be interviewing his predecessor while he was reading the descriptive passage. My first appointment with each student was set up by the guidance counselor; I would make the next appointment directly with the student and issue him the passes he needed to keep it. The student has no *open* time at his own disposal; he has to select the period he can miss with least loss to himself. Students well adapted to the school usually pick study halls; poorer or more trouble-some students pick the times of their most disagreeable classes; both avoid cutting classes in which the teacher is likely to respond vindictively to their absence. Most stu-dents, when asked when they would like to come for their next interview, replied, "I can come any time." When I pointed out to them that there must, after all, be some times that would be more convenient for them than others, they would say, "Well, tomorrow, fourth period," or what-ever. *But hardly anyone knew when this would be in clock time.* High-school classes emphasize the importance of punctuality by beginning at regular but uneven times like 10:43 and 11:27, which are, indeed, hard to remember; and the students did not know when this was.

How typical is all this? The elements of the composition —the passes, the tight scheduling, the reliance on threats of detention or suspension as modes of social control—are nearly universal. The complete usurpation of any possible *area* of student initiative, physical or mental, is about as universal. Milgrim forbids boys to wear trousers that end more than six inches above the floor, and has personnel fully capable of measuring them. But most high schools have some kind of dress regulation; I know of none that accepts and relies on the tastes of its students. There are differences, to be sure, in tone; and these matter. They greatly affect the impact of the place on students.

Take, for comparison and contrast, Hartsburgh. Not fif-teen miles from Milgrim, it is an utterly different commu-nity. It is larger; the school district is more compact and more suburban, more of a place. First impressions of Harts-burgh High are almost bound to be favorable. The building, like Milgrim, is new; unlike Milgrim, it is handsome. Exter-nal walls are mostly glass, which gives a feeling of light, air, and space. There is none of the snarling, overt hostility that taints the atmosphere at Milgrim. There are no raucous buzzers, no bells of any kind. Instead, there are little blinker lights arranged like the Italian flag. The green light blinks and the period is over; the white light signals a warning; when the red light blinks it is time to be in your classroom. Dress regulations exist but are less rigorous than at Milgrim. Every Wednesday, however, is dress-up day; boys are expected to wear ties and jackets; the girls, dresses rather than skirts and sweaters. On Wednesday the school day ends with an extra hour of required assembly and, the students explain, there are often outside visitors for whom they are expected to look their best.

Students at Hartsburgh seem much more relaxed than at Milgrim. In the grounds outside the main entrance, during lunch period, there is occasional horseplay. For ten minutes during one noon hour I watched three boys enacting a mutual fantasy. One was the audience who only sat and laughed, one the aggressor, and the third—a pleasant, inarticulate varsity basketball player—was the self-appointed victim. The two participants were portraying in pantomine old, silent-movie-type fights in slow motion. The boy I did not know would slowly swing at Paul, who would sink twisting to the ground with grimaces of anguish; then the whole sequence would be repeated with variations, though the two boys never switched roles. In my interviews with Paul I had never solved the problems arising from the fact that he was eloquent only with his arms and torso movements, which were lost on the tape recorder, and it was a real pleasure to watch him in his own medium. This was a pleasure Milgrim would never have afforded me. Similarly, in the corridors at Hartsburgh I would occasionally come upon couples holding hands or occasionally rather more, though it distressed me that they always broke guiltily apart as they saw me or any other adult. One of my subjects, who had completed the preliminary readings for his interview and was waiting outside for me to finish with the previous subject, was dancing a little jig by himself in the corridor when I got to him. This is all rather reassuring.

It is also contrary to policy. There is a regulation against couples holding hands and they are punished if caught by the kind of teacher who hates sexuality in the young. The air and space also, subtly, turn out to be illusions if you try to use them. Hartsburgh High is built around a large landscaped courtyard with little walks and benches. I made the mistake of trying to conduct an interview on one of these benches. When it was over we could not get back into the building except by disturbing a class; the doors onto this inviting oasis can only be opened from the inside, so nobody ever goes there. Since the courtyard is completely enclosed by the high-school building, this affords no additional protection from intruders; but it does sequester a possible place of informal refuge. The beautiful glass windows do not open enough to permit a body to squirm through and consequently do not open enough to ventilate the rooms, in which there are no individual controls for the fiercely effective radiators. Room temperature, at Hartsburgh, is a matter of high policy.

Teachers do not hide in the washrooms at Hartsburgh, but the principal recently issued to all students a letter warning that any student caught in the vicinity of the school with "tobacco products" on him would be subject to suspension; students were directed to have their parents sign the letter as written acknowledgment that they were aware of the regulation and return it to school. Staff, of course, are permitted to smoke.

A former teacher, promoted to assistant principal, is now a full-time disciplinarian, but students are not dragged to his office by infuriated teachers as sometimes happens at Milgrim. Instead, during the first period, two students from the school Citizenship Corps go quietly from classroom to classroom with a list, handing out summonses. The air at Hartsburgh is less rancorous and choleric than at Milgrim, and there seem to be more teachers there who like teaching and like kids. But the fundamental pattern is still one of control, distrust, and punishment.

. . . .

What is learned in high school, or for that matter anywhere at all, depends far less on what is taught than on what one actually experiences in the place. The quality of instruction in high school varies from sheer rot to imaginative and highly skilled teaching; but classroom content is often handled at a creditable level and is not in itself the source of much difficulty. Generally speaking, both at Milgrim and Hartsburgh, for example, the students felt that they were receiving competent instruction and that this was an undertaking the school tried seriously to handle. Throughout our sample of nine schools—though not necessarily in each of them—more than four-fifths of our pretest sample, aggregating nearly one thousand students, agreed that the following statements applied to their school:

> There are teachers here who, when they tell you your work is well done, you know it is good.

> Many of the teachers know a great deal about things other than what they cover in their subject in class.

> Some teachers surprise you by getting you interested in subjects you'd never really thought of before.

But important as it is to note that students generally recognize academic quality in the schools, and particularly the contributions of exceptional teachers, serious questions remain as to how the school affects the students' conception of either academic mastery or of themselves. For more than 80 percent also agree that:

> You have to be concerned about marks here; that is, if you are going to get anywhere and be anything.

> The school doesn't expect students to wear expensive clothes, but they do have to be neat and clean. Clothes that are too sporty or sexy are "out."

> The student newspaper here is pretty careful not to report things in such a way that they might make trouble for the school with other people.

> Keeping everybody quiet when they're in the library is a regular cause with the librarians here.

> A girl who went too far here and got into trouble would be suspended or expelled.

In my judgment, the kind of tutelage and status that the high school assigns students affects their lives and subsequent development far more crucially than the content and quality of formal instruction. What is learned most thoroughly by attendance at Milgrim or Hartsburgh is certain core assumptions that govern the conditions of life

of most adolescents in this country and train them to operate as adult, if not as mature, Americans. The first of these
is the assumption that the state has the right to compel
adolescents to spend six or seven hours a day, five days a
week, thirty-six or so weeks a year, in a specific place,
under the charge of a particular group of persons in whose
selection they have no voice, performing tasks about which
they have no choice, without remuneration and subject to
specialized regulations and sanctions that are applicable
to no one else in the community nor to them except in this
place. So accustomed are we to assuming that education is
a *service* to the young that this statement must seem fla-
grantly biased. But it is a simple statement of what the
law provides. Whether this provision is a service or a
burden to the young—and, indeed, it is both, in varying
degrees—is another issue altogether. Compulsory school
attendance functions as a bill of attainder against a particular age group, so the first thing the young learn in school
is that there are certain sanctions and restrictions that apply only to them, that they do not participate fully in the
freedoms guaranteed by the state, and that, *therefore, these
freedoms do not really partake of the character of inalienable rights.*

When services are to be provided to an individual whom
the law respects as it does the agency providing the services, the normal legal instrument is, of course, a contract,
which defines the rights and obligations of both parties and
provides each with legal remedies against the contract's
breach.

Compulsory school attendance, however, is provided by
a law which recognizes no obligation of the school that
the students can enforce. He cannot petition to withdraw if
the school is inferior, does not maintain standards, or
treats him brutally. There are other laws, certainly, that
set standards for school construction and maintenance, the
licensing of teachers, technics of discipline, and so forth;
and proceedings under these may be invoked if the school
does not abide by them. But they do not abate the student's
obligation to attend the school and accept its services. His
position is purely that of a conscript who is protected by
certain regulations but in no case permitted to use their
breach as a cause for terminating his obligation.

Of course not. The school, as schools continually stress, acts *in loco parentis;* and children may not leave home because their parents are unsatisfactory. What I have pointed out is no more than a special consequence of the fact that students are minors, and minors do not, indeed, share all the rights and privileges—and responsibilities—of citizenship. Very well. However one puts it, we are still discussing the same issue. The high school, then, is where you really learn what it means to be a minor.

For a high school is not a parent. Parents may love their children, hate them, or, like most parents, do both in a complex mixture. But they must, nevertheless, permit a certain intimacy and respond to their children as persons. Homes are not run by regulations, though the parents may think they are, but by a process of continuous and almost entirely unconscious emotional homeostasis, in which each member affects and accommodates to the needs, feelings, fantasy life, and character structure of the others. This may be, and often is, a terribly destructive process; I intend no defense of the family as a social institution. Salmon, actually, are much nicer than people: more dedicated, more energetic, less easily daunted by the long upstream struggle and less prudish and reticent about their reproductive functions, though inclined to be rather cold-blooded. But children grow up in homes or the remnants of homes, are in physical fact dependent on parents, and are too intimately related to them to permit their area of freedom to be precisely defined. This is not because they have no rights or are entitled to less respect than adults, but because intimacy conditions freedom and growth in ways too subtle and continuous to be defined as overt acts.

Free societies depend on their members to learn early and thoroughly that public authority is *not* like that of the family; that it cannot be expected—or trusted—to respond with sensitivity and intimate perception to the needs of individuals but must rely basically, though as humanely as possible, on the impartial application of general formulae. This means that it must be kept functional, specialized, and limited to matters of public policy; the meshes of the law are too coarse to be worn close to the skin. Especially in an open society, where people of very different backgrounds and value systems must function together, it would seem obvious that each must understand that he may not push others further than their common undertaking demands or impose upon them a manner of life that they feel to be alien.

After the family, the school is the first social institution an individual must deal with—the place in which he learns to handle himself with strangers. The school establishes the pattern of his subsequent assumptions as to which relations between the individual and society are appropriate and which constitute invasions of privacy and constraints on his spirit—what the British, with exquisite precision, call "taking a liberty." But the American public school evolved as a melting pot, under the assumption that it had not merely the right but the duty to impose a common standard of genteel decency on a polyglot body of immigrants' children and thus insure their assimilation into the better life of the American dream. It accepted, also, the tacit assumption that genteel decency was as far as it could go. If America has generally been governed by the practical man's impatience with other individuals' rights, it has also accepted the practical man's respect for property and determination to protect it from the assaults of public servants. With its contempt for personal privacy and individual autonomy, the school combines a considerable measure of Galbraith's "public squalor." The plant may be expensive—for this is capital goods; but nothing is provided graciously, liberally, simply as an amenity, either to teachers or students, though administrative offices have begun to assume an executive look. In the schools I know, the teachers' lounges are invariably filled with shabby furniture and vending machines. Teachers do not have offices with assigned clerical assistance and business equipment that would be considered satisfactory for, say, a small-town, small-time insurance agency. They have desks in staffrooms, without telephones.

To justify this shabbiness as essential economy and established custom begs the question; the level of support and working conditions customarily provided simply defines the status of the occupation and the value the community in fact places on it. An important consequence, I believe, is to help keep teachers timid and passive by reminding them, against the contrasting patterns of commercial affluence, of their relative ineffectiveness; and to divert against students their hostilities and their demands for status. Both teachers and students, each at their respective levels, learn to regard the ordinary amenities and freedoms of middle-class life as privileges. But the teacher has a few more of them. He hasn't a telephone, but he may make calls from a phone in the general office, while, in some schools, the public pay phone in the hallway has a lock on it and the student must get a key from the office before he can dial his call. Where a hotel or motel, for example, provides in its budget for normal wear and tear and a reasonable level of theft of linens and equipment and quietly covers itself with liability insurance, the school—though it may actually do the same thing—pompously indoctrinates its students with "respect for public property," "good health habits," and so forth before it lets them near the swimming pool. In a large city, the pool may have been struck out of the architect's plans before construction began, on the grounds that it would be unfair to provide students in a newer school with a costly facility that students in older schools do not have.

If the first thing the student learns, then, is that he, as a minor, is subject to peculiar restraints, the second is that these restraints are general, and are not limited to the manifest and specific functions of education. High school administrators are not professional educators in the sense that a physician, an attorney, or a tax accountant are professionals. They are not practitioners of a specialized *instructional* craft, who derive their authority from its requirements. They are specialists in keeping an essentially political enterprise from being strangled by conflicting community attitudes and pressures. They are problem-oriented, and the feelings and needs for growth of their captive and disfranchized clientele are the least of their problems; for the status of the "teenager" in the community is so low that even if he rebels, the school is not blamed for the conditions against which he is rebelling. He is simply a truant or juvenile delinquent; at worst the school has "failed to reach him." What high-school personnel become specialists in, ultimately, is the *control* of large groups of students even at catastrophic expense to their opportunity to learn. These controls are not exercised primarily to facilitate instruction, and, particularly, they are in no way limited to matters bearing on instruction. At several schools in our sample boys had, for example, been ordered by the assistant principal—sometimes on the complaint of teachers—to shave off beards. One of these boys, who had played football for the school all season, was told that, while the school had no legal authority to require this, he would be barred from the banquet honoring the team unless he complied. Dress regulations are another case in point.

Of course these are petty restrictions, enforced by petty penalties. American high schools are not concentration camps; and I am not complaining about their severity but about what they teach their students concerning the proper relationship of the individual to society. The fact that the restrictions and penalties are petty and unimportant in themselves in one way makes matters worse. Gross invasions are more easily recognized for what they are; petty restrictions are only resisted by "troublemakers." What matters in the end, however, is that the school does not take its own business of education seriously enough to mind it.

The effects on the students of the school's diffuse willingness to mind everybody's business but its own are manifold. The concepts of dignity and privacy, notably deficient in American adult folkways, are not permitted to develop here. The high school, certainly, is not the material cause of this deficiency, which is deeply rooted in our social institutions and values. But the high school does more than transmit these values—it exploits them to keep students in line and develop them into the kinds of people who fit the community that supports it.

A corollary of the school's assumption of custodial control of students is that power and authority become indistinguishable. If the school's authority is not limited to matters pertaining to education, it cannot be derived from educational responsibilities. It is a naked, empirical fact, to be accepted or controverted according to the possibilities of the moment. In this world power counts more than legitimacy; if you don't have power, it is naïve to think you have rights that must be respected; wise up. High-school students experience regulation only as control, not as protection; they know, for example, that the principal will generally uphold the teacher in any conflict with a student, regardless of the merits of the case. Translated into the high-school idiom, *suaviter in modo, fortiter in re* becomes "If you get caught, it's just your ass."

Students, I find, do not resent this; that is the tragedy. All weakness tends to corrupt, and impotence corrupts absolutely. Identifying, as the weak must, with the more powerful and frustrating of the forces that impinge upon them, they accept the school as the way life is and close their minds against the anxiety of perceiving alternatives. Many students like high school; others loathe and fear it. But even these do not object to it on principle; the school effectively obstructs their learning of the principles on which objection might be based; though these are among the principles that, we boast, distinguish us from totalitarian societies.

Yet, finally, the consequence of submitting throughout adolescence to diffuse authority that is not derived from the task at hand—as a doctor's orders, or the training regulations of an athletic coach, for example, usually are—is more serious than political incompetence or weakness of character. There is a general arrest of development. An essential part of growing up is learning that, though differences of power among men lead to brutal consequences, all men are peers; none is omnipotent, none derives his potency from magic but only from his specific competence and function. The policeman represents the majesty of the State, but this does not mean that he can put you in jail; it means, precisely, that he cannot—at least not for long. Any person or agency responsible for handling throngs of young people—especially if it does not like them or is afraid of them—is tempted to claim diffuse authority and snare the youngster in the trailing remnants of childhood emotion, which always remain to trip him. Schools are permitted to infantilize adolescence and control pupils by reinvoking the sensations of childhood punishment, effective because it was designed, with great unconscious guile, to dramatize the child's weakness in the face of authority. In fact, they are strongly encouraged to do so by the hostility to "teenagers" and the anxiety about their conduct that abound in our society.

In the process, the school affects society in two complementary ways. It alters individuals: their values, their sense of personal worth, their patterns of anxiety and sense of mastery and ease in the world on which so much of what we think of as our fate depends. But it also performs a Darwinian function. The school endorses and supports the values and patterns of behavior of certain segments of the population, providing their members with the credentials and shibboleths needed for the next stages of their journey, while instilling in others a sense of inferiority and warning the rest of society against them as troublesome and untrustworthy. In this way, the school contributes simultaneously to social mobility and social stratification. It helps to see to it that the kinds of people who get ahead are those who will support the social system it represents; while those who might, through intent or merely by their being, subvert it are left behind as a salutary moral lesson.

INDIVIDUALISM IN SUBURBIA

William H. Whyte, Jr.

[American society is increasingly dominated by giant bureaucracies which affect the individual autonomy of everyone in the society—but most directly those who are on the inside. Though different organizations operate in different ways, the experience of a middle-level executive in a large business organization is typical. William Whyte studied the impact of the organization on the life-styles of its employees in his now-classic *The Organization Man* and his portrayal has not been surpassed.

[William Whyte, Jr., is the author of *The Organization Man, Is Anybody Listening?,* and *Open Space Action.*]

To anyone who has ever worried over the contemporary collectivization of society, there is nothing quite so unnerving as a drive past one of the great new suburban villages rising outside our biggest cities. To the stranger from an older community or an older generation, the spectacle of superblock after superblock of ranch-type houses undulating off to infinity is overpowering. Even the diversity is standardized; drive by them at dusk, when the blue light of television shines out of the picture window, and you can speculate that if you were to blink your eyes like the shutter of a camera, the scene flashing by would freeze into one motionless picture.

The social pressures the television aerials portend are not peculiar to the new suburbia, nor are they peculiar to the United States; essentially they are the product of a universal trend toward the large-scale organization of society. In few places, however, are the results so immediately visible. In these suburbs the young people are concentrated, almost totally free from the traditions and restraints that would affect them elsewhere. Thrown into such propinquity, they bring out in each other—sometimes in caricature—tendencies not so easily observed in more conventional environments. Abnormal? One gets the feeling that the way of life here is likely to be the normality of not so many years from now.

To speak of individualism in terms of these new collectives may seem an arrant contradiction in terms. Yet, for the very reason there are so many pressures on the individual here, his struggle is all the more illuminating. Nowhere is it tougher; no panache can be waved in suburbia, and what would be only the mildest rebellion elsewhere requires real courage here. With considerable justification the young suburbanites can argue that they must pay a higher price for independence than their forebears ever did.

The key to the struggle is not to be found in the physical uniformity of the new suburbia that can so preoccupy the observer. Rows and rows of identical ranch houses are a dispiriting sight, but the uniformity is not the product of an inner spiritual urge. It is simple necessity, for modular construction is the price that must be paid for moderate cost of housing. And the price is not so very steep; unless one believes poverty is ennobling, the new housing is much less antithetical to the development of the individual than the rows and rows of drab tenements it helps supplant.

The key to the surburbanite's problem lies in the fact that he is primarily an organization man. Whether his organization allegiance is to one of the huge government agencies, the Atomic Energy Commission, the armed services, or, more frequently, the corporation, is of secondary importance.

In one great respect, these organizations are all of a piece; in a life increasingly divorced from fixed guideposts they have become the constant in the life of their transient members. This gives them a tremendous power over the individual for, benevolent or not, the organization allegiance has superseded to a large degree such formerly dominant ties as those of family and community.

The situation is one which the organization man thinks about a great deal more than his equable exterior would suggest. For though the terms of the organization man's relationship to society have changed, he is without a firm ethic that will rationalize the change. He confuses people because he still talks as if he were guided by the ethic of his fathers. Whatever his religion, it is essentially the old Protestant Ethic as defined by Max Weber, with its obeisance to the sanctity of property, thrift, competitive struggle, qualities which not so very long ago were called "rugged individualism."

But the old ethic no longer fits the facts of his existence. Thrift? The economic structure no longer allows him to accumulate wealth; instead of his being thrifty as an individual, the organization is thrifty for him. Hard work? He works as hard as people ever did but with less and less ideological comfort. Leisure is now coming to be venerated as an end in itself, and if, which is so often the case, he cares little for leisure, he must now worry that he does care so little. Self-help? While a person's future has always been determined to a great extent by the environment, the organization way of life no longer allows one the luxury of pretending to himself that it isn't. He knows very well that his area of choice is limited, and he will get nowhere, let alone survive, if he does not accept in large measure control of his destiny by others.

He can hardly be blamed if he is trying to reinterpret individualism in this new context. He senses well that the old one is in some respects incompatible with the reality he must face. For the common good, and not merely expediency, he must yield often to the group consensus, and what he is looking for is an ideological justification—a set of beliefs, to put it in another way, that will make a virtue of necessity. In his search he is coming to place far too much emphasis on the group, but before we can properly criticize him for this, we must at least try to comprehend how very difficult is his course.

The suburbanites are, for one thing, a mobile people. For some of them the move to suburbia was the most important they will ever make, for as they moved from the city ward they moved right into the middle class. For others, it is only one of a long succession of moves. The dominant group in these new communities are the organization people—the junior executive, the researchers, young corporation lawyers, engineers, and salesmen who have left home to join one of our great organizations, and who, for years to come, will keep on going. From community to community the proportions vary but they are strikingly alike in their basic statistics. What might be called the model man is a twenty-five- to thirty-five-year-old junior executive with a college degree, a salary between $6,000 and $7,000, a wife, one child, and another on the way.

As a result, high turnover is a built-in feature of these communities. For about a quarter of the residents this is the end of the line or, at least, a social step so high that it will be many years before they will think of moving away. For the bulk of the people, however, it is no more than a way station until the organization decides to shift them to another branch. In Park Forest, Illinois, the suburb where I spent the most time, roughly a quarter of its population of twenty thousand turns over every year. Over half of this turnover is virtually institutionalized; about 12 percent of the "move-outs" are army and navy couples, and 44 percent are couples being transferred by corporations. (These suburbs have been so convenient for corporations in this respect that some have standing arrangements with the developers, and as soon as one batch of junior executives have been taken away another will be brought in immediately to replace the quotas.)

Understandably, these people are highly aware of the power of the environment over them. Where once people hated to concede that their behavior was determined by anything except their own free will, there are few things which suburbanites talk so much about. At times it almost seems as though each man was his own resident sociologist; words like "permissive," "upward mobility," and "sociocultural groups" are thrown around in conversation quite readily, and one word, "outgoing," has become almost a synonym for "good" or "unselfish."

Or "necessary." In the fixed community of old, a man could afford not to worry over his adaptability to other people; his place was defined and so was that of everyone else, and as long as this tacit relationship obtained one didn't have to worry much about "belonging." Society itself had already attended to the matter. The young transient, however, is vouchsafed no such fix; no matter how comfortable his position is in a community, the position is only a small degree exportable, and when he moves he leaves behind the prestige and the support of the complex accumulation of relationships that defined his place. Wherever he now moves, he must reearn a place, and to do this, he must learn well how to acclimate himself to others and, in a sort of mutual assistance pact, help fellow transients to do the same. Let me illustrate with a couple we shall call Dot and Charlie Adams. Charlie, a corporation trainee, is uprooted from the Newark office, arrives at Apartment 8, Court M-12. It's a terrible day, the kids are crying, Dot is half sick with exhaustion, and the movers won't be finished until late. But soon, because M-12 is a "happy" court, the neighbors will come over to introduce themselves. In an almost inordinate display of decency, some will help them unpack, and around suppertime two of the girls will come over with a hot casserole and another with a percolator full of hot coffee. Within a few days the children will have found playmates, Dot will be *kaffeeklatsching* and sunbathing with the girls like an old-timer, and Charlie, who finds that Ed Robey in Apartment 5 went through officers' candidate school with him, will be enrolled in the Court Poker Club. The Adamses are, in a word, *in*—and someday soon, when another new couple, dazed and hungry, move in, the Adamses will make their thanks by helping them to be likewise.

In the court, they find, their life will be highly communal. Except for the $200 or $300 put aside for the next baby, few of the transients have as yet been able to accumulate much capital or earthly possessions, and so they share to make the best of it. One lawn mower (with each man doing his allotted stint) may do for the whole court. For the wives there is a baby-sitting "bank" (that is, when one wife baby-sits for another she is credited with the time, and when she wishes to draw on it, one of the wives who has a debit to repay will sit for her). To hoard possessions is frowned upon; books, silverware, and tea services are constantly rotated, and the children feel free to use each other's bicycles and toys without bothering to ask. "We laugh at how the Marxist society has finally arrived," one junior executive says, "but I think the real analogy is to the pioneers."

That this utopia is built on quicksand is a thought that they can never quite shut out. Much as they will joke about being "in a womb with a view" or a "sorority house with kids," the subject of their transiency strikes a very sensitive nerve in them. When I went back to Park Forest after our initial articles on it had appeared, I braced myself for complaints about its emphasis on their desire to get along. To my surprise, most of the people didn't cavil at this at all, but instead upbraided me for the attention paid to the turnover. Even those who were soon to move themselves seemed extraordinarily touchy about it. (The ex-sociologist in charge of signing rental apartments tried to demonstrate to me mathematically that as long as a percentage of the incoming people were people who were going to stay, each year there would be a declining number of vacancies for transients, and soon it would be stable just like any other town.)

Among those who planned to stay in Park Forest the touchiness is understandable enough; these people who have come from lower-middle-class backgrounds do not like to be reminded of the double social standard. But among the transients themselves, mobility is a desideratum. When a couple is transferred, their neighbors are vicariously proud of them, and the inevitable farewell party has a strong congratulatory note. Conversely, an organization man who does not move after several years soon feels impelled to explain to his friends why he hasn't lest they get the idea he has been passed over for promotion.

Yet the very transiency they aspire to unsettles them. To be reminded of it is to be reminded of the lack of fixed points in the life to which they have committed themselves. If everything and everybody else would stand still, their transiency would not abrade them; but as they so well realize, everyone else in their particular world is transient too. It is the fluidity of the whole society itself, rather than their own movement in it, which seems the rub to them.

They speak of home often, but it is with the same highly mixed feeling that they discuss the transiency. Most of the organization couples came from comfortable, upper-middle-class families in small towns, and in retrospect the place they left seems far more supportive, more rooted than it probably was. I was struck with how many times people would speak of trees: "We had a beautiful old oak tree right outside the house," one wife, rather typical of many, said. "There were squirrels and birds all around. I think I miss that tree more than anything else." She waved her hand in disgust at the small sapling outside the picture window. "You know, the birds don't come here yet."

But it is a world they can never recapture. The accidents of assignment might take them to a similar town—or, perhaps, even the old one—but they can never really belong again. They are transients, and between them and those who never left home there is a conflict of values not easily concealed. The transients feel that they have gone out into the world, and those who have not, know they feel that way. "Dave and I have thought often about going back to East Wells," a successful young lawyer's wife told me. "It's a beautiful old New England town, and both of us have had such happy times there. But there's a coolness now. All the people who have had anything on the ball seem to have left. Two boys who took over their father's business are still fun and alive, but the rest—I hate to sound snobbish, but we do feel superior to them."

In the old terms they seem almost completely adrift. Much of their rootlessness, however, lies in the eyes of the beholder, for he tends to equate roots with the fixed family and social relationships of the stable community. These, the transients will never have, but because they have been searching so very hard for compensation, they have developed what could almost be called a new kind of rootedness. In a sort of national cooperative, they have found it in one another.

Wherever they go, they will find themselves. The faces and the names change; the people do not. One du Pont couple put it to me this way: "We like it here in Deerhurst and we've made many wonderful friends. But moving isn't as bad as you think. I don't know whether we are going to be sent down to South Carolina or West Virginia, but we're sure to find a bunch just like the one we've left."

Sometimes their way of life is no more than a corporation version of army post life; in several large companies people can move all over the world and never meet anybody but other company people—and be quite happy that they don't. The important bond, however, is not company affiliation; when transients refer to people that "talk the same language," they mean other organization people. Whether they are with General Electric, the government, or the services is secondary; for the problems they talk over with each other—their next transfer, their children's reaction to changing schools, whether they should try and get out of their staff slot—are generic to organization life. They are all, as they so tirelessly repeat, "in the same boat."

This search for roots helps explain why the new suburbs are such hotbeds for civic participation. There are many reasons for this—the newness of the towns, for example, provides more problems to solve; and the turnover in leadership more opportunities for the newcomer to get included in them. But equally important is the function it performs for the individual. More than most, the transient wants to relate himself to others, and civic work is an ideal vehicle.

The result is often participation for participation's sake. The ease with which petition signatures are obtained, for example, is nothing short of startling, and no matter how many organizations they may belong to, transients generally feel impelled to deprecate their activity as a sort of idle folly. But the vitality is unmistakable. Because they are conscious that they personally are involved in a shift of values, they have a remarkable capacity for attributing undue significance to local issues. If you sit in on one of their meetings, you are likely to hear the matter under discussion—from a placement of a new water main to the most minor zoning restriction—described as the test case of America at the crossroads of democracy's crisis in microcosm.

Their desire for issues is insatiable. Several years ago the whole of Park Forest rose in arms against the developer because he wouldn't add a "multipurpose classroom" to one of the local schools. Financially he had an excellent case, as some of the village leaders conceded, but the issue got so wound up with the future of American education, the rights of free citizens under a "feudal barony," and so on that it overwhelmed everybody with a sense of community. And thus, though it got nowhere, it served its purpose. "I still don't know what it was all about," says an ex-Park Forest leader who led a mass march on the developer's office. "I suppose it was all a little silly—but I tell you, we were *living*."

In this search for roots lies the transient's dilemma. On one hand, he wants very much to maintain his autonomy against the pressures of the group, yet at the same time the group participation that he seeks to give meaning to his life puts a heavy premium on adaptability to the group. He cannot emphasize one except at the expense of the other. Which way is he to incline?

The question confronts him in very practical ways. Let me illustrate with the problem of the "happy" block. In the course of our study we found that, despite the high turnover, some blocks and rental courts remained very tightly knit socially, while others, owing in part to their design, never quite jelled into cohesive groups. Somewhat to our surprise, we found that when we plotted the location of the people most active in civic and cultural matters, a disproportionately small number came from the "happy" blocks. The more neighborly the group, it appeared, the more did it constrain its members from seeking outlets elsewhere.

And here we see the conflict. The couple in such a block who have other stirrings are inhibited from expressing them not merely for fear of the group but because they also feel a moral obligation to it. "Every once in a while I wonder," one such housewife told me, in an almost furtive moment of contemplation. "I would like to join the Players' Club, but if I did, it wouldn't help things here. It's not just that the people here would think I was getting snooty; I'd have to be away a good bit and others would have to double for me in watching the block playpen and it would, well, upset things. They're kind and decent people here, and we've made a big effort, all of us, to get along. I'd hate to be the first to break it up." She asked me if I thought she was being a coward, and she meant it as a question. Quite genuinely, she couldn't decide. So with many others; never quite sure whether the group is a tyrant or a friend, on they continue, imprisoned in brotherhood.

The "happy block" carries another price—and one, it should be added, that planners intent on bestowing social cohesion do not always recognize. If the socially functional design steps up the *Gemütlichkeit* of the group, it also steps up the misery of the deviate. Where in looser blocks no one pays much attention to the nonmixer, in the close-knit block the friction can become almost unbearable. Since the deviates upset the group's traditions, the group very easily becomes a monster. When people live only feet away from each other, their sanctions—the parties one's children don't get asked to, the hellos unspoken—can be an excruciating torment, and it is almost frightening to see the effect it has had on some couples.

Paradoxically, the best defense against the group is put up by those with the most social skill. It is easy to think of the isolate as the individualist, but this is not necessarily the case. Most of the alienated people I came across in suburbia didn't offend the group with unorthodox political views or disparate tastes; they offended because they didn't obey the basic rules of the game. These were the people who borrowed sugar and never repaid it, who ducked their turn in mowing the common lawn, or who gave a party and made a point of leaving out people on their side of The Line—that imaginary but most rigid line by which groups resolved the problem of hurt feelings. They were, in a word, socially inept.

Those least influenced by group pressures were hard to spot because they generally had a high amount of protective coloration. Whatever they may have thought of their neighbors, they were good about baby-sitting, returning borrowed things, and observing all the neighborly graces. They did not, furthermore, give the group a chance to isolate them; they didn't let it get that close. They were quite articulate on this point; like seasoned shipboard travelers, they explained that early in the transient life you learn that you must keep your neighbors at a certain distance and not allow propinquity to compromise the selection of your friends.

They liked to talk of themselves as deviates. With great relish they would tell how the purchase of a high-fidelity set instead of a TV set struck their neighbors as selfishness toward the children, or how their political stand in the last controversy shocked the whole block. Then, shaking their heads at the shame of it all, they would excuse themselves in order to attend some meeting. For they were the leaders, and not, as they would have you believe, the outcasts.

More than they realize it, it is these people who set the standards of the others. I remember one very intelligent woman who was certain that her preference for reading over the usual nonstop *kaffeeklatsching* had made neighbors think ill of her. One day, she told me, she had moved her beach chair to the front of the apartment as a signal that she wanted to read undisturbed. Though this was an accepted court convention, a wife new to the court came up to chat with her. " 'What you reading there?' she asked me. You might know that would be the day when I was rereading Plato's *Republic*. She was flabbergasted. Now everybody in the court is positively sure I'm a nut." As I was to learn later when I talked to the others, they thought no such thing. There was a hint of resentment that she hadn't become close with them, but they took pride that there was somebody so intellectual in the court. "A real educated group here," one told me, "not like that crew over in E-40. They don't do anything but have barbecues and watch television all the time."

The potential leaders differ, as we have noted, from most of their neighbors. But how much do they differ? They are more individualistic than the rest of their contemporaries, but this is only a relative comparison, for their values also indicate how very far the balance between the group and the individual has shifted. In a more muted fashion many of the leaders hold the same basic view of man as a social animal, and though they say it much more intelligently—and know that they are saying it—they, too, tend to equate the lone individual with psychic disorder. "We have learned not to be so introverted," one junior executive, and a very thoughtful and successful one, describes the lesson. "Before we came here we used to live pretty much to ourselves. On Sundays, for instance, we used to stay in bed until around maybe two o'clock reading the paper and listening to the symphony on the radio. Now we stop around and visit with people, or they visit with us. I really think Park Forest has broadened us."

For their children as well as themselves, they have elevated adaptability into a philosophy. Park Forest's high-school superintendent has given an unusual amount of encouragement to the "life-adjustment curriculum." "Ours is an age of group action," he says, and better prepare the children for it. He is much more intent upon courses like Family Group Living than upon the traditional academic disciplines. But this is exactly what the parents want. When they were asked in a questionnaire what they thought should be the primary purpose of the school, one answer came up more than all the others combined. The first job of the school, they wrote, is to teach people how to get along with others.

This same emphasis shows in church life as well. Park Forest's United Protestant Church emphasized the social function of church life in uniting people much more than theology. "We try not to offend anybody," says the minister who helped found it. "The business of doctrine should come later. The basic need is to belong to a group. You find this fellowship in a church better than anywhere else. Young people want a place to take their problems and someone to talk to about them. That's what we're after —a sense of community. We pick out the more useful part of the doctrine to that end."

What gives this social ethic its appeal is the way it seems geared to vital contemporary needs. It is, as the school superintendent says, an age of group action. But this is why their philosophy is so tremendously redundant. The very life they lead is such that they need no additional schooling in the ways of group life. What they need is the opposite.

Their own doubts indicate how very badly suited to the times is their ethic. For those who have tried hardest to rationalize adjustment are also those who complain the most bitterly about suburban conformity. They want very much to think of themselves as lone individualists surrounded by a sea of conformists and outdo one another in telling stories that show how herdlike everyone else is. But for all this, they also demonstrate considerable capacity for being honest about themselves. Inevitably, they will realize the effect the group has had on their own behavior, and they will concede that it has been far too great. They are not, they accuse themselves, the independents they should be.

But what is independence? Here is the heart of their problem. What bedevils them is not whether to conform but to know when they are conforming. To *belong* and to help others to belong is crucial to them, and thus much of what seems conformity to strangers is not mere submission to the group, but something much more active—a positive search for values, a *modus vivendi* by which they can accommodate themselves to the shifting loyalties and uncertainties of the transient life. To a large degree, to put it another way, their defects are the extension of what they consider virtues.

This goodwill does not make conformity any the less inhibiting; quite the contrary: it gives the group a moral sanction that makes it all the more powerful. The suburbanites sense this flaw in their social ethic and they are restive in their very sense of belonging. But what, they ask, is the alternative? Because it does not concede the moral base, the conventional damning of conformity is irrelevant to them. Not until their dilemma is conceded will they be vouchsafed the intellectual armor they so badly need.

THE INDIVIDUAL AT BAY

Vance Packard

[Advancing technology has provided new means of social control. Today, as never before, governmental and private agencies have the capability of keeping tabs on any individual and, consequently, discouraging or encouraging different behavior by granting or withholding jobs, credit, insurance, etc. The implications are ominous, as Vance Packard points out in this prescient piece, written in 1964.

[Vance Packard is the author of *The Hidden Persuaders*, *The Status Seekers*, *The Naked Society*, and *The Waste Makers*.]

Society is continually pushing in on the individual. He has only a few areas in which he can be himself, free from external restraint or observation.
—U.S. SENATOR EDWARD V. LONG OF MISSOURI

By telescoping time a bit let us look in on a reasonably successful family in a typical city of the Land of Liberty.

Mom is at the department store trying on a new dress in the dressing room. A closed-circuit TV camera hidden behind a mesh screen is recording her moves to make certain she does not pocket any of the store's merchandise.

Dad is at a conference table in his office talking to a group of colleagues about the operations of his department. The colleague sitting next to him is an undercover agent hired from a nationwide detective agency by the president of Dad's company to keep tabs on the performance of key subordinates. Elsewhere an investigator is on the telephone chatting with Dad's banker about the size of Dad's account and any outstanding loans. It seems that Dad recently applied for an insurance policy on his personal property.

Son John, just out of college, is seated in a chair with a pneumatic tube strapped across his chest and an electrode taped to his palm. John has applied for a job as a sales representative for an electronics concern. He is now undergoing the usual lie-detector test to probe his honesty, his possibly dangerous habits, and his manliness. Meanwhile an investigator is talking to one of John's erstwhile professors concerning any political opinions the boy may have expressed during class discussions.

Daughter Mary, sweet girl, is still only a sophomore in high school. She is in the classroom struggling with a 250-item questionnaire. It asks her to reveal whether her parents seem to quarrel a lot, whether they have ever talked to her about sex, and whether she is worried about menstrual disorders. If Mary's parents happen to hear about this probing, they would be denied any information as to her various responses and how they were scored.

All these things obviously would not happen on the same day to one family but all of them happen every day to a great many individuals. All have become common enough occurrences to raise somber questions about what the future holds for late twentieth-century society.

Are there loose in our modern world forces that threaten to annihilate everybody's privacy? And if such forces are indeed loose, are they establishing the preconditions of totalitarianism that could endanger the personal freedom of modern man?

These are the questions we must ponder as we explore the recent enormous growth in methods for observing, examining, controlling, and exchanging information about people. Individually the new social controls we are seeing are cloaked in reasonableness. And some perhaps have comic overtones. But when we view them collectively we must consider the possibility that they represent a massive, insidious impingement upon our traditional rights as free citizens to live our own lives.

Many of these new forces are producing pressures that intrude upon most of us where we live, work, shop, go to school, or seek solitude. Millions of Americans are living in an atmosphere in which peering electronic eyes, undercover agents, lie detectors, hidden tape recorders, bureaucratic investigators, and outrageously intrusive questionnaires are becoming commonplace, if often only suspected, facts of life.

Privacy is becoming harder and harder to attain, surveillance more and more pervasive. Mr. Justice William O. Douglas of the United States Supreme Court has commented: "The forces allied against the individual have never been greater."

The surveillance of citizens in the United States—and much of western Europe—has been growing year by year. One indication of its extent in the United States is seen in an analysis of our security system made a few years ago. It indicated that, even then, more than 13,500,000 Americans—or approximately one-fifth of all jobholders—were being scrutinized under some sort of security or loyalty program. In 1962 the Department of Defense alone conducted security investigations on 826,000 individuals.

Surveillance of individuals for security, loyalty, or general behavior is most rampant in Southern California. In this area the majority of the families have one or more members under some form of watch, either as defense workers, public employees, studio employees, or as recipients of welfare benefits. For most of these people, at least one investigator is bound to call on next-door neighbors to inquire about their backgrounds or living habits.

The United States Government employs more than 25,000 professional investigators, not including counter-intelligence and espionage operatives. Federal investigators, however, represent only a small fraction of the total number of people in the nation who earn their living investigating other people. There are hundreds of thousands of private, corporate, municipal, county, and state investigators.

Consider one private investigative firm that is little known to most Americans. Its world headquarters are in Atlanta. This firm bears the now outdated name of the Retail Credit Company. It offers a continent-spanning intelligence service with 6,000 full-time salaried "inspectors" on "constant call," who operate out of 1,500 offices in every state and

Canadian province. It has sixty-four offices in Ohio alone and has representatives in Mexico and Europe. The company's inspectors conduct about 90,000 investigations every working day, reporting mostly on individuals. They investigate applicants for insurance and claimants of insurance, they also check people's credit, and they conduct investigations of job applicants for clients. Their firm has 38,000 client-accounts that include many of the world's largest companies.

Much of the surveillance of individuals by trained investigators has been made easier by the proliferation of record-keeping in our increasingly bureaucratic society. I found it startling to learn how much information about one's private life is readily available to any skilled investigator who knows where to check accessible records and make a few routine inquiries. Detectives told me some of the presumably private information about myself—or just about any adult who is not a hermit—that an investigator could readily produce in most areas of the United States. They were referring just to an "easy" kind of checkout. An investigator in the New York State area could produce for a curious client most of the facts about you or me listed below, and it could be done within a few days. Here are the facts:

—Whether there are any significant blemishes on your record where you have worked.

—How much money you have in your checking account at the bank (roughly), whether you borrow money often and for what, whether you have been delinquent in paying back loans, and whether you have any outstanding loans.

—Whether you are a poor credit risk.

—Whether you have ever suffered from mental illness for which you were confined, been treated for a heart ailment, or been a victim of convulsive disorders. (This information can often be found in a public document—one's original application for a driver's license.)

—Whether you are a known sexual deviate.

—Whether you actually received that college degree, if you claim one.

—Whether you have ever been arrested, or had any lawsuits filed against you.

—A good surmise as to whether you were legitimately born, when and where, and the occupation of your parents at the time.

—Your net worth (provided you have a sizable unsecured bank loan), the value of your home, its layout and construction, its furnishings and upkeep, and what kinds of locks there are on your doors.

—Whether you have been involved in an automobile accident in recent years.

—Whether your loyalty has ever been questioned by any of the better-known investigative bodies, public or private.

—Whether you are a registered Democrat, Republican, or have failed to register a party preference.

When I expressed curiosity about my own credit rating one detective said, "Give me a couple of hours." Within that period he called and gave me data from a credit report on me. It contained a fairly thorough summary of my life, employers, agents, abodes, and offspring for the past two decades, and the precise assessed value of my home in Connecticut. He chuckled and added: "They say that, though you pay your bills, you occasionally take your time about it." He added that such reports often will provide a guess as to the person's annual income but that apparently my income was too erratic for a guess to be made.

Most American adults with jobs, cars, houses, charge accounts, insurance, and military or government records can assume that at least one specific dossier on them—more probably several—has been compiled. Most contain facts that are, by and large, relatively impersonal. But a great many hundreds of thousands of these dossiers contain thick reports with intimate details. Many also contain erroneous or adverse information.

The U.S. Civil Service Commission, which maintains a dossier on nearly everyone who has applied for federal employment since 1939, reportedly has nearly 250,000 dossiers that contain adverse information.

Its central index of approximately 7,500,000 dossiers is just one of the many central files on individuals that have grown to enormous proportions in recent years. The Defense Department maintains a central index of members of the armed forces, civilian employees, and a great many other people, including scientists working for defense contractors. The Federal Bureau of Investigation, of course, has its extensive central file. The House Un-American Activities Committee reportedly has accumulated a card file of more than a million names. The Association of Casualty and Surety Companies maintains a vast nationwide clearing-house of information regarding claimants. Very recently its file contained 18,200,000 entries on claimants for bodily injury or workmen's compensation. The bureau investigates or scrutinizes about one-fourth of all claims, which means it conducts about 500,000 investigations a year. And then, of course, there are the credit bureaus in every part of the United States as well as in Canada, England, and Australia that are affiliated with the Associated Credit Bureaus of America. Through rapid exchange arrangements any bureau can draw upon files kept on more than 100,000,000 individuals.

The private investigative firm Retail Credit Company has files on more than 42,000,000 individuals. These files consist of previous reports the firm has made on individuals, significant newspaper clippings, and available public records about individuals. The company points out to prospective clients that its massive files can strengthen and support any current investigations it makes.

A further indication of the increase in surveillance since the beginning of World War II is the tremendous amount of electronic eavesdropping that now occurs. An electronics expert familiar with the practices of U.S. intelligence agencies told me: "In all major cities" the government maintains hotel rooms with eavesdropping equipment already installed through a nearby wall. When a person under surveillance goes to such a hotel, "the proper authorities arrange for him to be put in the proper room," he said.

The United States, of course, is not the only country in which eavesdropping has been growing. The Russians have a very large head start. An American with Communist sympathies who had lived inside Russia a few years and then returned to America cited to acquaintances as one of his grievances about the Russian system that electronic listening devices were everywhere.

Of the many forms of electronic surveillance, wire-tapping has had the most public attention in the U.S., not because it is the most pernicious and rampant, but simply because it has generated the most political heat. Unlike the hiding of microphones and cameras, which is more in-vasive of privacy, wiretapping is a federal crime, although the Justice Department for its own good reasons takes a tortured view of the law and an interestingly lax approach to enforcing even its own view.

The Justice Department and law-enforcement officials in a few states are pressing hard for clear-cut permission to wiretap in investigating certain suspected criminal activities. At one Senate hearing the Attorney General explained: "We are balancing off the right of privacy versus the need for better law enforcement. . . ." Many Americans, par-ticularly those apprehensive about crime, would insist the "balance" tips far more heavily toward law enforcement.

During one session attended by the Attorney General, Senator John A. Carroll of Colorado raised a crucial point. He wondered if there was perhaps so much preoc-cupation with "racketeers, gamblers or prostitutes" that something far more fundamental to society was not being neglected: "the right of every citizen to his privacy."

. . . The Federal Communications Commission, after many years of virtually ignoring the mounting problem of electronic eavesdropping, invited comment on proposed rules seeking to curb one kind of electronic surveillance. That would be the kind requiring the use of radio trans-mitters, whether for bugging or wiretapping. Even if we as-sume the rules are issued, their enforcement probably will be delayed pending court challenges brought by manufactur-ers. This action is long overdue. However, it seems doubt-ful that these proposed rules would significantly diminish eavesdropping because of the broad exceptions written into them. For example they make an exception for ac-tions by law-enforcement agencies. They also except any situation where one party to the conversation knows of the eavesdropping.

Still another dimension of surveillance can be seen in the growing suspiciousness toward employees that has gripped much of U.S. industry. One of the nation's fastest-growing trade associations is the American Society for Industrial Security. Its membership grew from 1,800 to 2,500 in two recent years. And at a recent convention members were treated to a comprehensive display of bugging devices. A Washington newspaper called them "more frightening than any Black Widow spider." A spokesman for one of the displayers boasted that he didn't believe there was "any escape from this sort of equipment."

Along with the industrial espionage a new and more subtle surveillance is occurring throughout the land: psychological espionage of employees and schoolchildren.

The growing surveillance—and here I've just given a glimpse of its many manifestations—is inevitably exerting a significant impact upon the behavior patterns and value systems of the millions of citizens involved. The person who finds he is not trusted tends to strike back by becoming indeed untrustworthy. And the person who finds himself being watched, electronically or otherwise, tends unwittingly to become careful in what he does and says. This breeds not only sameness but a watchfulness completely untypical of the exuberant, freewheeling American so commonly accepted as typical of this land in earlier decades. The American Civil Liberties Union has observed (correctly, I believe), "A hallmark of totalitarian societies is that the people are apprehensive of being overheard or spied upon."

The former district attorney of Philadelphia, Mr. Samuel Dash, who made an exhaustive survey of eavesdropping in several states during the fifties, told a Senate committee:

> In cities where wiretapping was known to exist there was generally a sense of insecurity among professional people and people engaged in political life. Prominent persons were constantly afraid to use their telephones despite the fact that they were not engaged in any wrongdoing. It was clear that freedom of communication and the atmosphere of living in a free society without fear were handicapped by the presence of spying ears.

The closing in upon the privacy of the individual comes not only from the outright scrutiny of individuals but also from multiplying rules and regulations and from ever mounting requirements for licenses. There is the new insistence that one be traceable from cradle to grave. Bess E. Dick, staff director of the House Committee on the Judiciary, complained to me: "There is a crowding in." You are required to "live just this way and no other way." She felt the typical citizen is robbed of eccentricity.

Among the numerous rights heretofore considered characteristically American that we seem to be in danger of scuttling are:

—The right to be different.

—The right to hope for tolerant forgiveness or overlooking of past foolishnesses, errors, humiliations, or minor sins—in short, the Christian notion of the possibility of redemption.

—The right to make a fresh start.

America was largely settled, and its frontiers expanded, by people seeking to get away from something unpleasant in their pasts, either oppression, painful episodes, poverty, or misdemeanors.

Today it is increasingly assumed that the past and present of all of us—virtually every aspect of our lives —must be an open book; and that all such information about us can be not only put in files but merchandised freely. Business empires are being built on this merchandising of information about people's private lives. The expectation that one has a right to be let alone—the whole idea that privacy is a right worth cherishing—seems to be evaporating among large segments of our population.

There appears to be little awareness today among the complacent that no one is secure unless everyone is secure from the overeager constable, the overzealous investigator, and the overnosy bureaucrat. Totalitarianism typically begins when a would-be tyrant—whether a Hitler or a Castro —plays upon the anxieties of the majority to institute repressive measures against despised or troublesome minorities. Gradually the repressive measures are extended, perhaps inexorably, to larger and larger segments of the populace.

It was to protest the possibility of such an eventuality in the U.S.A. that Mr. Justice Brandeis issued his eloquent dissent in a case in 1928 involving surveillance. He said:

> The makers of our Constitution . . . sought to pro-
> tect Americans in their beliefs, their thoughts, their
> emotions and their sensations. They conferred as
> against the Government, the right to be let alone—the
> most comprehensive of the rights of man and the
> right most valued by civilized men.

Today, as we shall see, the Bill of Rights is under assault from many directions. Thomas Jefferson's vow that
he had sworn eternal hostility to every form of tyranny
over the mind of man has a quaint ring to many people
in 1964. Aldous Huxley commented that the classic cry of
Patrick Henry that he wanted either liberty or death now
sounds melodramatic. Instead today, Huxley contended, we
are more apt to demand, "Give me television and ham-
burgers but don't bother me with the responsibilities of
liberty."

It is worth noting that Mr. Huxley's prophetic book,
Brave New World, written way back in the thirties about
a technological society living in doped-up bliss under a
watchful tyrant six centuries from now, has been banned
from several U.S. schools. Also among the banned is
George Orwell's *1984*, depicting life under the ever-present
electronic eye and ear of a tyrannical Big Brother a bare
two decades from now. When the U.S. Commissioner of
Education was asked about the banning of these two clas-
sics from a Miami high school, he declined to comment because he said he had never heard of either of the books!

Many of the present invasions of our privacy originate
in the kinds of life the citizens have chosen to pursue.
Often such intrusions can be checked only by an aroused
concern about individual rights. Other of the invasions, as
we shall see, are susceptible to legal restraint. In general
the legal checks are in a state of lamentable confusion,
vagueness, or neglect. One judge has described the state
of the law of privacy, for example, as "still that of a hay-
stack in a hurricane."

Let us then try to understand what is happening to our
privacy—and our freedom—as individuals in the face of

the new kinds of pressure generated by our violently changing world. We might bear in mind a haunting comment made to me by Representative Robert Kastenmeier of Wisconsin, who has led several battles for individual rights on the floor of Congress. He said:

> Basically I am not hopeful about the pressures that will in time make our country something of a police state. Unless we can bring a release from the prolonged Cold War and can check the inward drift of our country, I sense a losing game.

WOMEN'S LIBERATION

Vivian Gornick

[The collective constraints on a suppressed class of
people drastically affect the prospects for individuals
within that class. Women achieved the right to vote
years ago, but have progressed little since then. They
are still expected to be the homemakers, cooking for
their families and following their husbands wherever
they may go. When women do venture into the job
market, they receive lower salaries and fewer advancement opportunities than men. This kind of discrimination is similar to the discrimination that faces blacks
and can have the same debilitating psychological effects.
Recently, a widespread and active women's liberation
movement has emerged to redress the situation. It may
well have an impact in the 1970s comparable to the
civil-rights movement in the 1960s.

[Vivian Gornick is a writer for *The Village Voice*.]

One evening not too long ago, at the home of a well-
educated and extremely intelligent couple I know, I mentioned the women's liberation movement and was mildly
astonished by the response the subject received. The man
said: "Jesus, what *is* all that crap about?" The woman, a
scientist who had given up ten working years to raise her
children, said: "I can understand if these women want to
work and are demanding equal pay. But why on earth do
they want to have children, too?" To which the man re-
joined: "Ah, they don't want kids. They're mostly a bunch
of dykes, anyway."

Again: Having lunch with an erudite, liberal editor,

trained in the humanist tradition, I was struck dumb by his reply to my mention of the women's liberation movement: "Ah shit, who the hell is oppressing them?"

And yet again: A college-educated housewife, fat and neurotic, announced with arch sweetness, "I'm sorry, I just don't *feel* oppressed."

Over and over again, in educated, thinking circles, one meets with a bizarre, almost determined ignorance of a fact of unrest that is growing daily, and that exists in formally organized bodies in nearly every major city and on dozens of campuses across America. The women of this country are gathering themselves into a sweat of civil revolt, and the general population seems totally unaware of what is happening; or, indeed, that anything is happening; or that there is a legitimate need behind what is happening. How is this possible? Why is it true? What relation is there between the peculiarly unalarmed, amused dismissal of the women's rights movement and the movement itself? Is this relation only coincidental, only the generally apathetic response of a society already benumbed by civil rights and student anarchy and unable to rise to yet one more protest movement, or is it more to the point in the case of women's rights, is it not, in fact, precisely the key to the entire issue?

Almost invariably, when people set out to tell you there is no such thing as discrimination against women in this country, the first thing they hastily admit to is a *minor* degree of economic favoritism shown toward men. In fact, they will eagerly, almost gratefully, support the claim of economic inequity, as though that will keep the discussion within manageable bounds. Curious. But even on economic grounds or grounds of legal discrimination most people are dismally ignorant of the true proportions of the issue. They will grant that often a man will make as much as $100 more than a woman at the same job, and yes, it *is* often difficult for a woman to be hired when a man can be hired instead, but after all, that's really not *so* terrible.

This is closer to the facts:

Women in this country make 60 cents for every $1 a man makes.

Women do not share in the benefits of the fair employment practices laws because those laws do not specify "no discrimination on the basis of sex."

Women often rise in salary only to the point at which a man starts.

Women occupy, in great masses, the "household tasks" of industry. They are nurses but not doctors, secretaries but not executives, researchers but not writers, workers but not managers, bookkeepers but not promoters.

Women almost never occupy decision- or policy-making positions.

Women are almost nonexistent in government.

Women are subject to a set of "protective" laws that restrict their working hours, do not allow them to occupy many jobs in which the carrying of weights is involved, do not allow them to enter innumerable bars, restaurants, hotels, and other public places unescorted.

Women, despite 100 years of reform, exist in the domestic and marriage laws of our country almost literally as appendages of their husbands. Did you know that rape by a husband is legal but that if a woman refuses to sleep with her husband, she is subject to legal suit? Did you know that the word "domicile" in the law refers to the husband's domicile and that if a woman refuses to follow her husband to wherever he makes his home, legal suit can be brought against her to force her to do so? Did you know that in most states the law imposes severe legal disabilities on married women with regard to their personal and property rights? (As a feminist said to me: "The United Nations has defined servitude as necessarily involuntary, but women, ignorant of the law, put themselves into *voluntary* servitude.")

Perhaps, you will say, these observations are not so shocking. After all, women *are* weaker than men, they do need protection, what on earth is so terrible about being protected, for God's sake! And as for those laws, they're never invoked, no woman is dragged anywhere against her will; on the contrary, women's desires rule the middle-class household, and women can work at hundreds of jobs; in fact, a great deal of the wealth of the country is in their hands, and no woman ever goes hungry.

I agree. These observed facts of our national life are not so shocking. The laws and what accrues from them are not so terrible. It is what's behind the laws that is so terrible. It is not the letter of the law but the spirit determining the law that is terrible. It is not what is explicit but what is implicit in the law that is terrible. It is not the apparent condition but the actual condition of woman that is terrible.

"The woman's issue is the true barometer of social change," said a famous political theoretician. This was true 100 years ago; it is no less true today. Women and blacks were and are, traditionally and perpetually, the great "outsiders" in Western culture, and their erratic swellings of outrage parallel each other in a number of ways that are both understandable and also extraordinary. A hundred years ago a great abolitionist force wrenched this country apart and changed its history forever; many, many radical men devoted a fever of life to wrecking a system in which men were bought and sold; many radical women worked toward the same end; the abolitionist movement contained women who came out of educated and liberal nineteenth-century families, women who considered themselves independent, thinking beings. It was only when Elizabeth Cady Stanton and Lucretia Mott were not allowed to be seated at a World Anti-Slavery Conference held in the 1840s that the intellectual abolitionist women suddenly perceived that their own political existence resembled that of the blacks. They raised the issue with their radical men and were denounce' furiously for introducing an insignificant and divisive i.   one which was sure to weaken the movement. Let's win   ar first, they said, and then we'll see about women's right.   the women had seen, in one swift visionary moment, t. he very center of the truth about their own lives, and they knew that first was *now*, that there would never be a time when men would willingly address themselves to the question of female rights, that to strike out *now* for women's rights could do nothing but strengthen the issue of black civil rights because it called attention to all instances of rights denied in a nation that prided itself on rights for all.

Thus was born the original Women's Rights Movement, which became known as the Women's Suffrage Movement because the single great issue, of course, was legal political recognition. But it was never meant to begin and end with the vote, just as the abolitionist movement was never meant to begin and end with the vote. Somehow, though, that awful and passionate struggle for suffrage seemed to exhaust both the blacks and the women, especially the women, for when the vote finally came at the end of the Civil War, it was handed to black males—but not to women; the women had to go on fighting for 60 bitterly long years for suffrage. And then both blacks and women lay back panting, unable to catch their breath for generation upon generation.

The great civil-rights movement for blacks in the 1950s and 1960s is the second wind of that monumental first effort, necessary because the legislated political equality of the 1860s was never translated into actual equality. The reforms promised by law had never happened. The piece of paper meant nothing. Racism had never been legislated out of existence; in fact, its original virulence had remained virtually untouched, and, more important, the black in this country had never been able to shake off the slave mentality. He was born scared, he ran scared, he died scared; for 100 years after legal emancipation, he lived as though it had never happened. Blacks and whites did not regard either themselves or each other differently, and so they in no way lived differently. In the 1950s and 1960s the surging force behind the renewed civil-rights effort has been the desire to eradicate this condition more than any other, to enable the American black to believe in himself as a whole, independent, expressive human being capable of fulfilling and protecting himself in the very best way he knows how. Today, after more than 15 years of unremitting struggle, after a formidable array of reform laws legislated at the federal, state, and local levels, after a concentration on black rights and black existence that has traumatized the nation, it is still not unfair to say that the psychology of defeat has not been lifted from black life. Still (aside from the continuance of crime, drugs, broken homes, and all the wretched rest of it), employers are able to say: "Sure, I'd love to hire one if I could find one who qualified," and while half the time this is simply not true, half the time it *is,* because black life is still marked by the "nigger mentality," the terrible inertia of spirit that accompanies the perhaps irrational but deeply felt conviction that no matter what one does, one is going to wind up a thirty-five-year-old busboy. This "nigger mentality" characterizes black lives. It also characterizes women's lives. And it is this, and this alone, that is behind the second wave of feminism now sweeping the country and paralleling precisely, exactly as it does 100 years ago, the black rights movement. The fight for reform laws is just the beginning. What women are really after this time around is the utter eradication of the "nigger" in themselves.

Most women who feel "niggerized" have tales of overt oppression to tell. They feel they've been put down by their fathers, their brothers, their lovers, their bosses. They feel that in their families, in their sex lives, and in their jobs they have counted as nothing, they have been treated as second-class citizens, their minds have been deliberately stunted and their emotions warped. My own experience with the condition is a bit more subtle, and, without bragging, I do believe a bit closer to the true feminist point.

To begin with, let me tell a little story. Recently, I had lunch with a man I had known at school. He and his wife and I had all been friends at college; they had courted while we were in school and immediately upon graduation they got married. They were both talented art students, and it was assumed both would work in commercial art. But shortly after their marriage she became pregnant, and never did go to work. Within five years they had two children. At first I visited them often; their home was lovely, full of their mutual talent for atmosphere; the wife sparkled, the children flourished; the husband rose in the field of commercial art; I envied them both their self-containment, and she especially her apparently contented, settled state. But as I had remained single and life took me off in various other directions, we soon began to drift apart, and when I again met the husband, we had not seen each other in many years. We spoke animatedly of what we had both been doing for quite a while. Then I asked about his wife. His face rearranged itself suddenly, but I couldn't quite tell how at first. He said she was fine, but didn't sound right.

"What's wrong?" I asked. "Is she doing something you don't want her to do? Or the other way around?"

"No, no," he said hastily. "I want her to do whatever she wants to do. Anything. Anything that will make her happy. And get her off my back," he ended bluntly. I asked what he meant and he told me of his wife's restlessness of the last few years, of how sick she was of being a housewife, how useless she felt, and how she longed to go back to work.

"Well," I asked, "did you object?"

"Of course not!" he replied vigorously. "Why the hell would I do that? She's a very talented woman, her children are half grown, she's got every right in the world to go to work."

"So?" I said.

"It's *her*," he said bewilderedly. "She doesn't seem able to just go out and get a job."

"What do you mean?" I asked. But beneath the surface of my own puzzled response I more than half knew what was coming.

"Well, she's scared, I think. She's more talented than half the people who walk into my office asking for work, but do what I will, she won't get a portfolio together and make the rounds. Also, she cries a lot lately. For no reason, if you know what I mean. And then, she can't seem to get up in the morning in time to get a baby-sitter and get out of the house. This is a woman who was always up at seven A.M. to feed everybody, get things going; busy, capable, doing ten things at once." He shook his head as though in a true quandary. "Oh well," he ended up, "I guess it doesn't really matter any more."

"Why not?" I asked.

His eyes came up and he looked levelly at me. "She's just become pregnant again."

I listened silently, but with what internal churning! Even though the external events of our lives were quite different, I felt as though this woman had been living inside my skin all these years, so close was I to the essential nature of her experience as I perceived it listening to her husband's woebegone tale. I had wandered about the world, I had gained another degree, I had married twice, I had written, taught, edited, I had no children. And yet I knew that in some fundamental sense we were the same woman. I understood exactly—but exactly—the kind of neurotic anxiety that just beset her, and that had ultimately defeated her; it was a neurosis I shared and had recognized in almost every woman I had ever known—including Monica Vitti, having her Chiaparellied nervous breakdown, stuffing her hand into her mouth, rolling her eyes wildly, surrounded by helplessly sympathetic men who kept saying: "Just tell me what's *wrong*."

I was raised in an immigrant home where education was worshiped. As the entire American culture was somewhat mysterious to my parents, the educational possibilities of that world were equally unknown for both the boy and the girl in our family. Therefore, I grew up in the certainty that if my brother went to college, I too could go to college; and, indeed, he did, and I in my turn did too. We both read voraciously from early childhood on, and we were both encouraged to do so. We both had precocious and outspoken opinions and neither of us was ever discouraged from uttering them. We both were exposed early to unionist radicalism and neither of us met with opposition when, separately, we experimented with youthful political organizations. And yet somewhere along the line my brother and I managed to receive an utterly different education regarding ourselves and our own expectations from life. He was taught many things, but what he learned was the need to develop a kind of inner necessity. I was taught many things, but what I learned, ultimately, was that it was the prime vocation of my life to prepare myself for the love of a good man and the responsibilities of homemaking and motherhood. All the rest, the education, the books, the jobs, that was all very nice and of course, why not? I was an intelligent girl, shouldn't I learn? *make* something of myself! but oh dolly, you'll see, in the end no woman could possibly be happy without a man to love and children to raise. What's more, came the heavy implication, if I *didn't* marry, I would be considered an irredeemable failure.

How did I learn this? How? I have pondered this question 1,000 times. Was it really that explicit? Was it laid out in lessons strategically planned and carefully executed? Was it spooned down my throat at regular intervals? No. It wasn't. I have come finally to understand that the lessons were implicit and they took place in 100 different ways, in a continuous day-to-day exposure to an *attitude*, shared by all, about women, about what kind of creatures they were and what kind of lives they were meant to live; the lessons were administered not only by my parents but by the men and women, the boys and girls, all around me who, of course, had been made in the image of this attitude.

My mother would say to me when I was very young, as I studied at the kitchen table and she cooked: "How lucky you are to go to school! I wasn't so lucky. I had to go to work in the factory. I wanted so to be a nurse! But to be a nurse in Williamsburg in 1920! Maybe you'll be a nurse. . . ." I listened, I nodded, but somehow the message I got was that I was like her and I would one day be doing what she was now doing.

My brother was the "serious and steady" student, I the "erratic and undisciplined" one. When he studied, the house was silenced; when I studied, business as usual.

When I was fourteen and I came in flushed and disarrayed, my mother knew I'd been with a boy. Her fingers gripped my upper arm; her face, white and intent, bent over me: What did he do to you? *Where* did he do it? I was frightened to death. What was she so upset about? What could he do to me? I learned that I was the keeper of an incomparable treasure and it had to be guarded: it was meant to be a gift for my husband. (Later that year when I read *A Rage to Live,* I knew without any instruction exactly what all those elliptical sentences were about.)

When I threw some hideous temper tantrum my mother would say: "What a little female you are!" (I have since seen many little boys throw the same tantrums and have noted with interest that they are not told they are little females.)

The girls on the street would talk forever about boys, clothes, movies, fights with their mothers. The 1,000 thoughts racing around in my head from the books I was reading remained secret, no one to share them with.

The boys would be gentler with the girls than with each other when we all played roughly; and our opinions were never considered seriously.

I grew up, I went to school, I came out, wandered

around, went to Europe, went back to school, wandered again, taught in a desultory fashion, and at last! got married!

It was during my first marriage that I began to realize something was terribly wrong inside me, but it took me ten years to understand that I was suffering the classic female pathology. My husband, like all the men I have known, was a good man, a man who wanted my independence for me more than I wanted it for myself. He urged me to work, to do something, anything, that would make me happy; he knew that our pleasure in each other could be heightened only if I was a functioning human being too. Yes, yes! I said, and leaned back in the rocking chair with yet another novel. Somehow, I couldn't do anything. I didn't really know where to start, what I wanted to do. Oh, I had always had a number of interests but they, through an inability on my part to stick with anything, had always been superficial; when I arrived at a difficult point in a subject, a job, an interest, I would simply drop it. Of course, what I really wanted to do was write; but that was an altogether ghastly agony and one I could never come to grips with. There seemed to be some terrible aimlessness at the very center of me, some paralyzing lack of will. My energy, which was abundant, was held in a trap of some sort; occasionally that useless energy would wake up roaring, demanding to be let out of its cage, and then I became "emotional"; I would have hysterical depressions, rage on and on about the meaninglessness of my life, force my husband into long psychoanalytic discussions about the source of my (our) trouble, end in a purging storm of tears, a determination to do "something," and six months later I was right back where I started. If my marriage had not dissolved, I am sure that I would still be in exactly that same peculiarly nightmarish position. But as it happened, the events of life forced me out into the world, and repeatedly I had to come up against myself. I found this pattern of behavior manifesting itself in 100 different circumstances; regardless of how things began, they always seemed to end in the same place. Oh, I worked, I advanced, in a sense, but only erratically and with superhuman effort. Always the battle was internal, and it was with a kind of paralyzing anxiety at the center of me that drained off my energy and retarded my capacity for intellectual concentration. It took me a long time to perceive that nearly every woman I knew exhibited the same symptoms, and when I did perceive it, became frightened. I thought, at first, that perhaps, indeed, we were all victims of some biological deficiency, that some vital ingredient had been deleted in the female of the species, that we were a physiological metaphor for human neurosis. It took me a long time to understand, with an understanding that is irrevocable, that we are the victims of culture, not biology.

Recently I read a marvelous biography of Beatrice Webb, the English socialist. The book is full of vivid portraits, but the one that is fixed forever in my mind is that of Mrs. Webb's mother, Laurencina Potter. Laurencina Potter was a beautiful, intelligent, intellectually energetic woman of the middle nineteenth century. She knew 12 languages, spoke Latin and Greek better than half of the classics-trained men who came to her home, and was interested in everything. Her marriage to wealthy and powerful Richard Potter was a love match, and she looked forward to a life of intellectual companionship, stimulating activity, lively participation. No sooner were they married than Richard installed her in a Victorian fortress in the country, surrounded her with servants and physical comfort, and started her off with the first of the 11 children she eventually bore. He went out into the world, bought and sold railroads, made important political connections, mingled in London society, increased his powers, and relished his life. She, meanwhile, languished. She sat in the country, staring at the four brocaded walls; her energy remained bottled up, her mind became useless, her will evaporated. The children became symbols of her enslavement and, in consequence, she was a lousy mother: neurotic, self-absorbed, increasingly colder and more withdrawn, increasingly more involved in taking her emotional temperature. She became, in short, the Victorian lady afflicted with indefinable maladies.

When I read of Laurencina's life, I felt as though I were reading about the lives of most of the women I know, and it struck me that 100 years ago sexual submission was all for a woman, and today sexual fulfillment is all for a woman, and the two are one and the same.

Most of the women I know are people of superior intelligence, developed emotions, and higher education. And yet our friendships, our conversations, our lives are not marked by intellectual substance or emotional distance or objective concern. It is only briefly and insubstantially that I ever discuss books or politics or philosophical issues or abstractions of any kind with the women I know. Mainly, we discuss and are intimate about our Emotional Lives. Endlessly, endlessly, we go on and on about our emotional "problems" and "needs" and "relationships." And, of course, because we are all bright and well educated, we bring to bear on these sessions a formidable amount of sociology and psychology, literature and history, all hoked out so that it sounds as though these are serious conversations on serious subjects, when in fact they are caricatures of seriousness right out of Jonathan Swift. Caricatures, because they have no beginning, middle, end, or point. They go nowhere, they conclude nothing, they change nothing. They are elaborate descriptions in the ongoing soap opera that is our lives. It took me a long time to understand that we were talking about nothing, and it took me an even longer and harder time, traveling down that dark, narrow road in the mind, back, back to the time when I was a little girl sitting in the kitchen with my mother, to understand, at last, that the affliction was cultural not biological, that it was because we had never been taught to take ourselves seriously that I and all the women I knew had become parodies of "taking ourselves seriously."

The rallying cry of the black civil-rights movement has always been: "Give us back our manhood!" What exactly does that mean? Where is black manhood? How has it been taken from blacks? And how can it be retrieved? The answer lies in one word: responsibility; therefore, they have been deprived of serious work; therefore, they have been deprived of self-respect; therefore, they have been deprived of manhood. Women have been deprived of exactly the same thing and in every real sense have thus been deprived of womanhood. We have never been prepared to assume responsibility; we have never been prepared to make demands upon ourselves; we have never been taught to expect the development of what is best in ourselves because no one has ever expected *anything* of us—or for us. Because no one has ever had any intention of turning over any serious work to us. Both we and the blacks lost the ballgame before we ever got up to play. In order to live you've got to have nerve; and we were stripped of our nerve before we began. Black is ugly and female is inferior. These are the primary lessons of our experience, and in these ways both blacks and women have been kept, not as functioning nationals, but rather as operating objects, but a human being who remains as a child throughout his adult life is an object, not a mature specimen, and the definition of a child is: one without responsibility.

At the very center of all human life is energy, psychic energy. It is the force of that energy that drives us, that surges continually up in us, that must repeatedly spend and renew itself in us, that must perpetually be reaching for something beyond itself in order to satisfy its own insatiable appetite. It is the imperative of that energy that has determined man's characteristic interest, problem-solving. The modern ecologist attests to that driving need by demonstrating that in a time when all the real problems are solved, man makes up new ones in order to go on solving. He must have work, work that he considers real and serious, or he will die, he will simply shrivel up and die. That is the one certain characteristic of human beings. And it is the one characteristic, above all others, that the accidentally dominant white male asserts is not necessary to more than half the members of the race, i. e., the female of the species. This assertion is, quite simply, a lie. Nothing more, nothing less. A lie. That energy is alive in every woman in the world. It lies trapped and dormant like a growing tumor, and at its center there is despair, hot, deep, wordless.

It is amazing to me that I have just written these words. To think that 100 years after Nora slammed the door, and in a civilization and a century utterly converted to the fundamental insights of that exasperating genius, Sigmund Freud, women could still be raised to believe that their basic makeup is determined not by the needs of their egos but by their peculiar childbearing properties and their so-called unique capacity for loving. No man worth his salt does not wish to be a husband and father; yet no man is raised to be a husband and father and no man would ever conceive of those relationships as instruments of his prime function in life. Yet every woman is raised, still, to believe that the fulfillment of these relationships is her prime function in life and, what's more, her instinctive choice.

The fact is that women have no special capacities for love, and when a culture reaches a level where its women have nothing to do but "love" (as occurred in the Victorian upper classes and as is occurring now in the American middle classes), they prove to be very bad at it. The modern American wife is not noted for her love of her husband or of her children; she is noted for her driving (or should I say driven?) domination of them. She displays an aberrated, aggressive ambition for her mate and for her offspring which can be explained only by the most vicious feelings toward the self. The reasons are obvious. The woman who must love for a living, the woman who has no self, no objective, external reality to take her own measure by, no work to discipline her, no goal to provide the illusion of progress, no internal resources, no separate mental existence, is constitutionally incapable of the emotional distance that is one of the real requirements of love. She cannot separate herself from her husband and children because all the passionate and multiple needs of her being are centered on them. That's why women "take everything personally." It's all they've got to take. "Loving" must substitute for an entire range of feeling and interest. The man, who is not raised to be a husband and father specifically and who simply loves as a single function of his existence, cannot understand her abnormal "emotionality" and concludes that this is the female nature. (Why shouldn't he? She does too.) But this is not so. It is a result of a psychology achieved by cultural attitudes that run so deep and have gone on for so long that they are mistaken for "nature" or "instinct."

A good example of what I mean are the multiple legends of our culture regarding motherhood. Let's use our heads

for a moment. What on earth is holy about motherhood?
I mean, why motherhood rather than fatherhood? If anything is holy, it is the consecration of sexual union. A man
plants a seed in a woman; the seed matures and eventually
is expelled by the woman; a child is born to both of
them; each contributed the necessary parts to bring about
procreation; each is responsible to and necessary to the
child; to claim that the woman is more so than the man
is simply not true; certainly it cannot be proven biologically
or psychologically; all that can be proven is that some
one is necessary to the newborn baby; to have instilled in
women the belief that their childbearing and housewifely
obligations supersedes all other needs, that indeed what
they fundamentally *want* and need is to be wives and
mothers as distinguished from being anything else, is to
have accomplished an act of trickery, an act which has
deprived women of the proper forms of expression necessary to that force of energy alive in every talking creature,
an act which has indeed mutilated their natural selves and
deprived them of their womanhood, what*ever* that may be,
deprived them of the right to say "I" and have it mean
something. This understanding, grasped whole, is what
underlies the current wave of feminism. It is felt by
thousands of women today, it will be felt by millions
tomorrow.

MODERN ECONOMIC REALITIES
AND INDIVIDUALISM[1]

Paul A. Samuelson

[Ever since the publication of Adam Smith's *The Wealth of Nations,* economic arguments have figured heavily in the definition of American individualism. Paul Samuelson examines the role of individualism in the marketplace and argues, wittily, that nothing is so simple as it seems.

[Paul Samuelson is professor of economics at Massachusetts Institute of Technology and the author of *Foundations of Economic Analysis, Economics: An Introductory Analysis, Readings in Economics,* and *Linear Programming and Economic Analysis.*]

To an economist the word "individualism" is tied up with laissez-faire. Or with liberalism in the nineteenth-century Manchester School sense, as distinct from the modern American connotation of a liberal as a kind of New Dealer who is just to the left of the moving center but not quite over the brink into radicalism. Perhaps John Stuart Mill is the archetype of an individualist. And

[1] Acknowledgment is made to Felicity Skidmore for research assistance. Part of this discussion was adapted from my contribution to a Swarthmore symposium and from research for a workshop sponsored by the Industrial Relations Division of the University of California at Berkeley. See George J. Stigler and Paul A. Samuelson, "A Dialogue on the Proper Economic Role of the State," *Selected Papers,* No. 7 (Graduate School of Business, University of Chicago, 1963); also P. A. Samuelson, "Personal Freedoms and Economic Freedoms in the Mixed Economy," *The Business Establishment,* Earl F. Cheit (ed.), (New York: John Wiley & Sons, Inc., 1964), Chap. 6, pp. 193–227.

perhaps the apotheosis of individualism is that social order which Thomas Carlyle contemptuously dismissed as "anarchy plus the constable." In this last century the world has obviously moved away from rugged individualism. Presumably, in the century before that, the Western world had been moving toward a greater degree of individualism. Yet it would be a mistake to think that there was ever a golden age of unadulterated individualism.

EDEN IN EQUILIBRIUM

Physicists have a model of a dilute gas. The air in this hypothetical balloon I hold in my hand is supposed to consist of a number of hard little atoms in continuous motion. So small is each atom as to make the distances between them very large indeed. It is a lonely life, and the encounters between atoms are very few and far between—which is indeed fortunate since the encounters are envisaged by the physicist as involving collisions with elastic rebounds. Something like this is pictured by the extreme individualist. Daniel Boone, who moved farther west when he could begin to hear the bark of his neighbor's dog, would regard this model of a dilute gas as very heaven. Those who cherish family life, or at the least have an interest in biological survival, will gladly extend the notion of an individual to include the family group. Nor will this daunt the physicist, who is happy to think of the air in this balloon as consisting of molecules, which in their turn consist of clusters of parent-and-children atoms rather than detached bachelors.

I will tell you a secret. Economists are supposed to be dry-as-dust, dismal fellows. This is quite wrong, the reverse of the truth. Scratch a hard-boiled economist of the libertarian persuasion and you find a Don Quixote underneath. No lovesick maiden ever pined for the days of medieval chivalry with such sentimental impracticality as some economists long for the return to a Victorian marketplace that is completely free. Completely free? Well, almost so. There must, of course, be the constable to ensure that voluntary contracts are enforced and to protect the property rights of each molecule which is an island unto itself.

Where Carlyle envisaged an anarchy that was veritable

chaos, a jungle red in tooth and claw, the antiquarian economist sees Newtonian order—an impersonal system of competitive checks and balances. Life in this other Eden is neither nasty, brutish, nor short. Law, labor, and capital end up getting combined in an optimal way, so that the best menu of apples, automobiles, Picasso paintings, comic books, gin, applesauce, xylophones, and zebras is offered to the consumer. He chooses from the lot what pleases him best. As Bentham said, all pleasures are one: pushpin is as good as poetry provided individuals deem it so. Applejack gives a less pure pleasure than apple juice, but not for the reason that alcohol is morally bad. Rather only for the reason that its positive pleasure tonight must be carefully adjusted for the negative pleasure of tomorrow's hangover; if the net balance yields more utils than apple juice, then bottoms up! If at some midpoint between tonight's revelry and tomorrow's hangover, you decide to walk over Niagara Falls on a tightrope, that is just your way of maximizing utility. Should the enterprise turn out in some altitudinal way to have been a mistake—well, each man who is free and twenty-one is entitled to make his own mistakes without the nosy interference of his neighbor or of artificial government.

Special allowance might have to be made for lunatics and minors. While most Benthamites would certify women as "competents"—i.e., free-wills whose tastes should be respected—few of them would go as far as Albert Schweitzer and extend the felicific calculus to animals, insects, and plants. The formula, each to count for one and only one, was not expected to include chimpanzees or amoebae. The total utility which the Universe was to minimize apparently did not include an algebraic contribution from the likes of them.

On the other hand, Bentham would not have recognized an inferior caste of slaves whose pleasures were not to count. What would he think of a person who sold himself into perpetual slavery in order to give a weekend potlatch? I am not sure, but if it were a sober, arms-length transaction at the going competitive market price, I dare say Bentham would have wanted such contracts to be legally enforceable.

WHAT SMITH HATH WROUGHT

The first human was Adam. The first economist (if one can make the distinction) was Adam Smith. The year 1776 was a vintage one: it gave us the Declaration of Independence, the work of Thomas Jefferson and a committee; and it gave us *The Wealth of Nations*, the work of an individual. Smith was an urbane and skeptical Scot nurtured on the same branch water as his friend David Hume. No zealot he, Smith gave two resounding cheers for individualism; but for state interference of the prenineteenth-century type, he could muster up only a Bronx cheer.

And make no mistake about it: Smith was right. Most of the interventions into economic life by the State were then harmful both to prosperity and freedom. What Smith said needed to be said. In fact, much of what Smith said still needs to be said: good intentions by government are not enough; acts do have consequences that had better be taken into account if good is to follow. Thus, the idea of a decent real wage is an attractive one. So is the idea of a low interest rate at which the needy can borrow. Nonetheless, the attempt *by law* to set a minimum real wage at a level much above the going market rates, or to set a maximum interest rate for small loans at what seem like reasonable levels, inevitably does much harm to precisely the persons whom the legislation is intended to help. Domestic and foreign experience—today, yesterday, and tomorrow—bears out the Smithian truth. Note that this is not an argument against *moderate* wage and interest fiats, which may improve the perfection of competition and make businessmen and workers more efficient.

Smith himself was what we today would call a pragmatist. He realized that monopoly elements ran through laissez-faire. When he said that Masters never gather together even for social merriment without plotting to raise prices against the public interest, he anticipated the famous Judge Gary dinners at which the big steel companies used to be taught what every oligopolist should know. Knowing the caliber of George III's civil service, Smith believed the government would simply do more harm than good if it tried to cope with the evil of monopoly. Pragmatically, Smith might, if he were alive today, favor the Sherman Act and stronger antitrust legislation or even public-utility regulation generally. He might even, in our time, be a Fabian. Certainly Jeremy Bentham, with his everlasting concern for maximizing utility, would in our nonindividualistic age be a social activist—at the very least a planner of the present French type.

THE INVISIBLE HAND

One-hundred-percent individualists skip these pragmatic lapses into good sense and concentrate on the purple passage in Adam Smith where he discerns an Invisible Hand that leads each selfish individual to contribute to the best public good. Smith had a point; but he could not have earned a passing mark in a Ph.D. oral examination in explaining just what that point was. Until this century, his followers—such as Bastiat—thought that the doctrine of the Invisible Hand meant one of two things: (*a*) that it produced maximum feasible total satisfaction, somehow defined; or (*b*) that it showed that anything which results from the voluntary agreements of uncoerced individuals must make them better (or best) off in some important sense.

Both of these interpretations, which are still held by many modern libertarians, are wrong. This is not the place for a technical discussion of economic principles, so I shall be very brief and cryptic in showing this. First, suppose some ethical observer—such as Jesus, Buddha, or for that matter John Dewey or Aldous Huxley—were to examine whether the total of social utility (as that ethical observer scores the deservingness of the poor and rich, saintly and sinning individuals) was actually maximized by 1860 or 1962 laissez-faire. He might decide that a tax placed upon yachts, the proceeds to go to cheapen the price of insulin to the needy, might increase the total of utility. Could Adam Smith prove him wrong? Could Bastiat? I think not. Of course, they might say that there is no point in trying to compare different individuals' utilities because they are incommensurable and can no more be added together than can apples and oranges. But if recourse is made to this argument, then the doctrine that the Invisible Hand maximizes total utility of the universe has already been thrown out the window. If they admit that the Invisible Hand will truly maximize total social utility *provided the state intervenes so as to make the initial distribution of dollar votes ethically proper,* then they have abandoned the libertarian's position that individuals are not to be coerced, even by taxation.

In connection with the second interpretation that anything which results from voluntary agreements is in some sense, *ipso facto,* optimal, we can reply by pointing out that when I make a purchase from a monopolistic octopus, I have performed a voluntary act, for I can always go without Alka-Seltzer or aluminum or nylon or whatever product you think is produced by a monopolist. Mere voluntarism, therefore, is not the root merit of the doctrine of the Invisible Hand: what is important about it is the system of checks and balances that comes under perfect competition; and its measure of validity is at the technocratic level of efficiency, not at the ethical level of freedom and individualism.[2] That this is so can be seen from the fact that such socialists as Oscar Lange and A. P. Lerner have advocated channeling the Invisible Hand to the task of organizing a socialistic society efficiently.

[2] What perfectly competitive equilibrium, the Invisible Hand, achieves is this: if production functions satisfy appropriate returns conditions, if all externalities of production and tastes are appropriately absent (which includes the absence of public goods and of neighborhood effects), then competitive equilibrium is such that not *everyone* can be made better off by any intervention. This is not a theorem about ideal laissez-faire, for it holds just as valid after good or bad (lump-sum) interferences have determined the initial distribution of wealth and earning powers. There are literally an infinite number of equilibrium states just as "efficient" as that of laissez-faire individualism. Such an efficiency state is a necessary but not sufficient (repeat, not) condition for maximization of a social-welfare function that respects individuals' tastes. It is a tribute to competitive pricing that under the severe returns and externality conditions specified, and only then, it can maximize an ethically prescribed social-welfare function, provided the initial "distribution of resources" has been rectified so as to make of equal social deservingness each consumer dollar which votes in the market. All this is complex and was not understood until this century at the earliest. A. Bergson, P. Samuelson, and O. Lange can, I think fairly,

In summary, these individualistic atoms of the rare gas in my balloon are not isolated from the other atoms. Adam Smith, who is almost as well known for his discussion of the division of labor and the resulting efficiency purchased at the price of interdependence, was well aware of that. What he would have stressed was that the contacts between the atoms were *organized* by the use of markets and prices.

THE IMPERSONALITY OF MARKET RELATIONS

Just as there is a sociology of family life and of politics, there is a sociology of individualistic competition. It is not a rich one. Ask not your neighbor's name; inquire only for his numerical schedules of supply and demand. Under perfect competition, no buyer need face a seller. Haggling in a Levantine bazaar is a sign of less than perfect competi-

---

be cited for the present formulation; but parts of it had been understood, and sometimes misunderstood, by such distinguished economists as V. Pareto, E. Barone, A. P. Lerner, N. Kaldor, J. R. Hicks and T. Scitovsky. Mention should be made of the useful intuitions of the neoclassical economists L. Walras, K. Wicksell, A. Marshall, F. von Wieser, A. C. Pigou, A. Young, J. B. Clark, P. Wicksteed, F. Edgeworth, F. Taylor, F. Knight, H. Hotelling, J. Viner, and still others. For a partial review of doctrine, see P. Samuelson, *Foundations of Economic Analysis,* Chapter Eight (Cambridge, Massachusetts: Harvard University Press, 1947).

An economist might wonder whether the later work of K. Arrow does not cast doubt on the concept of a social-welfare function. Valuable as it is in its own right as a contribution to mathematical politics, Arrow's demonstration, that it is impossible to have a "constitutional function" that compromises differing tastes of individuals and at the same time satisfies certain plausible requirements, does not rob the Bergson formulation of its validity. A constitutional function is not a social-welfare function, even if it is given the same name as one. I should mention that Harsanyi, in the last decade, has made the notable contribution that the Bergson Social-Welfare Function can be written as additive in individuals' utilities provided certain plausible postulates about social choice in the presence of probabilities are accepted. The view that R. Coase has shown that externalities—like smoke nuisances—are not a logical blow to the Invisible Hand and do not call for coercive interference with laissez-faire is not mine. I do not know that it is Coase's. But if it had not been expressed by someone, I would not be mentioning it here. Unconstrained self-interest will in such cases lead to the insoluble bilateral monopoly problem with all its indeterminacies and nonoptimalities.

tion. The telephone is the perfect go-between to link buyers and sellers through the medium of an auction market, such as the New York Stock Exchange or the Chicago Board of Trade for grain transactions. Two men may talk hourly all their working lives and never meet. It is alleged that many women have developed affection for the local milkman, but few romances have blossomed over a Merrill Lynch teletype.

These economic contacts between atomistic individuals may seem a little chilly or, to use the language of wine tasting, "dry." They remind one of those nunneries which receive sustenance from the outside world only through a contrivance like a dumbwaiter which bars all human confrontation. Or they are like the anthropological custom in which certain tribes trade with their neighbors by laying out, at dead of night, gifts which the others pick up and reciprocate. Presumably custom keeps the balance of trade about even, which is more than custom has been doing for the weak American balance of international payments in recent years.

This impersonality has its good side. If money talks, you and I do not have to fabricate conversation. That is one reason my wife buys our toothpaste at the self-service supermarket rather than at the corner drugstore—which as a matter of fact is no longer there, for reasons that are obvious. The prices have been equalized by Massachusetts law, and she is liberated from talking about the New England weather, being able to save her energies for our dialogues about Plato and Freud. On the other hand, that Southern editor, Harry Golden of North Carolina, claims he has never bought an entire box of cigars in his life, since that would deprive him of pleasurable daily contacts. Under perfect laissez-faire, those who want to talk about the weather have only to put their money in the telephone slot and dulcet tones will present the latest betting odds. I understand you already can call for a spiritual message each day; and if the demand warrants it, you will be able to dial for a set of random digits whenever your statistical work has soiled the old ones and calls for a fresh set.

Believe me, I do not wish to jest. Negroes in the South learned long ago that their money was welcome in local department stores. Money can be liberating. It corrodes the cake of custom. Money does talk. Sociologists know that replacing the rule of status by the rule of contract loses something in warmth; it also gets rid of some of the bad fire of olden times.

Impersonality of market relations has another advantage, as was brought home to many "liberals" in the McCarthy era of American political life. Suppose it were efficient for the government to be the one big employer. Then if, for good or bad, a person becomes in bad odor with government, he is dropped from employment and is put on a black list. He really then has no place to go. The thought of such a dire fate must in the course of time discourage that freedom of expression of opinion which individualists most favor. Many of the people who were unjustly dropped by the federal government in that era were able to land jobs in small-scale private industry. I say small-scale industry because large corporations are likely to be chary of hiring names that appear on anybody's black list. What about people who were justly dropped as security risks or as members of political organizations now deemed to be criminally subversive? Many of them also found jobs in the anonymity of private industry. Many conservative persons, who think that such men should not remain in sensitive government work or in public employ at all, will still feel that they should not be hounded into starvation. Few want for this country the equivalent of Czarist Russia's Siberia, or Stalin Russia's Siberia either. It is hard to tell on the Chicago Board of Trade the difference between the wheat produced by Republican or Democratic farmers, by teetotalers or drunkards, Theosophists or Logical Positivists. I must confess that this is a feature of a competitive system that I find attractive.

Moreover, no law prevents people from falling in love over the brokerage telephone. And the warm personal relationships that are lacking in the economic sphere can be pursued in after hours. Medieval guild crafts are not the only human associations that are worthwhile, and the price to retain them may be too high in terms of their inefficiency.

EDEN COLLAPSED

I have now finished describing the ideal equilibrium of the gas which has individual atoms in dilute form. We have seen how a perfect model of competitive equilibrium might behave if conditions for it were perfect. The modern world is not identical with that model. As mentioned before, there never was a time, even in good Queen Victoria's long reign, when such conditions prevailed.

To elucidate, let us ask what happens when we squeeze the balloon. Or, what is the same thing, if we permit a Malthusian proliferation of molecules within the same space. The gas is no longer dilute, the atoms no longer lonely.[3] The system heats up. Now the collisions are frequent and uncomfortable. It is no longer a question of hearing our neighbor's dog; we toss with insomnia while his TV blares. In revenge, our electric shaver distorts his morning symphony. For better or worse the human race has been joined.

Whatever may have been true on Turner's frontier, the modern city is crowded. Individualism and anarchy will lead to friction. We now have to coordinate and cooperate. Where cooperation is not fully forthcoming, we must introduce upon ourselves coercion. Now that man must obey the stoplights he has lost his freedom. But has he really? Has he lost something that he had? Was he free to race his car at the speed he wished and in the direction he wished? Of course not. He had only the negative freedom of sitting

---

[3] Density of population produces what economists recognize as external economies and diseconomies. These "neighborhood effects" are often dramatized by smoke and other nuisances that involve a discrepancy between private pecuniary costs and social costs. They call for intervention: zoning, fiats, planning, regulation, taxing, and so forth.

But too much diluteness of the gas also calls for social interfering with laissez-faire individualism. Thus, the frontier has always involved sparse populations in need of "social overhead capital," which in terms of technical economics jargon has the following meaning: when scale is so small as to lead to unexhausted increasing returns, free pricing cannot be optimal and there is a prima-facie case for cooperative intervention.

in a traffic jam. We have, by cooperation and coercion, although the arch individualist may not like the new order, created for ourselves greater freedom.

The principle of unbridled freedom has been abandoned; it is now just a question of haggling about the terms. Few will deny that it is a bad thing for one man, or a few men, to impose his will on the vast majority of mankind, particularly when that will involves terrible cruelty and terrible inefficiency. Yet where does one draw the line? At a 51-percent majority vote? Or, should there be no actions taken that cannot command unanimous agreement—a position which such modern exponents of libertarian liberalism as Professor Milton Friedman are slowly evolving toward. Unanimous agreement? Well, virtually unanimous agreement, whatever that will come to mean.

The principle of unanimity is, of course, completely impractical. My old friend Milton Friedman is extremely persuasive, but not even he can keep his own students in unanimous agreement all the time. Aside from its practical inapplicability, the principle of unanimity is theoretically faulty. It leads to contradictory and intransitive decisions. By itself, it argues that just as society should not move from laissez-faire to planning because there will always be at least one objector—Friedman if necessary—so society should never move from planning to freedom because there will always be at least one objector. Like standing friction, it sticks you where you are. It favors the status quo. And the status quo is certainly not to the liking of arch individualists. When you have painted yourself into a corner, what can you do? You can redefine the situation, and I predicted some years ago that there will come to be defined a privileged status quo, a set of natural rights involving individual freedoms, which alone will require unanimity before it can be departed from.

At this point the logical game is up. The case for "complete freedom" has been begged, not deduced. So long as full disclosure is made, it is no crime to assume your ethical case. But will your product sell? Can you persuade others to accept your axiom when it is in conflict with certain other desirable axioms?

NOT BY REASONING ALONE

The notion is repellent that a man should be able to tyrannize over others. Shall he be permitted to indoctrinate his children into any way of life whatsoever? Shall he be able to tyrannize over himself? Here, or elsewhere, the prudent-man doctrine of the good trustee must be invoked, and in the last analysis his peers must judge—i.e., a committee of prudent peers. And may they be peers tolerant as well as wise!

Complete freedom is not definable once two wills exist in the same interdependent universe. We can sometimes find two situations in which Choice A is more free than Choice B in apparently every respect and at least as good as B in every other relevant sense. In such singular cases I will certainly throw in my lot with the exponents of individualism. But few situations are really of this simple type; and these few are hardly worth talking about, because they will already have been disposed of so easily. In most actual situations we come to a point at which choices between goals must be made: Do you want this kind of freedom and this kind of hunger, or that kind of freedom and that kind of hunger? I use these terms in a quasi-algebraic sense, but actually what is called "freedom" is really a vector of almost infinite components rather than a one-dimensional thing that can be given a simple ordering.

Where more than one person is concerned, the problem is thornier still. My privacy is your loneliness, my freedom to have privacy is your lack of freedom to have company. Your freedom to "discriminate" is the denial of my freedom to "participate." There is no possibility of unanimity to resolve such conflicts.

The notion (so nicely expounded in a book I earnestly recommend to you, Milton Friedman, *Capitalism and Freedom* [Chicago, 1962]) that it is better for one who deplores racial discrimination to try to persuade people against it than to do nothing at all, but, failing to persuade, it is better to use no democratic coercion in these matters—such a notion as a general precept is arbitrary and gratuitous. Its absurdity is perhaps concealed when it is put abstractly in the following form: If free men follow Practice X that you and some others regard as bad, it is wrong in principle to coerce them out of that Practice X; in principle, all you ought to do is try to persuade them out of their ways by "free discussion." One counterexample suffices to invalidate a general principle. An exception does not prove the rule; it disproves it. As a counterexample I suggest we substitute for "Practice X" the "killing by gas of five million suitably specified humans." Who will agree with the precept now?

Only two types would possibly agree to it: (1) those so naïve as to think that persuasion can keep Hitlers from cremating millions; or (2) those who think the status quo achievable by what can be persuaded is a pretty comfortable one after all, even if not perfect. I exclude a third type who simply accept an axiom without regard to its consequences or who do not understand what its consequences are. The notion that any form of coercion whatever is in itself so evil a thing as to outweigh all other evils is to set up freedom as a monstrous shibboleth. In the first place, absolute or even maximum freedom cannot even be defined unambiguously except in certain special models. Hence one is being burned at the stake for a cause that is only a slogan or name. In the second place, as I have shown, coercion can be defined only in terms of an infinite variety of arbitrary alternative stati quo.

The precept "Persuade if you can but in no case coerce" can be sold only to those who do not understand what it is they are buying. This doctrine sounds a little like the "Resist not evil" precepts of Jesus or Gandhi. But there is absolutely no true similarity between the two doctrines, and one should not gain in palatability by being confused with the other.

MARKETPLACE COERCION,
OR THE HEGELIAN FREEDOM OF NECESSITY

Libertarians fail to realize that the price system is, and ought to be, a method of coercion. Nature is not so bountiful as to give each of us all the goods he desires. We have, by the nature of things, to be coerced out of such an expectation. That is why we have policemen and courts. That is why we charge prices which are high enough relative to limited money, to limit consumption. The very term "rationing by the purse" illustrates the point. Economists defend such a form of rationing, but they have to do so primarily in terms of its efficiency and its fairness. Where it is not efficient—as in the case of monopoly, externality, and avoidable uncertainty—it comes under attack. Where it is deemed unfair by ethical observers, its evil is weighed pragmatically against its advantages, and modifications of its structure are introduced.

Classical economists, like Malthus, always understood this coercion. They recognized that fate dealt a hand of cards to the worker's child that was a cruel one, and a favorable one to the well-born. John Stuart Mill in a later decade realized that mankind, not Fate with a capital F, was involved. Private property is a concept created by and enforced by public law. Its attributes change in time and are man-made, not Mother Nature-made.

Nor is the coercion a minor one. Future generations are condemned to starvation if certain supply-and-demand patterns rule in today's market. Under the freedom that is called laissez-faire, some worthy men are exalted; and so are some unworthy ones.[4] Some unworthy men are cast down; and so are some worthy ones. The Good Man gives the system its due, but reckons in his balance its liabilities that are overdue.

Anatole France said epigrammatically all that needs to be said about the coercion implicit in the libertarian economics of laissez-faire. "How majestic is the equality of the Law, which permits both rich and poor alike to sleep under the bridges at night." I believe no satisfactory answer has yet been given to this. It is certainly not enough to say, "We made our own beds and let us each lie in them."[5] For, once democracy rears its pretty head, the

[4] "I am kept from attending college because my family is————." To discern the coercion implicit in a competitive pricing system, note that any of the following can be substituted into the blank space: Negro, bourgeois, Jewish—or, poor.

[5] If one disagrees with Malthus and France and thinks that we all had equal opportunities and *have* made the beds we are to lie in, our judgment of laissez-faire improves—as it should. But note it

voter will think: "There, but for the Grace of God and the Dow Jones averages, go I."

HOW UNEQUAL IS EQUAL? IS UNEQUAL?

The game is up for abnegation of all social decision making. To "do nothing" is not really to do nothing but to continue to do what has been done. Since coercion is willy-nilly involved, and there is no algebraic magnitude of it that can be minimized in the interests of maximizing algebraic freedom of n men, what can abstract reasoning deduce concerning the "equitable" exercise of coercion, or, what may be the same thing, concerning the setting up of optimal arrangements for cooperation? Very little, as experience has shown and as reason itself confirms.

"Equals are to be treated equally." Who could disagree with this sage precept? But what does it mean? And how far does it carry us? No two anythings are *exactly* equal. In what respect are they to be treated as essentially equal? What differences are to be ignored? Here are two organisms, each with a nose. Should they be treated equally, and what does it mean to do so? If the state taxes a brunette a dollar, then few will argue it should tax a redhead two. That seems discriminatory. But what if the redhead has a million dollars of income or wealth and the brunette has a thousand? Many would consider it indiscriminate to treat them as equals, to tax them each the same number of dollars or the same percentage of dollars.

A true story points up the problem of defining equality as a guide to "equity." In the Second World War, Professor Ragnar Frisch, a world-famous economist and a brave Norwegian patriot, was put into a concentration camp by the Nazis. Food was scarce there and rationed. Frisch, according to legend, raised the question: Is equal rations per man equitable? Or, since nutritional need depends on metabolism, which depends on body area and size, should not bigger men get larger allotments—their fair share, but no more? (If the result seems circular, a case of giving

is because of its fine welfare results, and *not because the kind of freedom embodied in it is the end-all of ethics.*

to him who hath, Frisch would no doubt be able to devise a measure of "inherent bigness." In any case, no important vicious circle would be involved since the infinite series would be a rapidly converging one, as in the case where Gracie Allen found that the heavier a package was, the more stamps she had to put on it, and the heavier still it became.) This is not a trifling matter. Colin Clark has pointed out that 1,800 daily calories for a small-boned man in the tropics is not quite so bad as it sounds.

"Do unto others as you would have them do unto you." Shaw has not so much improved on this Golden Rule as given its antidote. "Do not do unto your neighbor as you would have him do unto you; his tastes may be different." This is, of course, the Anatole France point about asymmetry made general. It illustrates how little guidance can be derived from Kant's Categorical Imperative: Act (or create institutions that will lead to acting) in such a way that if your action were generalized to all, the total welfare and welfare of each would be maximized. Such a precept has meaning only in a perfect symmetry situation; in real life even approximate axes of symmetry cannot be found and agreed upon.

The whole matter of proper tax policy involves issues of ethics, coercion, administration, incidence, and incentives that cannot begin to be resolved by semantic analysis of such terms as "freedom," "coercion," or "individualism."

MINE, THINE, AND OUR'N

Life consists of minimizing multiple evils, of maximizing multiple goals by compromise. Inevitably involved is a "rule of reason." But this kind of rule is misnamed, for it cannot be generated by abstract reason. It depends on ethics and experience. I shall not labor the point but merely give some examples of the inability of deductive reasoning to infer what is the optimal pattern of freedom and coercion, of individualism and cooperation.

Mill, and anyone, will agree: You are to be as free as possible so long as you do not interfere with the freedom of others. Or as Mrs. Pat Campbell, Bernard Shaw's pen pal, put it: Anyone can do whatever he likes so long as he does not scare the horses in the street. In an interdependent world the horses scare easily.

In practice, as recent reports in Britain illustrate, the gist of these modes of reasoning leads to the view that the law should not interfere with, say, the relationships between homosexuals so long as these are carried on in private. But, as these reports say, certain special issues are connected with the problem of enticement of the young or simply enticement in general. Quite similar problems exist in connection with heterosexuality but almost escape notice in our post-Victorian world.

Let me leave this whole issue by reminding you of a well-told anecdote. A gay young blade is blithely swinging his umbrella and is told off by an irate oldster.

GAY YOUNG BLADE: What's the matter, this is a free country, isn't it?

IRATE OLDSTER: Yes, young man, but your freedom ends where my nose begins.

Actually, this is an understatement. Just as we have the rule of a three-mile limit, so there is intrinsically involved here a six-inch rule of nasal *Lebensraum*. And life is much more complicated even than this, for, just as we live by taking in each other's washing, we live by breathing in each other's breath. Abstract reasoning cannot *find* a line between individuals, nor *draw* a line.

FINALE

We live in an interdependent world. Just as God knows about every sparrow that falls, Einstein's theory of general relativity shows that everything does depend on everything else: when that sparrow falls, it creates a wrinkle in space-time which changes space everywhere. The doughnut which is an individual man is a collection of cells, each of which is a collection of smaller individuals. The skin that surrounds us is thin skin.

My body is remaking itself every moment: the "I" who is talking is the heir to the "I's" that were and the sire to those that will be. Radioactive isotopes show that even our teeth are tenants on a short lease; they are remaking themselves every day, and the half-life of the charter-member calcium is measured in weeks, not years. Only our serial number has soullike persistence.

Before Rousseau, people made the mistake of treating children as merely adults shrunk small. The Bible and Freud go farther and tell us that an adult is merely a child grown large. Man is imperfect, and so is woman. And so is We, Incorporated, who paternalistically put restraints upon ourselves. Not even an individual's perfections are his alone; like his imperfections, they are group-made. We entered a world we never made, and leave one we did not unmake.

Carry the notion of the individual to its limit and you get a monstrosity, just as you do if you carry the notion of a group to its limit. You get not Nietzsche's superman, nor even Mill's imperfect-perfect Victorian entitled to his own mistakes. You get Wolf Boy.

The Edward Everett Hale story of *The Man Without a Country* made a lasting impression on the boy that was I. You recall that Lieutenant Philip Nolan said in a fit of temper that he wanted never to hear the name of his country again. Fate gave him his wish; and how cruel his fate was. It would be a cruel fate likewise, I have thought, should an extreme individualist be given the wish of every child: to be able to travel anywhere with the gift of being invisible, inaudible, untouchable, and for that matter, inedible. To be condemned to dwell with mankind and never experience the interaction of others—I almost said other individuals—would be misery enow. It is not human to be such a human, and he would soon beg to join some committee, any committee.

Perhaps what I have been saying comes to this. Wherever the true home of man is, it certainly is not in Coventry.

INDIVIDUALISM AND THE COMMUNES

William B. Hedgepeth

[Young people are reacting against contemporary American life in a number of ways—through politics, drugs, rock music, etc. But their most potentially revolutionary impulse is the growing movement to create new life-styles. Communes are springing up, in the deserts and in the cities, attempting to find a manner of living which enhances, not destroys, individualism. The fate of the movement is uncertain, but what it represents—young people trying to find new ways of expressing individuality in what they think is a repressive society—will be with us for some time.

[William Hedgepeth, a staff writer for *Look* magazine, is the author of *The Alternative: Communal Life in New America*.]

I. OPENING MOVEMENT

But I reckon I got to light out for the Territory ahead of the rest, because Aunt Sally she's going to adopt me and sivilize me, and I can't stand it. I been there before.

—HUCKLEBERRY FINN

They left. Not in a mass, organized way or because some dark figure came to town and told them to, but rather left because they sensed some itch in the back of the teeth or in the root of the brain that put upon them each, singly, an awful awareness that wherever they had come from was no longer now the place to stay. Somehow it was just no longer home. So they up and drifted doggedly outward from the settings they had known: out of suburban ranch-style two-car-garage cottages; out of high-rise condominiums and anonymous urban rat-warrens and sensible Southern middle-class brick bungalows and grain-belt clapboard dwellings. Up and out the door now and down the path, beyond the gate and—slam—they'd gone.

They are bits of everything from everywhere. They are service-station attendants from Cleveland or bank tellers from Boston or farmhands from West Virginia or secretaries or waitresses or ex-GIs or dropouts, drug heads, fatties, fragile faces, pimpled skin, dreamy-eyed, angry, scared-of-the-draft, artistic and undiscovered, looking for the Holy Grail, been-in-school-too-long, or just gnawingly aware of something big being missed. The chief features they hold in common are that they are young, that they are the children of contemporary American technology and that—like all American migrants back through history—they feel that somewhere there must surely be something better a way way off down the road and over the hills, westerly.

To whatever extent they have a shared and at least semicoherent philosophy, it's one whose origins lay in the blossoming, and subsequent wilting, of the "flower children" phase of the hippie revolution: so carefully scrutinized, analyzed, and televised in the Haight-Ashbury district of San Francisco while it was still titillating the public—and so diligently documented and filed away as a faintly disagreeable historical event when it began to bore.

The Haight, like most other valuable social phenomena, probably reached its creative peak before people anywhere else were able to learn what was going on. What *was* going on prior to, say, the legendary summer of 1967, was the beginning of an intensely gentle, profoundly subversive shift in the whole system. And it started with a mutation. At some point along the catabolic course of Haight-Ashbury's decomposition into what would have ordinarily terminated in black ghetto status (the standard fate of older urban neighborhoods), the district suddenly began to transform along a totally abnormal line. Starting slowly at first, around 1960, it developed, first, into a small gathering point for postgrad "beats," truth-seekers and hopeful talents; next, into an epicenter for the creatively alienated; and then into an unofficial Mecca for sincerely dissident young people, mostly in their early or mid-twenties.

It came to represent not merely a place but a state of mind, a different approach to the world—and eventually a full-scale testing tank for whole fresh shapes of human life and new reasons for doing things. Something wildly radical was being awakened: the senses—feeling, seeing, hearing, smelling, soaking up, "grokking." People rediscovered here the perfect wholeness of their own bodies; in the doing of which, it dawned on them for the first time, too, just how ungodly fragmented and sealed off from themselves they had always lived before. And not only that, but along with beholding their innermost selves there grew a revelation of each other in a different perspective. With the combined influences of the large, Victorianesque houses in the Haight and meager funds for renting them on an individual basis, the new settlers hit upon a completely pragmatic, commonsense, wild-ass notion: pooling resources and living collectively in fairly large numbers. This, in turn, soon led each group of six, ten, twelve, twenty or so people who might jointly occupy a house, to think and relate and refer to themselves as a communal "family," whose brothers and sisters shared and sensed all things together with an intricate rapport most of them had never known.

The Haight became a *feeling* place, a renaissance of human purpose. A painting, for example, wasn't something you did to hang on a wall or in a hall or to sell; it was for the sunburst spontaneous joy of *doing,* right out there in the open where people could see. Or maybe smeared on your own body. Or perhaps painstakingly composed in pastels on the sidewalk for others to touch and to walk on and for the first hard rain to wash away. And music. Music here didn't mean preachy folksinging; it meant strong, bonged-out, gut-stomp-twang-crash complex acid-rock rhythms electronically amplified to the brink of the transcendental, with real-life lyrics beamed not nearly so much to the cerebral cortex as to the viscera. Feel. Feel. Everyday living as an exhaustless art form.

Haight-Ashbury became a place for arousing and exploring your sensory awareness—as well as for sensing a swelling estrangement from all the sinister forces that had held you so out-of-reach from yourself up until this very moment. It was a tight-woven community of people newly awakened to all of this, and in open revolt against that unspoken, all-pervasive Calvinist notion that pain is somehow better for you than pleasure. It was a basin where these young souls—sensing their own incompleteness—came together not only to free themselves from the awesome moral weight of everything that sat upon them in straight society but also to make themselves whole, and then to feel their own part in a whole, harmonious humanity: a Universal Consciousness kindled by way of astrology or mysticism or music or Eastern religions or chanting or rare chemical concoctions—or anything else that was either immoral or of "no practical value" back where they'd come from. But here it all seemed to work. Breakthrough. Man in Eden, sharing shelter, love, language, perceptions, values, each other, and the total freedom to experiment endlessly with any other remotely plausible or freaky way of doing anything else.

In time, the members of this new-pattern coalition found a group identity. But they also found themselves affixed with a brassy identity tag for purposes of outside consumption, courtesy of *San Francisco Chronicle* columnist Herb Caen, who one day brightly branded the whole lot of them "hippies." Hippies. Hippies. Ahhh. A name to focus upon. A neat label to be pinned with. And pointed out with on the street. And called by in the press.

This name tag and these first bare bursts of local notoriety naturally brought in small streams of brand-new dropouts and converts and joiners. But not until 20,000 such turned-on kids turned up in Golden Gate Park in January of 1967 for the "World's First Human Be-In" did the national press begin taking serious notice—as did still thousands more disgruntled youngsters throughout the land, who soon turned those small streams into swollen torrents: the advance guard of the hallucination generation.

The Haight grew into a place of constant coming and going. It was now a refuge for ex-students, overprivileged children, curiosity seekers and restless questers. And it became, as well, a symbolic center for (among other idealist causes) a sweeping youthful revulsion toward all private property, American materialism, ecological rape, The

Bomb, and the War in Vietnam. In due course, the streets and curbs and stairwells began to clot with the garish plumage of new youth, newly arrived and desperately groping for someplace to belong—freaks, gypsies, nomads, spades, acid-heads, motorcycle outlaws, barely pubescents, beads, beards, amulets, anklets, cowbells, shag hair, headbands, hepatitis, gonorrhea, rimless glasses and hope-wide, moony eyes. Hashbury offered a little of everything for everyone. It had a newspaper, a clinic, a legal service, a free store, head shops, crash pads, free food, grassy hills to roll down in Golden Gate Park, and, inevitably, an audience.

The Haight became a hot thing for the media. And before long—lo and behold—by means of media exposure all those brightly flowing, kaleidoscopic, amoebic shapes and paisley curlicues and eye-blowing designs of hip garb turned into fast-moving marketable items in straight society: image of dour-faced Arkansas farmer asquat in his outhouse, thumbing through Sears, Roebuck's cataloged offerings of psychedelic shirts and bell-bottom trousers: image of uniformed lines of dowdy, hair-netted women members of ILGWU seated at their sewing machines in some drab New Jersey garment plant, dutifully cranking out racksful of swirly, flashy-toned, freaked-out hippie fashions. Officially, socially, morally, America didn't like hippies. Commercially, it ate them up.

Yet the hip movement in Haight-Ashbury not only turned out to be a larger insurgency than those before (such as the "lost generation" or the Beatnik flurry of the late fifties), but unlike the others, it posed a relatively well-thought-out alternative to established institutions. It was a new kind of revolution, with "transformation by example" its chief tactic. As a group, the revolutionaries asked only for the freedom to do their own thing—to create, nonviolently, their own parallel culture and social system, whose success, so they assumed, would naturally inspire a similar value shift throughout the rest of society. But, as can sometimes happen, the major danger of trying to appear as an example lies in appearing simply as a fool; and while there were plenty of hippies willing to be fools for a good cause, there were plenty more who succumbed to the encouragement of the media to appear plain foolish.

The Haight had been self-styled street theater. But by

mid-1967, the sheer size of its audience (and by this time it had an international reputation) changed many of the actors into star-struck children eager to pose and pontificate before TV cameras or pour forth ga-ga Utopian prose for reporters, and then wait impatiently to clip their quotes or photos in the next day's papers. They began, in short, to romanticize themselves in the very terms of the straight world they had supposedly forsaken. So, along about this time—though it passed unnoticed in all the fanfare—the *original* community began to disintegrate in the face of the TV crews, narcotics agents, and ambling droves of vacant-faced teenies fresh on the scene and eagerly sniffing around for drug-fantasy freak-outs and pussy galore and a place to hide out from parents or their parents' private detectives.

And then, too, came the tourists. Carloads. Busloads. Bumper-to-bumper gawkers creeping slowly up Haight Street with windows tightly rolled up, doors locked, and eyeballs and Instamatics primed for the delightfully disgusting sight of unlimited perversions: Oh, Momma, look at that! *(Flash)* All that hair. All those colors. *(Flash)* Oh, pretty. Oh, dirty. Ugh! Ooooh, look, no underwear! *(Flash)*

Dirty. That was the ultimate jab. Once the glitter of bizarre newness began to fade and all the colorful accouterments of hip culture had been absorbed into straight society there remained with the hippies only that distinction: Dirty. Dirty flesh. The one epithet in America against which there simply can be no defense. It can overshadow anything else.

The hippies had struck out a style of life for themselves that seemed more humane and certainly preferable to what they'd known before. They saw their schools, churches and all other old institutions as masses of cold social machinery geared to preparing and placing a person in an occupational role. The goal of such a role is to earn the means for purchasing those things society says are vital for "the good life." Yet, if society's conception of "good life" suddenly appears horrifically barren and irrelevant to reality, then there's no longer the blaring internal pressure to play the game to amass the money to purchase that life. So the hippies devalued money in their own minds and tried instead to relate to people in terms of human needs. And it worked. They tried, too, to pull off that very important feat no one had ever taught them back home: the molding of a community. A community, in this sense, is a gathering of individuals whose certain shared goals and values create, for each, a real feeling of personal involvement for the common good. A ghetto, on the other hand, doesn't have this sort of common purpose or positive sense of identity. A ghetto is also, almost by definition, dirty. Haight-Ashbury began as a community and devolved into a ghetto. Dirty.

One year after 1967's "summer of love," Hashbury was acknowledged as a violent, animalized slum, awash with hard-drug pushers, old junkies, Hell's Angels, hot-eyed spades, hoods, stumble-drunk Indians, assaultive speed freaks, ageless derelicts—and with drifting clumps of disillusioned young runaways who hadn't gotten the word before they left home that this was no longer the "love capital of the world," and who still felt obliged, therefore, to wander the streets trying sadly to generate something colorful, or at least suitably eccentric.

"Bad vibes," said Felix, and shook his head. The year before, Felix Supersalesman had been a small-scale hip tycoon in the head drug trade. Now here he stood like a defeated heap on the curb, hustling bad grass cut with oregano to kids either too young or too stoned to know the difference, and carrying a tire chain stuck away in his shirt for self-defense. "Bad vibes," he explained. Halfway up the hill on Belvedere, just off Haight, an old, rumpled, sotty wino and a toothless adolescent—both of them stoned wild-eyed on their respective potions—clutched a large dog the kid was trying his frantic best to ball there on the sidewalk.

Actually, forebodings of the district's downfall had been sensed by some of the original hip types—and foretold in the omens of gurus—back in early 1967. And it was these premonitions which, at that time, led many of them away from the Haight and out into the less publicized, uncommercialized atmosphere of the northern California countryside. Here, they could abide in tribal-style communes, in essentially the same multipersonal life-shape they'd developed back in the city, but with the added comfort now of knowing they were at least a little harder for others to get to. For the purposes of these young people, this new rural obscurity was pure salvation. In media eyes, hipness was Haight-Ashbury, and the death of the latter obviously meant the gradual extermination of the former. Finally, the omniscient *New York Times* felt secure enough to hoot forth the headline "LOVE IS DEAD," over a last-word-on-the-subject sort of story which let it be known: "The hippie movement is over—the alternative to the 'computerized society' has proved to be as unsatisfactory to its adherents as the society that gave birth to it."

So . . . with that and a few other such pronouncements, the press and the public retooled for new explorations into fresh areas of social outrage, and the Haight was allowed to continue its slow rot in relative privacy. And that seemed to be that. And just as well! It was something of a relief not to have to think anymore about hippiness and lovey-doveyness, because nobody had really known what to think of the whole business in the first place. "The way Americans deal with anything that seems unmanageable," said Margaret Mead, "is to run it into the ground by overuse. . . . We exaggerate, we caricature, we overemphasize and then we eliminate."

Missing in all of the epitaphs, though—and totally overlooked—was the fact that these young people's mass readjustment to their parents' world simply didn't take place. Another, and quieter, alternative had appeared. Even while hippie stories were fading from the headlines to the back pages and then out of the public eye altogether, hip communes of every genre imaginable were silently cropping out of the earth by the hundreds. And in time, the faint word-of-mouth murmurations about their whereabouts had swollen into enough of a knowledgeable whisper among alienated young folk to set them off in collective exodus once again. This time, however, the young migrants were a little less noisy, a little more sophisticated and a damn sight more serious about why they were leaving and what they were headed for.

It was not just displaced-veteran hip gypsies who set forth on this second wave; now they were joined by the thousands more hippie-symps and until-just-recently straight kids who were finally sensing the *Angst* of living in official

America. Each was, in his own way, either originally motivated or now propelled by some set of ineffable but strong vibrations—by a vague interplay of biologic, geographic, social, historical and mystical forces. More importantly, there was a vibrant sense of something shared in the separate and uncoordinated driftings of all these individuals. As children, they had been quietly coaxed along with the blind, carrot-on-a-stick faith that someday, someday when they were older, they might be able to make sense out of things. And now here they were, and they couldn't. It was as if they'd become infected somehow *en masse* with the germ of the death of their own childhood, whose symptoms erupted in varying shades of the amorphous yearning that finally pushed them, wordless, outwards, out the door and away. And so it was—not quite certain as to the origins of their motives or specific goals, but eyes bright with stone-serious fantasy—they left. And their leaving seemed to satisfy, for the moment at least that unquenchable itch that had grown up within them to run way the hell off beyond the farthest highway somewhere and start their own country.

But to get to the new country they still had to travel across the vast expanse of the old. Out now beyond the confines of their cities they found themselves immersed in raw mystery they had neither foreseen nor ever imagined themselves capable of entering. With Washington, D.C., on the East Coast and San Clemente, California, on the West, America today (like the late Roman Empire) has two capitals. And, again like Rome, what lies between the two can therefore be considered the provinces, dotted here and there with a large metropolis. Linking the provinces and lacing up the entire landscape like sterile stone ribbons are the 3,800,000 miles of the country's highways. For all practical purposes, they're omnipresent. They criss and recross every type of terrain and poke into everything in an efficiently aloof, peculiarly American way. The country is cities and highways. Nothing else really counts.

In the Middle Ages, maps of the world outlined all the known land masses in ornately ignorant detail, dismissing everything as yet undiscovered which lay beyond the maps' edges with the warning: "Beyond this Place there be Dragons!" It's almost that way with our highways. A highway is to deposit oneself upon to zip as cleanly and single-mindedly as possible from one place to another place, with the clear implication being that to veer off the road at any point in between is to enter a hostile, uncharted realm of wooly desolation filled with darkly gleeful, leaping specters, and with trees that have eyes and long claws for limbs and go, "WOOOooo," just like in the cartoons. Leave the highway and that's it for you. You simply won't be heard from again.

Highways are concrete projections of the American character, on which the idea is to get somewhere else quickly and painlessly without experiencing the actual act of going and without becoming any more personally involved in whatever may lie between origin and destination than if the whole expanse were a projected image flickering on a screen. Interstate highways are the ultimate in such detachment. They are monumental masterpieces of cold stone splendor over which citizens can roar 70 miles per hour in closed-up, air-conditioned projectiles across rivers, deserts, valleys and mountains, and not sense a single distraction; on which they can girdle towns without touching; can refresh and refuel at uniformly bland "rest areas"; can, in fact, hurtle from one end of the national land mass to the other without being jarred by beauty along the way and without establishing any human contact whatever. It's the next best thing to traveling in a sealed vacuum tube. Long-distance multilaned freeways and superhighways and interstates—more cruelly so than anything else Americans have built, achieve that fine, unspoken middle-class goal of keeping people separate from their environment and remote from each other: the sought-after, porcelain, passionless quality that sooner or later leads to deranged frustration or indifference.

However, there are other kinds of highways that require a different pace and frame of reference altogether; and it's these lesser roads which bear the tidal drift of the nation's young expatriates. These are the largely unlighted, narrower routes that, in some measure, *do* touch whatever span of countryside they straddle: oil-streaked concrete lanes or asphalt, tarry-shining, worn from the dull weight of big trucks that grunt along day and night, and from tractors and pickups and dust-caked old sedans chock-

full of farmers with their women and younguns. These are
the roads built years ago by men in not so much of a
hurry, who were not afraid to let you drive for a while
alongside the gentle wash of a river or parallel to railroad
tracks on which, if you were lucky, the loud rattly-bang
of iron wheels might meld in syncopation with the pneumatic clack of your tires over the even-spaced joins in the
concrete. These are the windswept, outback byways flecked
with gunky truck stops and the kind of motels people still
call "tourist courts."

To be young and a traveler along these roads is to define, without words, the kind of person you are. You've
broken the bonds, packed your gear, and left the nest. And
now—some hundred or so miles beyond the belching smoke
of city factories—you find yourself far out into the
stretched immenseness and solitude of the earth, all alone
now with your little life of some few teen or twenty years,
with the awesome prospect on up ahead of a whole vast
continent to escape into and develop. And the way to get
there is along these hinterland highways that run past
the minor glories and uncensored spoils of this native
land that is no longer home to you.

Turning back at this or at any point is out of the question—as unthinkable as it would have been never to leave.
For remaining at home now would be outright hurtful to
the soul once it has become aware that all those delicate
vibrations which had always spelled "home" are simply no
longer there. We are losing touch with home. Western civilization—particularly in its amplified American form—has
finally manufactured a race of fragmented men tragically
out of touch even with their own bodies. It happens that
this generation now adrift on these roads is the first to
defy, in large numbers, the relentlessly dehumanizing direction in which ordinary life seems headed. It is the first to
break loose in a mass manner and simply refuse to "succeed."

So the nation's internal exodus continues, and the paved
paths and byroads out in the boondocks bear the further
flow of alienated youth—angular faces, matted hair, lanky-
boned bodies—following their noses to nowhere in particular, as long as that eventual stopping point turns out to be
someplace where nothing whatsoever is the same. Those

who can't catch rides plod by foot, perfectly undeterred, along the swoops and lifts of their own chosen highways, and on past the myriad images of life in this fast, fat land. In the beginning, they may have sensed only bitter defiance, but this feeling slowly mellows into a spirit of growing detachment as the newly alien features of America flow by—and as they realize, more and more, that they are finally beyond all those things now. With each new mile put behind them, the blurry visions in their minds of sports cars and stereos and Position and popular acclaim for some sort of once-hoped-for big achievement become ever more dim and distasteful.

They pass the placid farms and tiny, tree-shaded towns of an older America, now brought abruptly up-to-date with the odd stares, snarls and occasional oaths flung at them by mid-class citizens who perceive, through softly lobotomized eyes, the profound threat implied in their passing through. They press on past the material dregs of U.S. society: tar-paper shacks, slums, hugely heaped carcasses of rusted cars, sanitary land-fills stuffed with rubbish, and vulgar mountains of miscellaneous plunder or polluted waste—part of the 3½ billion tons dumped each year onto the land. And every so often—no matter how remote or untraveled the special stretch of countryside—their ears pick up the dully savage *choonk-a, choonk-a, choonk-a, choonk-a* bumping growl and ghastly bray that grows in volume with the approach of massive, tread-tracked yellow earth-rending machines chomping away irreparably at the green landscape. It's hard to leave this particular image behind, for just a few more miles on up ahead is likely to lurk more mechanical creatures with more remorseless engines chugging and straining at their notable little role in the casual pillage and spoliation of the continent. Packs of huge metallic hogs forever rooting up the loam.

In moments, it seems to young people as if the whole country had been plopped, with a shrug, into the metal paws of a billion machines which coldly divided up chores between the cerebral sort (computers and calculators) and the brutish lot (bulldozers, drills, scrapers, scoopers and such) and have since gone grimly on about the business of picking us all to pieces in one way or another. In the eyes of these migrants, America itself has long since been transmogrified into a machine: a vast, off-balanced centrifuge which has flung them out to exist now as deracinated, displaced fugitives on their own land.

Yet they continue, confident, unperturbed, beyond the jostlings of those machines visible from the road; on along, hopefully, to the lands of communes that lie somewhere out there—and to the embryonic rise of the entirely fresh counterculture they feel they must be part of now. And if ever their spirits droop momentarily, the highway can be counted upon to spur them on with added inspiration. Here it comes—larger and larger as it nears—The Billboard: headshot of a rueful-looking, shag-haired boy beneath the huge message:

KEEP AMERICA BEAUTIFUL
GIVE A HIPPIE A HAIRCUT

And with this, the pace quickens. This is still straight and narrow America. We gotta get away.

The town of Sibley sits astride state route 60 on the western edge of Iowa. Iowa is a lot of things rolled up into a single something or other. It is sweeping fields with endless rows of crops and limitless, unquestioning, grim-faced labor to tend those crops—the paradigm of U.S. productivity, the Protestant work ethic gone wild. Iowa is other things, too: not only is it the living archetype for what once passed as Anglo-Saxon wholesomeness, but it's also just about the last outpost for the rudimental remains of serene, warm, hi-neighbor, loll around the courthouse steps, ice-cream-parlor centered, God-fearin', classic American small-towniness, now gone rank.

Late in an autumn afternoon, a part of the collective drift of young discontent flowed into Sibley in the form of two longhairs from the East, who trudged silently, respectfully through the town and on down route 60, due southwest. Placidly gazing through the plate-glass window from his perch in the swivel chair in Kiuper's Barber Shop, the middle-aged man, a feed-and-seed dealer, spotted the kids as they passed, all beaded and rucksacked, down Main Street. The barber noticed, too, and the both of them fol-

*lowed with their eyes until the boys were well on out of
sight. As the chair swiveled back to face the mirror, the
man opened his mouth to comment, then caught himself
and remained mute. The barber muttered a low little something about "irresponsible, no-good brats"; but he, too,
fell silent, as each uncomfortably sensed within himself
again the unspoken dreams of escape in the minds of ordinary men.*

Mobility has always been an unofficially admired feature
of American life. Over 40 million people, one-fifth of the
population, change their places of residence every year.
This perpetual fluidity may be prompted, in each individual
case, by surface economic factors—like job offers, trans-
fers, the demands of technology, rumors of work opportunities or whatever else—but the deeper cause has always
been rooted in the nation's spiritual heritage of restive discontent. The country was discovered and settled by disgruntled transients, and their ancestors have been discov-
ering it ever since. There has persisted in people's minds
the sensation that the nation is always right on the brink
of something bigger. And along with this, Americans have
forever sensed a mystic beckoning from the sheer enormity
of the land itself, whose boundless newness seems to offer
constant hope of ever better things beyond, just up ahead.
There's an ebb and flow to this moon-tidal restlessness,
governed perhaps by the official atmosphere of the moment,
or by whatever flavor of social malaise it is that causes
people to pause and to realize once more their own essential isolation and loneliness, no matter where they may be.
And some of them up and take off. In the 1930s, the roads
were filled with thousands of respectable young men who,
out of mass national disenchantment or outright feelings of
betrayal, joined the drifting, free, freight-hopping ranks of
bindle stiffs and hobos. There's something in this kind of
life or in this nomadic type of mind which, at once, fas-
cinates and repells those souls who yield to society's pressure to stay put. The most recurring characters in American mythology are usually landless, "tempest-toss'd," or
just footloose: the pioneer, the trail blazer, frontiersman,
immigrant, refugee, migrant worker, cowboy, Oakie, hobo,
Daniel Boone, John Dillinger, James Dean. They may be

oppressed or naïve or self-exiled strangers on their own home soil, or perhaps, as today, once-hopeful young people in full flight from the stark prospect of becoming "personnel."

They are on the roads again now, mostly shaggy-haired, bearded and, of course, dirty—with wind-blown faces, gay or grave, that call up old recollections of the Dustbowl. They are like an infestation of Tom Joads or hordes of drifting young Jesuses. And they move on, in perfect Huck Finn freedom, past the cultural outskirts of America. Past high-spired churches, now deserted or redesigned as dwellings or restaurants; past weather-beaten, patched-up gospel tents plonked down in rural pastures; and past those semi-kindred spirited persons who live portably in the country's growing colonies of trailers and mobile homes.

Still, to those who watch them pass, they evoke gnawing discomfort or a disquieting mixture of envy and nostalgia and simultaneous resentment, for few things seem to arouse more anguish than the actual sight of other people's freedom. But not only that. There is, in these young people's presence and in their passing by, an unmistakable impression and the beginnings of a realization: a vague stirring inside that clearly says something in this nation is terribly wrong. Their passing touches upon the tribal reservoirs of traditional American footlooseness and restive discontent. But something new and far more frightening is also touched, as each of these uprooted adolescents appears, with his passing, like a fresh harbinger of social decay.

Logansport, Louisiana, is a bare mile east of the Texas line. At his desk in his office above the drugstore, where he's been stuck away since passing the bar exam a generation ago, the lawyer—pale, pear-shaped, soft-bottomed from years of sitting—rubbed his temples and then swirled abruptly to the open window behind him. A soft jingle. Up the nearly empty sidewalk, a girl and a boy, westbound, floated warmly. The girl was simultaneously ratty and beatific. She flowed to the even beat of an ankle bell, with chin thrust up and bleached-out eyes that gaped blandly frontwards. The boy, blond and barely old enough to shave, alternately walked and waltzed in slow spins, arms

*stretched out, doing lazy loops and smiling all the while
like an angelic marshmallow, dreamy, loony, stoned as a
goose.*

*The lawyer's eyes tightened. He toyed with the flash
thought of throwing something. They're not from 'round
here, that's for sure. Where'd they be comin' from, though?
East of here? Alabama? Mississippi? Mississippi hippies?
Gawd! The mind reels. The stomach turns. Gawdamighty!*

*And now, from the opposite direction, a fat, super-
straight short-hair bounced down the street in a rhythmic
jiggle-waddle-plod, with ear jammed into pocket-size tran-
sistor radio. Nasal country tones of li'l' Tammy Wynette
blurred into the approaching ankle-bell beat until—converge, merge, emerge—all three passed without a blink,
oblivious, each aswirl in some sea of purely private glee.
The lawyer compressed his nostrils and let go a long
breath. Separate sounds into each ear trailing away: plod-
plod-plod and Tammy Wynette yowl off left; off right, a
faint jangle plus the passionate scrape of sandal on pave-
ment and leather tassel-booted feet, leaving. Texas, one
mile. Hoo, hah. Somebody'll crack down on 'em there for
damn sure.*

But the members of this migratory tribe persist in pop-
ping up, like the magical broomsticks in "The Sorcerer's
Apprentice," and continue to tramp, trot, lope, hitch, cycle,
float, fly, drive or drift or propel themselves forward in
every possible fashion, with all the dead-level intensity of
aliens or of lemmings. It's Haight-Ashbury and New York's
East Village turned loose on the land: wildly dressed children moving now across the countryside with all their tragi-
cal intuitions in tow. The unwritten hip gospel seems every
bit as demon-filled and apocalyptic as the Old Testament,
and its young believers all carry that quality within them
like an emblem affixed to their vital organs. They are, in
varying degrees, doom-ridden, claustrophobic, paranoiac,
occult . . . and hopeful. They are also without guile. And
guilelessly they tend to place their faith and base their hope
in a few simple gut-felt profundities of grave purity: that
(1) somewhere along the evolutionary line civilization
slipped up, freaked out and grew into a self-consuming,
arthritic gargoyle; that (2) we've got to go "back to the

land," where things are clean, and start from almost scratch again; and that (3) in time, and with God on our side and with honorable intentions and hard work and honesty among ourselves and faith in beauty's righteousness, the whole world's eventually going to turn on or blow up.

So there is, then, a serious, mass-level motive behind this migration—in a sense, something of a public-spirited attitude. And those communes lying out there somewhere in the fierce, snaky reaches of the wilderness are by no means seen as hideouts—copouts—from the world. Rather they are outposts, testing grounds, self-experimental laboratories, starting points for whole hallucinatory metropolises: Super turn-on—a culture shaped, at last, as a physical extension of the way people really are: a wildly different pattern of social life that more rightly fits the human form.

Some of the communes that have stuck it out for more than a year or so are regarded as little cities along the hip circuit, complete with cryptic or charismatic names like Olympali, Drop City, Libre, The Hog Farm, The New Buffalo, Lama, Wheeler's Free, etc. Others—not necessarily less durable or serious-purposed—may exist as simple groupings of like-minded souls, known (if known at all) not by a name but rather by vague sets of verbal directions as to how to reach them (or at least how to get within, say, 20 square miles of where they might be—or once were), if, in fact, they haven't meanwhile upped and moved off or been chased away or else just disbanded, with their various members latching, purely at random, onto any of the 500-plus *other* communes scattered throughout the open countryside.

Obviously, then, finding the exact community you may have heard of and set out for is an uncertain hope. Even once you've found a particular one (and no two are alike), the rigors of adjusting your own inner rhythms to the tempo of that specific communal family may set you off on the roads again in quest of some other group with more compatible vibrations. This kind of internal flux and interchange manages to create a sort of pan-communal communications network for sharing those ideas on new ways of living that seem to be proving successful in action. And, too, it makes a little easier each individual's personal search for the ideal site and circumstances and all the right chemical and mystical combinations needed in order for him to know for sure, at long last, the place where he will make a stand. Since there is a high turnover both in communitarians and in communes themselves, lasting success in that search is a gamble. But a gamble is at least hopeful. In the awakened eyes of those people already ensconced in communes (as well as those who are out on the road in quest of one) the possibility for success in the ossified world they left behind isn't even a risk. It's a sure-fire losing proposition—nil, zilch, zero, and a calamitous waste of time besides. For to these young refugees, "straight" America weighs success on a fraudulent scale— a scale by which they, too, once would have been content to measure out their workadays and generally rate the worth of their lives.

As it happened, though, something somehow seemed to go askew fairly early in their upbringing and grew more uncomfortably out of kilter, almost in direct proportion to their growing awareness of the world and of the pace of its events. That, in fact, was one thing right there: pace. With the post-World War II burst in population, individuals were in more frequent elbow-rubbing, idea-sharing contact. This phenomenon, matched with incredibly fast and constant technological change and with more urbanization, more education, construction, production, destruction, reproduction, fluxion and incessant introduction of new notions into people's heads via mass media hyped the pace of America almost beyond the ability of older minds to keep up with.

All of these elements added up to a new reality. And it was this frantic, fast-paced version of the world into which these young people were born. But meanwhile, the social structure (the traditional living patterns, values, culture totems, the myths men need to live by and all the other various, vital mental gimmicks that people use for making official sense out of their environment) hadn't received a similar jolt. In other words, reality changed without a corresponding change in the way people were supposed to regard it. And with evermore instantaneous awareness of the cosmos available through electronic media, children were placed in the awkward stance of perceiving the world as it presently exists—all while their elders were working to indoctrinate their minds with the old mythologies and methods of seeing and acting that related to the way the world used to be.

The more this went on, the more uneasy many young people became. They saw that the rewards of society—its judgments of success, its Good Conduct medals, and so forth—were conferred upon those who managed either to ignore or to be least true to their own actual senses and perceptions. They saw that to get by in *this* society you've got to act and think and talk *this* way, no matter what you imagine that you see and feel to be right. For the young, middle-class existence became an endless matter of trying to orient themselves around an enormous anachronism. Like the annual Miss America Pageant on a grand scale. (In recent years, the sponsors of this contest have had to special-order both the far-out-of-fashion ultra-high-heeled shoes as well as the quaint one-piece swimsuits the contestants must wear, since these are items no longer mass-produced, sold or worn anymore, either in this country or anywhere else. If you balk about the suit, shoes or the special makeup *à la* early 1940s Rita Hayworth, hubba-hubba, you not only don't get a crack at the crown, you don't even get to play the game—the game being, one must assume, the sad, ceaseless perpetuation of absurdity.)

Young people are implicitly called upon to make a choice of that sort: fit the new realities you live with into the old molds of thought and conduct, and you're an acceptable citizen; try anything else and you're out; you don't play the game. With options like these, more and more of the young were finding they just plain couldn't play.

Many began to realize, too, that their unorthodox outlooks and approaches actually seemed to function rather well in the new real world. And this led to something else. So long as society changed slowly, older people could honestly claim to know—and be able to teach—the major share of what was useful in the world and how to live with it. But many young people grew to discover that the old roles were reversing. This wasn't a smug boast; it was a frightening realization. It was jarring to learn not only that the old tunes just wouldn't do for dancing anymore, but also that the old dance teachers didn't know any new steps. All sorts of home-bred Truths gradually seemed to take on strange and troubling hues that clashed with the vivid colors they saw each time they opened their eyes. Notions of national life, once regarded every bit as impregnable and unimpeachable as the laws of geometry, now appeared not merely seedy but a little ridiculous—even slightly sinister: worship of technology as the panacea for any planetary woe; reverence for "rugged individualism," nationalism, materialism, competitivism and cold-eyed rationality; belief in "objectivity" as the only avenue to honesty; and total flag-waving faith in the *ipso facto* Rightness of America (as expressed by her political leaders or her armed might) as well as in the goodness of our Cause (or Causes) no matter what it might be at any given hour of the night or day. Every one of these and still other such labored Fables and American Home Truths were either dismissed outright with total contempt or, at the very least, called into serious question. Whole legions of articles of national sacrosanctimosity, once imbibed along with Mother's Milk, trooped forward for new inspection and limped away in Judas-like disrepute: You let us down. You lied. You've left us with no home, no guides, no comforts, no place to come in from the cold, nothing to clutch onto and wrap our minds around. Total . . . utter . . . abysmal . . . betrayal!

And then—SHAZAM!—somebody dropped acid.

Zam! Blam! Shot like streams of fiery violets out the skull and up the walls and twice around the moon. Scores of little Billy Batsons burst into red, flashy-suited Captain Marvels by the millions—*whooosh!* Purple-eyed fang-toothed flower-petally things flutter to the floor and expand and explode in a swirly glory of silver fish-scale sequins. Erupting torrents of red rust boil up and gush forth from long choked-off, cobweb-tangled corners of the brain —then run off in a pulsing crimson dazzle past the insides of the eyelids. We've become *unfolded!* Opened up. Cleaned out. Magicalized. We are washed in the Blood of the Lamb!

LSD was the super set-breaker, time-rearranger and head-turner—the shared spiritual experience that demythologized young minds *en masse.* For many, it marked their point of awakening and the release of human impulses stored way down deep in the psychic underground.

It took young trippers on an 180-degree turn into their own senses and rekindled their bodies with the childlike glow of crystal-pure enchantment which Western society tries its best to extinguish. It was the chemical counterbalance to overcivilization and to everything high-pressure, loud-volume, cutthroat, other-directed, aggressive Americanese. An acid voyage could mean a momentary suspension of the ego and a sense of extension into the whole world. For thousands of young Americans it was an original experience with gentleness. And while it may have filled trippers with visions, it filled them, more importantly, with a vision. They viewed existence now not as a linear beam, but as part of a timeless wholeness with the cosmos. Instant satori. A way for people to see beyond the limits of the intellect and to become imbued, at the same time, with a real sense of "us-ness" among themselves.

America now looked even more gouty and deformed than before. Suddenly these adolescents found themselves aghast, in retrospect, at what they'd been doing, where they'd been and where they would otherwise be headed. "It once occurred to me," wrote Dostoyevski, "that if it were desired to crush a man completely, to punish him so severely that even the most-hardened murderer would quail, it would only be needed to make his work absolutely pointless and absurd." Now, thank God, they were beyond that.

They were beyond mindless tedium. They were beyond anger. Beyond the social anguish that produces picket lines and nicely liberal protest marches and movements and naïve linking up of arms with saintly-solemn, moist-eyed blacks to demonstrate a cause, to right a bottomless wrong, or to intone the words of "We Shall Overcome" to a society of obese workaday daddies incapable of manifesting a concern for other mortals except perhaps under pressure of fear-crazed physical duress. They were beyond all that now. Their malaise transcended any hopes of attempting to "redress their woes" within a social system so irredeemably corrupt and fundamentally misdesigned.

"Manipulated for national goals they cannot believe in, the young are alienated," wrote Paul Goodman. "On every continent there is excessive urbanization and the world is headed toward ecological disaster. Under these conditions, the young reject authority, for it is not only immoral but functionally incompetent." They are, he suggests, "in an historical situation to which Anarchism is the only possible response."

The current anarchism among the young, though, is expressed not as a wild quest for chaos, but as an urgent attempt to build counterinstitutions that reflect their own highly principled, highly humanized ideas about how things should be. ("It's just not real back there," the one-time city boy said as he sat down to milk one of the communal goats. "But here we're learning what really is and what isn't. And now, by God," he nodded, groping around for a goat tit, "we're gonna run things *our* way.")

Maybe it's necessary every few generations or so for people to sever themselves from the comforts and the whole behavioral pattern of their society in order to update the knowledge of what it takes to survive. "A man is rich in proportion to the number of things he can do without," as Thoreau found out (and as the Haight-Ashbury hippies went around quoting to each other). However, the business of living severed from social comforts—and learning from that condition—is only rarely the result of a voluntary cut-off, as with people like Thoreau and the current communitarians. Usually it's very involuntary, and sometimes cataclysmic. The generation, for example, that became the parents of today's youth learned from the Great Depression. Overlearned, in fact. The stain of deprivation—the where-is-the-next-meal-coming-from kind of agony—settled so deeply in men's minds that they became, almost by instinct, hell-bent materialistic, maniacally job-focused and eternally frantic about their future security. And they learned to be highly successful in these pursuits, so much so that any other goals in life began to seem inconceivable to them. But not necessarily to their children (most of whose minds weren't afflicted with the Depression Syndrome), who grew, therefore, less and less able to comprehend their parents' irrational worship of well-being. So, many of them began to react by detaching themselves or dropping out in one way or another.

Currently, the rumblings from a sort of inner estrangement are being heard even among older people, as straight society itself begins to lap at the edges of its newest anguish: a sense of personal impotence and aimlessness. Out of the Depression came the idea that bigger institutions—government, business, labor, church, etc.—would naturally mean bigger, better machinery for producing and protecting individual comfort. Since that time, though, these same machines, on their own momentum, have grown so monolithic and impersonal that suddenly they're scary. Worse still, they're forcing older people today to feel their own relative inadequacy: "I don't even amount to the tiniest cipher in the GNP. . . . My vote doesn't count for a thing. . . . I've worked all my life to provide for my kids and now they don't want it. . . . I stall on the freeways . . . I gag on the smog . . . nothing hears me . . . nothing needs me . . . where am I?"

Many Americans are perceiving that beyond the scope of their own workaday murk they have no real purpose. And with no sense of purpose, they feel less free—for being free means that one has a choice of actions or directions, and a direction requires some idea of a goal. In this sort of spiritual limbo, and with only a minimal sense of participation in the forces that shape his environment, life to the Middle American grows more and more indifferent. The machines continue to whirr away. Plasticity aplenty. Retail emotions readily available on the shelf. The computers in control have manipulated national life to the point where the continued boominess of the economy ("And God knows, we can't afford another Depression") hangs upon the incessant creating and satisfying of synthetic demands: *"Hey, buddy, you mean you haven't yet got one of THESE?* [Some hitherto unnecessary thing.] *That's inexcusable! Your life would be better. Every erotic fantasy will come true. Your kids need it. Everyone else has one. Remember your grandmother. Remember the Maine! Jesus went and died for your sins and yet you still haven't bought this thing. OK? Here's where you can get it. Just ask for . . . etc. . . . etc. . . . Whir . . . Click"*

It's become so that even the smallest choices are taken out of the individual's hands. Many older folk are realizing, however vaguely, how little they, as people, fit into all of this. They sense America hardening now into a mechanical land of dissipated energies, dissolved dreams, and a diminishing confidence in Man himself. And out of their resulting frustration and hazy malaise, many become frightened of further change—and sullenly hostile, therefore, to their own changing children. Like the young, they feel the loss of comforting contact with many of the old myths. But *their* response has been a more frantic clinging and a more frequent drawing up into pugnacious poses.

Meanwhile, more and more young people continue to become totally demythologized and untotemed. They are beyond and away from all that now—away, away on down the roads, as far as the mind can imagine. Away from city stench and brick-sandwiched urban megalife. Away from all the supercharged hokum and humdrum, from American Ideals enshrined in soap commercials, pulpits, billboards, and *Time* magazine. Away from the Protestant work ethic, the senseless worship of the "practical," premarital chastity, deferred rewards for today's efforts, filial gratitude for parental sacrifice, the family car, the tooth fairy. They are far away, as well, from the dark prospect of white-collar jobs and the plight of lives like so many comic-strip Dagwoods endlessly fawning and imploring stern bosses for "that raise" or "that promotion." They're away from pollution and political pandering and Santa Claus and Howard Johnson's and Huntley-Brinkley and Richard Burton & Elizabeth Taylor and "brush your teeth three times a day" and the daily tallies of war dead. They're beyond all that. It has all become vestigial to them. For now they're on their way to cleanse themselves, to reassess old assumptions, to discover and create *new* myths, to groove with Nature, to prepare for The Bomb—and to insure, along with all this, the continuity of the human race. They are long gone away now, off down the roads into the wilds and sticks searching for someone's version of the Big Rock Candy Mountain. Or looking for the odd-colored domes or zomes or shapes or adobe huts or teepees or whatever else they will live in. Or perhaps just probing along for someplace far out of reach—*Oh Jubilee!*—where they can at last etch their own signatures upon the earth's face.

It was toward this that the young migrants were moving as they flowed along down those miles of cold macadam roads that lay between where they had been and what they hope to be. And America, meanwhile—caught up in its incessant frenetic pace and commercial contrivances and international struggles *ad infinitum*—remained too preoccupied to notice much of its own internal bleeding down these arteries.

By then it was 1:30, and time for lunch, and here we were standing around shift-footed, shrug-shouldered in the muddy, rutty driveway up to Drop City, hemming and hawing with a weedy-faced eighteen-year-old Texas kid who'd got the old wander itch up his ass again but suddenly needed somebody to aim him off in some direction. He had dragged himself up to this little Colorado hilltop commune to crash for a few days. And now, on leaving, he seemed struck by the apprehension (which I'm sure had probably followed him ever since he was born) that nobody and noplace else would want him. After all, he *did* look awful—like a Lon Chaney makeup job: old 1930s-style, frazzle-edged, wide-brim hat; tattered tweed coat; no-color pants; garishly malformed teeth; weak ice-blue eyes and a pimply squinched-up face like a pitted prune. He had the kind of back-country flavor of somebody who'd be named "Festus" or "Rufus" or "J.L." He was the sort of awful-looking person you feel sorry for and yet sense that any impulse to offer a comforting embrace would turn —*snap!*—into a desperate effort to kick and stomp him into the ground.

But Larry Lard—as permanent a resident as they have here—stopped tinkering with a hopelessly defunct auto engine long enough to get across just the right words needed to send the kid tramping happily down the slick mud driveway and off into the west. And then, after he'd shrunk out of sight and it was possible to feel compassion for him again, Jalal (who had taken her name from the Persian word for "glory") shrugged and said, "Eventually, everyone who splits from a community winds up back in a community. You just get to like the way of life."

Among all those communes that have bloomed since the start of the "psychedelic movement," the only feature common to their way of life is the near total absence of people at each other's throats. This is no small thing. There thrives within each community a genuinely shared sense of self among the individual members—or, at the very least, a conscious group effort to cultivate it. Most of the communitarians are aware that the disembodied culture they broke out of didn't seem to value—and therefore didn't teach—the concept of people really and truly living and being and relating together at close quarters. Aside from this common quality, however, the ways of life among the communes are as varied as the kinds of communities themselves.

Out along the unofficial network of communes, that stretches from New England to California (with most of them found west of the Mississippi), something well over 10,000 out-and-out hippies as well as just generally disaffected young people are either settled or still shifting from one sort of community to another. The types range from highly transient urban crash pads to those that are fairly large, self-contained and rural. And within that range is a vast variation.

The simplest of the urban type, for example, usually consists of an apartment or house where a steady turnover of new dropouts may exist in a loosely cooperative arrangement before either (*a*) going back home or (*b*) contracting some disease (and going back home) or (*c*) pushing onward to a more stable commune. The more stable of those communes that are able to function in cities generally tend toward a sort of space-age religious zealotry, complete with their own built-in avatars, fanatical-eyed young followers and well-ordered sets of loony notions about how to avoid the Apocalypse. Other of the city-centered type may be single-purpose communal groupings: collections of individuals who live together to share some special passion or practical function, such as rock music, art, draft resistance, printing posters, putting out underground newspapers, or subsisting philosophically on indiscriminate screwing.

The most radical departures from straight civilization, though, are the communes lying out in the open country. These can be "classified" according to their chief activity. Some, like the New Buffalo in northern New Mexico, are tribal alliances of mostly city-born young people determined to farm and generally befriend the earth. A few, like the Lama Foundation, also in New Mexico, resemble semi-religious retreats or Hindu ashrams, bent on teaching new styles of perception with, most usually, a strict ban on drug use. A few more are bizarre-exploratory like the Animal Farm in upper New York State, which takes in members willing to self-experiment creatively with human eugenics. Others, like Drop City, conceive themselves as rural "decompression chambers" for overurbanized kids fresh off the road. And still more, like Wheeler's Free near Occidental, California, (and countless other of the communes that don't have names) are wildly primitive stretches of rude landscape where unorganized agglomerations of hip gypsies live in scattered tents or in caves or abandoned cars or out under the trees.

In whatever form it may take, the new communal movement, on the whole, is an updated attempt to practicalize an ancient ideal—the pooling of souls and resources with some special vision in mind. And, too, regardless of how estranged from straight society they may feel, the new communitarians bring with them their ingrained Americanistic impulses to make things work. Along with this, they bring a mystical sort of faith that through work and through their anarchical mode of life they can rediscover their own functionalism as human beings. ("Now, by God, we're gonna do things *our* way.") Though many of them aren't aware of it, their visionary and migratory impulses form a common bond with the early Christians, who themselves were guided—as almost all communal efforts since then have been inspired—by Acts 2:44–46: "And all that believed were together, and had all things in common; and sold their possessions and goods and parted them to all men, as every man had need . . . and did eat their meat with gladness and singleness of heart."

Closer to home, the young people's communal approach to society, along with their predisposition toward a pragmatic strain of radicalism, fits within the heritage of America dating back as far as the country goes—back to the Pilgrims, even, who lived every bit as communally as most hippies today. Utopian experiments are both natural and even traditional in a country that started existence off as one itself. In addition—and no less traditional— there is here the influence of an immense land so unendingly new that it has always served both as an idealistic inspiration and as a very real challenge to its people's improvisational talents for survival. Historically, the land has been a vital element in the American's outlook on the world: a man on his own land by God, could stand off all the evils of the universe. Fundamental to Thomas Jefferson's thinking was the agrarian notion that a man must have enough land and control of his own subsistence to be free from external pressures. Then, too, the personalized politics of Thoreau were built upon his working relationship with the land and "essential facts of life" he learned there.

With this kind of philosophical foundation—and, of course, with the added fire of their own exotic religious visions, or views of the goals of human life—over a hundred and thirty utopian-minded communes, involving tens of thousands of people, cropped up and withered away during the course of the nineteenth century. Among the ultrareligious variety were the Harmonites, whose main settlement was in Economy, Pennsylvania; the Perfectionists in Oneida, New York; and the Zoarites in Zoar, Ohio. These had all faded into oblivion by the beginning of the twentieth century. But a few of this type have continued to exist, though in considerably diluted form: The Shakers (United Society of True Believers in Christ's Second Appearing) in New York; the Amana Society (Society of True Inspiration) in Iowa; and the Huterian Brethren, with settlements throughout the northern Midwest and in Canada.

The nonreligious communes of the nineteenth century were generally founded on the belief in the perfectability of man and in the viability of communal life as a universal social order. New Harmony, Indiana, and nine other communes were set up in 1825, basing themselves on the utopian world views of Robert Owen, a rich Scot who forsook the experiment three years later. Between 1844 and 1856, at least thirty-three other communities sprang up, all of them designed around the modified communistic principles of Fourierism, as preached by, among others, Horace Greeley. Still other communes with nonreligious leanings were the New England transcendentalist types such as Brook Farm in West Roxbury, Massachusetts, formed in 1841, whose members were perhaps the first organized group of Americans to probe around in the philosophies of Eastern religions. For a time, too, there were communal-style anarchist "villages" in Equity and Utopia, Ohio, and in Modern Times, Long Island—as well as some semi-anarchist-socialist communes such as the Ruskin Commonwealth in Georgia and New Llano in Louisiana.

Most of the settlers in both the religious and secular communes were prompted, at the outset, by their moral horror over the new industrialism and overspecialization, and by an urge to return to simpler modes of living out on the land. They folded for multifarious reasons: some because their rules on strict celibacy curtailed their continuation; some because the members couldn't pass their inspiration along to the next generation; and some because of pious pressure from those in straight society of that time, who were outraged by sermons and lip-smacking news stories about free love and sexual perversions "and God knows what all."

The nineteenth-century communitarians shared among themselves—and share with those today—the belief that theirs was a pattern for the reorganization of society which all people would eventually desire to follow. Also held in common with present-day young people was an intensity of commitment (religious or otherwise) that conventional society couldn't comprehend or accept. For commitment, then as now, always scares other people—particularly when those people have only woozy ideas as to what they themselves are supposed to be committed to. But more strongly than anything else, there dwelt among those older Americans, as with their spiritual descendants today, that strain of deeper discontent which generates movement and lays the seeds for eventual fundamental change: "Surely somewhere somehow there's another way of living—there has to be."

And so it is that the contemporary wanderers—propelled by an incredibly convoluted mixture of private and tribal impulses—silently flow forth on highways stretching mostly westward toward those fabled places they've heard of where nothing's supposed to be quite the same, where no ecstasies are alien. They are borne along by these prospects or by their personal muses or their horoscopes, or maybe even by the swift currents of unseen rivers in the sky—or the dark-flowing waters beneath the earth—with their destinies determined at each crossroads often by nothing more than a three-coin cast and consultation with the *I Ching*.

They continue in this pattern past shifting images of America. Past a young farmhand astride a John Deere tractor all customized-up with his own style of art nouveau shapes and psychedelic swirls in bright, chrome-orange Day Glo. Past ranchlands where long-haired cowboys—rough, not too much learning—smoke hash around campfires in the evening. Past and past all this. ("And now, by God, we're gonna do things *our* way.")

Historically and biologically it's no freak thing that's happening now. When a person senses, even subconsciously, a deprivation of some particular dimension to his life he silently craves it, like the dietary needs of pregnant women that so often seem irrational. These young migrants quietly sense the cruelly shattered status of a society erected on a cult of rigid, nonemotional "individualism." And in response, they hunger now for community. They crave the sensation of becoming whole with other human beings, of being a part of a larger thing. Rather than wanting to continue splitting up, specializing, pigeonholing the entire planet, they have upon them the urgent urge to put things back together.

They are socialist almost by instinct, for the shape of existence they seek is a living repudiation of the cash nexus among people. And they're completely cut loose and free now to make their visions a part of their actual lives, to go find out what means something and then create entire new definitions for what they discover. ("Now, by God, we're gonna do things *our* way.") "Good and bad," wrote Emerson, "are but names very readily transferable to that or this; the only right is what is after my constitution; the only wrong what is against it."

Their collective outflow into the land is a phenomenon of the innocence, unfettered impulses and the mad, magnetic energy of children. And on they go, with all the persistence of wild vines, hopping fences and happily trespassing on property called "private"—off into untrammeled territory, virgin fields, grass flow, flowers, trees sway, untrod meadows, see a cow. Their whole life-style is a statement: a commitment to recover those human relationships that make existence make sense—and to reclaim, as well, the lost realms within themselves.

"Out of the net"; that's one of the meanings of Nirvana. This is Nirvana Now. Exploding colors. Experimental people. Drawn, hairy faces, Jesuses galore. A passing bumper sticker: KING KONG DIED FOR YOUR SINS. Life is a trip. As aliens on their home soil they are, says the sociologist, "the last free Americans." And their passing down these roads leaves an indelible message, like the silvery trail of a snail, that tells custodians of the status quo: the world has switched its rules on you. Your life has been a vast psychosis.

Sundown on whatever day it was they left, the three of them, walking, reached the outskirts of the Kansas town, casting strangely scattered shadows backward in the direction from which they'd come. The wind quickened, and the air blew cool in their noses. It ruffled, too, the afghan lying across the lap of the old man seated, frail, in his wheelchair on the wide white porch of his house on his plot of once proudly tended land.

He looked out, and the three, at a distance, passed, with the shuffle of their sandals and Indian boots breaking momentarily—or so it seemed—into a sort of muted dance step. And then they were on past and on up the slight rise just beyond, getting smaller, with the janglings of their beads and trappings blended into a single softening haunting sound, like the vibrations of a fading bell carried on the wind. And they trod on, out into the unharmed body of the open earth. And the old man's fragile jaw worked up and down, and he squinted to keep sight of them as they filtered off more distant to his weakening eyes. Now, in this mellowing, muddy light they were suddenly period pieces: pioneers, coolies, drifters, tramps and uprooted images of Oakies all at once, all merging and fuzzing like old blurred photos fading into sepia. Gone. And the old man, still gazing outward, called to his middle-aged daughter on the porch swing. She appeared instantly at his side, and he said to her, offering his arm, "Feel my pulse."

FROM THE
"PORT HURON STATEMENT"

Students for a Democratic Society

[The New Left has already made a dramatic impact on American life, and the movement is extending downwards from the colleges to the high schools. The Port Huron Statement, the founding charter of the Students for a Democratic Society, is a vivid assertion of the student left's commitment to individual opportunity.]

We are people of this generation, bred in at least modest comfort, housed in universities, looking uncomfortably to the world we inherit.

. . .

Our work is guided by the sense that we may be the last generation in the experiment with living. But we are a minority—the vast majority of our people regard the temporary equilibriums of our society and the world as eternally functional parts. In this is perhaps the outstanding paradox: We ourselves are imbued with urgency, yet the message of our society is that there is no viable alternative to the present. Beneath the reassuring tones of the politicians, beneath the common opinion that America will "muddle through," beneath the stagnation of those who have closed their minds to the future, is the pervading feeling that there simply are no alternatives, that our times have witnessed the exhaustion not only of Utopias, but of any new departures as well. Feeling the press of complexity upon the emptiness of life, people are fearful of the thought that at any moment things might thrust out of control. They fear change itself, since change might smash whatever invisible framework seems to hold back chaos for them now. For most Americans, all crusades are suspect, threatening. The fact that each individual sees apathy in his fellows perpetuates the common reluctance to organize for changes. The dominant institutions are complex enough to blunt the minds of their potential critics, and entrenched enough to swiftly dissipate or entirely repel the energies of protest and reform, thus limiting human expectancies. Then, too, we are a materially improved society, and by our own improvements we seem to have weakened the case for change.

Some would have us believe that Americans feel contentment amidst prosperity—but might it not better be called a glaze above deeply felt anxieties about their role in the new world? And if these anxieties produce a developed indifference to human affairs, do they not as well produce a yearning to believe there *is* an alternative to the present, that something *can* be done to change circumstances in the school, the workplaces, the bureaucracies, the government? It is to this latter yearning, at once the spark and engine of change, that we direct our present appeal. The search for truly democratic alternatives to the present, and a commitment to social experimentation with them, is a worthy and fulfilling human enterprise, one which moves us and, we hope, others today. . . .

VALUES

Making values explicit—an initial task in establishing alternatives—is an activity that has been devalued and corrupted. The conventional moral terms of the age, the politician moralities ("free world," "peoples democracies") reflect realities poorly, if at all, and seem to function more as ruling myths than as descriptive principles. But neither has our experience in the universities brought us moral enlightenment. Our professors and administrators sacrifice controversy to public relations; their curriculums change more slowly than the living events of the world; their skills and silence are purchased by investors in the arms race; passion is called unscholastic. The questions we might want raised—what is really important? can we live in a different and better way? if we wanted to change society, how would we do it?—are not thought to be questions of a "fruitful, empirical nature," and thus are brushed aside.

Unlike youth in other countries, we are used to moral leadership being exercised and moral dimensions being clarified by our elders. But today, for us, not even the liberal and socialist preachments of the past seem adequate to the forms of the present. Consider the old slogans: Capitalism Cannot Reform Itself, United Front Against Fascism, General Strike, All Out on May Day. Or, more recently, No Cooperation with Commies and Fellow Travelers, Ideologies Are Exhausted, Bipartisanship, No Utopias. These are incomplete, and there are few new prophets. It has been said that our liberal and socialist predecessors were plagued by vision without program, while our own generation is plagued by program without vision. All around us there is astute grasp of method, technique—the committee, the *ad hoc* group, the lobbyist, the hard and soft sell, the make, the projected image—but, if pressed critically, such expertise is incompetent to explain its implicit ideals. It is highly fashionable to identify oneself by old categories, or by naming a respected political figure, or by explaining "how we would vote" on various issues.

Theoretic chaos has replaced the idealistic thinking of old—and, unable to reconstitute theoretic order, men have condemned idealism itself. Doubt has replaced hopefulness, and men act out a defeatism that is labelled realistic. The decline of utopia and hope is in fact one of the defining features of social life today. The reasons are various: The dreams of the older left were perverted by Stalinism and never recreated; the congressional stalemate makes men narrow their view of the possible; the specialization of human activity leaves little room for sweeping thought; the horrors of the twentieth century, symbolized in the gas ovens and concentration camps and atom bombs, have blasted hopefulness. To be idealistic is to be considered apocalyptic, deluded. To have no serious aspirations, on the contrary, is to be "tough-minded."

In suggesting social goals and values, therefore, we are aware of entering a sphere of some disrepute. Perhaps matured by the past, we have no sure formulas, no closed theories—but that does not mean values are beyond discussion and tentative determination. A first task of any social movement is to convince people that the search for orienting theories and the creation of human values is complex but worthwhile. We are aware that to avoid platitudes we must analyze the concrete conditions of social order. But to direct such an analysis we must use the guideposts of basic principles. Our own social values involve conceptions of human beings, human relationships, and social systems.

We regard *men* as infinitely precious and possessed of unfulfilled capacities for reason, freedom, and love. In affirming these principles we are aware of countering perhaps the dominant conceptions of man in the twentieth century: that he is a thing to be manipulated, and that he is inherently incapable of directing his own affairs. We oppose the depersonalization that reduces human beings to the status of things. If anything, the brutalities of the twentieth century teach that means and ends are intimately related, that vague appeals to "posterity" cannot justify the mutilations of the present. We oppose, too, the doctrine of human incompetence because it rests essentially on the modern fact that men have been "competently" manipulated into incompetence. We see little reason why men cannot meet with increasing skill the complexities and responsibilities of their situation, if society is organized not for minority participation but for majority participation in decision-making.

Men have unrealized potential for self-cultivation, self-direction, self-understanding, and creativity. It is this potential that we regard as crucial and to which we appeal— not to the human potentiality for violence, unreason, and submission to authority. The goal of man and society should be human independence: a concern not with image or popularity but with finding a meaning in life that is personally authentic; a quality of mind not compulsively driven by a sense of powerlessness, nor one which unthinkingly adopts status values, nor one which represses all threats to its habits, but one which has full, spontaneous access to present and past experiences, one which easily unites the fragmented parts of personal history, one which openly faces problems which are troubling and unresolved

—one with an intuitive awareness of possibilities, an active sense of curiosity, an ability and willingness to learn.

This kind of independence does not mean egoistic individualism; the object is not to have one's way so much as it is to have a way that is one's own. Nor do we deify man—we merely have faith in his potential.

Human relationships should involve fraternity and honesty. Human interdependence is contemporary fact; human brotherhood must be willed, however, as a condition of future survival and as the most appropriate form of social relations. Personal links between man and man are needed, especially to go beyond the partial and fragmentary bonds of function that bind men only as worker to worker, employer to employee, teacher to student, American to Russian.

Loneliness, estrangement, isolation describe the vast distance between man and man today. These dominant tendencies cannot be overcome by better personnel management, nor by improved gadgets, but only when a love of man overcomes the idolatrous worship of things by man.

As the individualism we affirm is not egoism, the selflessness we affirm is not self-elimination. On the contrary, we believe in generosity of a kind that imprints one's unique individual qualities in the relation to other men, and to all human activity. Further, to dislike isolation is not to favor the abolition of privacy; the latter differs from isolation in that it occurs or is abolished according to individual will.

• • •

In the last few years, thousands of American students demonstrated that they at least felt the urgency of the times. They moved actively and directly against racial injustices, the threat of war, violations of individual rights of conscience and, less frequently, against economic manipulation. They succeeded in restoring a small measure of controversy to the campuses after the stillness of the McCarthy period. They succeeded, too, in gaining some concessions from the people and institutions they opposed, especially in the fight against racial bigotry.

The significance of these scattered movements lies not in their success or failure in gaining objectives—at least not yet. Nor does the significance lie in the intellectual "competence" or "maturity" of the students involved—as some pedantic elders allege. The significance is in the fact that the students are breaking the crust of apathy and overcoming the inner alienation—facts that remain the defining characteristics of American college life.

If student movements for change are rarities still on the campus scene, what is commonplace there? The real campus, the familiar campus, is a place of private people, engaged in their notorious "inner emigration." It is a place of commitment to business-as-usual, getting ahead, playing it cool. It is a place of mass affirmation of the Twist, but mass reluctance toward the controversial public stance. Rules are accepted as "inevitable," bureaucracy as "just circumstances," irrelevance as "scholarship," selflessness as "martyrdom," politics as "just another way to make people, and an unprofitable one, too."

Almost no students value activity as a citizen. Passive in public, they are hardly more idealistic in arranging their private lives; Gallup concludes they will settle for "low success, and won't risk high failure." There is not much willingness to take risks (not even in business), no setting of dangerous goals, no real conception of personal identity except one manufactured in the image of others, no real urge for personal fulfillment except to be almost as successful as the very successful people. Attention is being paid to social status (the quality of shirt collars, meeting people, getting wives or husbands, making solid contacts for later on); much, too, is paid to academic status (grades, honors, the med-school rat race). But neglected generally is real intellectual status, the personal cultivation of the mind.

.   .   .

Look beyond the campus, to America itself. That student life is more intellectual, and perhaps more comfortable, does not obscure the fact that the fundamental qualities of life on the campus reflect the habits of society at large. The fraternity president is seen at the junior manager levels; the sorority queen has gone to Grosse Pointe; the serious poet burns for a place, any place, to work; the once-serious and never-serious poets work at the advertising agencies. The desperation of people threatened by forces about which they know little and of which they can say less, the cheerful emptiness of people giving up all hope of changing things, the faceless ones polled by Gallup who listed "international affairs" fourteenth on their list of problems but who also expected thermonuclear war in the next few years—in these and other forms, Americans are in withdrawal from public life, from any collective effort at directing their own affairs.

Some regard these national doldrums as a sign of healthy approval of the established order, but is it approval by consent or by manipulated acquiescence? Others declare that the people are withdrawn because compelling issues are fast disappearing; perhaps there are fewer breadlines in America, but is Jim Crow gone, is there enough work and is work more fulfilling, is world war a diminishing threat, and what of the revolutionary new peoples? Still others think the national quietude is a necessary consequence of the need for élites to resolve complex and specialized problems of modern industrial society. But, then, why should business élites help decide foreign policy, and who controls the élites anyway, and are they solving mankind's problems? Others finally shrug knowingly and announce that full democracy never worked anywhere in the past—but why lump qualitatively different civilizations together, and how can a social order work well if its best thinkers are skeptics, and is man really doomed forever to the domination of today?

There are no convincing apologies for the contemporary malaise. . . . The apathy is, first, subjective—the felt powerlessness of ordinary people, the resignation before the enormity of events. But subjective apathy is encouraged by the objective American situation—the actual separation of people from power, from relevant knowledge, from pinnacles of decision-making. Just as the university influences the student way of life, so do major social institutions create the circumstances in which the isolated citizen will try hopelessly to understand his world and himself.

The very isolation of the individual—from power and community and ability to aspire—means the rise of a democracy without publics. With the great mass of people structurally remote and psychologically hesitant with respect to democratic institutions, those institutions themselves attenuate and become, in a fashion of the vicious circle, progressively less accessible to those few who aspire to serious participation in social affairs. The vital democratic connection between community and leadership, between the mass and the several élites, has been so wrenched and perverted that disastrous policies go unchallenged time and again. . . .

The first effort, then, should be to state a vision: What is the perimeter of human possibility in this epoch? . . . The second effort, if we are to be politically responsible, is to evaluate the prospects for obtaining at least a substantial part of that vision in our epoch: What are the social forces that exist, or that must exist, if we are to be successful? And what role have we ourselves to play as a social force?

[*The "Port Huron Statement" was adopted by the Students for a Democratic Society at their convention in Port Huron, Michigan, in 1962. While not at present the official policy statement of SDS, it remains extremely influential, especially among those students just entering the movement.*]

CHANNELING

The Selective Service

[The power of the federal government has grown enormously in recent decades, bringing increased danger of governmental oppression. The most notable example is the Selective Service System, which is not simply a mechanism for conscription, but is designed to channel young people into various occupations. This text, excerpted from an internal Selective Service memorandum, illustrates how the government attempts to manipulate individual choices.

["Channeling" is one of ten documents in an "Orientation Kit" put out by the Selective Service. It was issued in July 1965 and has recently been withdrawn. The following are excerpts from that document.]

One of the major products of the Selective Service classification process is the channeling of manpower into many endeavors, occupations and activities that are in the national interest. . . .

The line dividing the primary function of armed forces manpower procurement from the process of channeling manpower into civilian support is often finely drawn. The process of channeling by not taking men from certain activities who are otherwise liable for service, or by giving deferment to qualified men in certain occupations, is actual procurement by inducement of manpower for civilian activities which are manifestly in the national interest.

While the best known purpose of Selective Service is to procure manpower for the armed forces, a variety of related processes take place outside delivery of manpower to the active armed forces. Many of these may be put under the heading of "channeling manpower." Many young men would not have pursued a higher education if there had not been a program of student deferment. Many young scientists, engineers, tool and die makers, and other possessors of scarce skills would not remain in their jobs in the defense effort if it were not for a program of occupational deferments. Even though the salary of a teacher has historically been meager, many young men remain in that job, seeking the reward of a deferment. The process of channeling manpower by deferment is entitled to much credit for the large number of graduate students in technical fields and for the fact that there is not a greater shortage of teachers, engineers and other scientists working in activities which are essential to the national interest. . . .

The System has also induced needed people to remain in these professions and in industry engaged in defense activities or in the support of national health, safety or interest. . . .

This was coupled with a growing public recognition that the complexities of future wars would diminish further the distinction between what constitutes military service in uniform and a comparable contribution to the national interest out of uniform. Wars have always been conducted in various ways, but appreciation of this fact and its relationship to preparation for war has never been so sharp in the public mind as it is now becoming. The meaning of the word "service," with its former restricted application to the armed forces, is certain to become widened much more in the future. This brings with it the ever increasing problem of how to control effectively the service of individuals who are not in the armed forces.

In the Selective Service System the term "deferment" has been used millions of times to describe the method and means used to attract to the kind of service considered to be most important, the individuals who were not compelled to do it. The club of induction has been used to drive out of areas considered to be less important to the areas of greater importance in which deferments were given, the individuals who did not or could not participate in activities which were considered essential to the defense of the Nation. The Selective Service System anticipates further evolution in this area. . . .

No group deferments are permitted. Deferments are granted, however, in a realistic atmosphere so that the fullest effect of channeling will be felt, rather than be terminated by military service at too early a time.

Registrants and their employers are encouraged and required to make available to the classifying authorities detailed evidence as to the occupation and activities in which the registrants are engaged. . . . Since occupational deferments are granted for no more than one year at a time, a process of periodically receiving current information and repeated review assures that every deferred registrant continues to contribute to the overall national good. This reminds him of the basis for his deferment. . . .

Patriotism is defined as "devotion to the welfare of one's country." It has been interpreted to mean many different things. Men have always been exhorted to do their duty. But what that duty is depends upon a variety of variables, most important being the nature of the threat to national welfare and the capacity and opportunity of the individual. Take, for example, the boy who saved the Netherlands by plugging the dike with his finger.

At the time of the American Revolution the patriot was the so-called "embattled farmer" who joined General Washington to fight the British. The concept that patriotism is best exemplified by service in uniform has always been under some degree of challenge, but never to the extent that it is today. In today's complicated warfare, when the man in uniform may be suffering far less than the civilians at home, patriotism must be interpreted far more broadly than ever before.

This is not a new thought, but it has had new emphasis since the development of nuclear and rocket warfare. Educators, scientists, engineers and their professional organizations, during the last ten years particularly, have been convincing the American public that for the mentally qualified man there is a special order of patriotism other than service in uniform—that for the man having the capacity, dedicated service as a civilian in such fields as engineering, the sciences and teaching constitute the ultimate in their expression of patriotism. A large segment of the American public has been convinced that this is true.

It is in this atmosphere that the young man registers at age 18 and pressure begins to force his choice. He does not have the inhibitions that a philosophy of universal service in uniform would engender. The door is open for him as a student if capable in a skill badly needed by his nation. He has many choices and he is prodded to make a decision.

The psychological effect of this circumstantial climate depends upon the individual, his sense of good citizenship, his love of country and its way of life. He can obtain a sense of well-being and satisfaction that he is doing as a civilian what will help his country most. This process encourages him to put forth his best effort and removes to some degree the stigma that has been attached to being out of uniform.

In the less patriotic and more selfish individual it engenders a sense of fear, uncertainty and dissatisfaction which motivates him, nevertheless, in the same direction. He complains of the uncertainty which he must endure; he would like to be able to do as he pleases; he would appreciate a certain future with no prospect of military service or civilian contribution, but he complies. . . .

Throughout his career as a student, the pressure—the threat of loss of deferment—continues. It continues with equal intensity after graduation. His local board requires periodic reports to find out what he is up to. He is impelled to pursue his skill rather than embark upon some less important enterprise and is encouraged to apply his skill in an essential activity in the national interest. The loss of deferred status is the consequence for the individual who has acquired the skill and either does not use it or uses it in a nonessential activity.

The psychology of granting wide choice under pressure to take action is the American or indirect way of achieving what is done by direction in foreign countries where choice is not permitted. Here, choice is limited but not denied, and it is fundamental that an individual generally applies himself better to something he has decided to do rather than something he has been told to do.

The effects of channeling are manifested among student physicians. They are deferred to complete their education through school and internship. This permits them to serve in the armed forces in their skills rather than in an unskilled capacity as enlisted men.

The device of pressurized guidance, or channeling, is employed on Standby Reservists of which more than 2½ million have been referred by all services for availability determinations. The appeal to the Reservist who knows he is subject to recall to active duty unless he is determined to be unavailable is virtually identical to that extended to other registrants.

The psychological impact of being rejected for service in uniform is severe. The earlier this occurs in a young man's life, the sooner the beneficial effects of pressured motivation by the Selective Service System are lost. He is labeled unwanted. His patriotism is not desired. Once the label of "rejectee" is upon him all efforts at guidance by persuasion are futile. If he attempts to enlist at 17 or 18 and is rejected, then he receives virtually none of the impulsion the System is capable of giving him. If he makes no effort to enlist and as a result is not rejected until delivered for examination by the Selective Service System at about age 23, he has felt some of the pressure but thereafter is a free agent.

This contributed to establishment of a new classification of I-Y (registrant qualified for military service only in time of war or national emergency). That classification reminds the registrant of his ultimate qualification to serve and preserves some of the benefit of what we call channeling. Without it or any other similar method of categorizing men in degrees of acceptability, men rejected for military service would be left with the understanding that they are unfit to defend their country, even in wartime.

An unprejudiced choice between alternative routes in civilian skills can be offered only by an agency which is not a user of manpower and is, therefore, not a competitor. In the absence of such an agency, bright young men would be importuned with bounties and pirated like potential college football players until eventually a system of arbitration would have to be established.

From the individual's viewpoint, he is standing in a

room which has been made uncomfortably warm. Several doors are open, but they all lead to various forms of recognized, patriotic service to the Nation. Some accept the alternatives gladly—some with reluctance. The consequence is approximately the same.

The so-called Doctor Draft was set up during the Korean episode to insure sufficient physicians, dentists and veterinarians in the armed forces as officers. The objective of that law was to exert sufficient pressure to furnish an incentive for application for commission. However, the indirect effect was to induce many physicians, dentists and veterinarians to specialize in areas of medical personnel shortages and to seek outlets for their skills in areas of greatest demand and national need rather than of greatest financial return.

Selective Service processes do not compel people by edict as in foreign systems to enter pursuits having to do with essentiality and progress. They go because they know that by going they will be deferred.

The application of direct methods to effect the policy of every man doing his duty in support of national interest involves considerably more capacity than the current use of indirection as a method of allocation of personnel. The problem, however, of what is every man's duty when each individual case is approached is not simple. The question of whether he can do one duty better than another is a problem of considerable proportions and the complications of logistics in attempting to control parts of an operation without controlling all of it (in other words, to control allocation of personnel without controlling where people eat, where they live and how they are to be transported), adds to the administrative difficulties of direct administration. The organization necessary to make the decisions, even poor decisions, would, of necessity, extract a large segment of population from productive work. If the members of the organization are conceived to be reasonably qualified to exercise judgment and control over skilled personnel, the impact of their withdrawal from war production work would be severe. The number of decisions would extend into billions.

Deciding what people should do, rather than letting them do something of national importance of their own choosing, introduces many problems that are at least partially avoided when indirect methods, the kind currently invoked by the Selective Service System, are used.

Delivery of manpower for induction, the process of providing a few thousand men with transportation to a reception center, is not much of an administrative or financial challenge. It is in dealing with the other millions of registrants that the System is heavily occupied, developing more effective human beings in the national interest. If there is to be any survival after disaster, it will take people, and not machines, to restore the Nation.

July 1965

PART IV
TOWARD THE FUTURE

POWER AND THE INDIVIDUAL

Richard N. Goodwin

[Power is central to individualism, for without real power choice is meaningless. Richard Goodwin incisively examines why people lack power today and how political action can help them achieve it.

[Richard Goodwin, a former aide to John F. Kennedy and Robert Kennedy, is the author of *The Sower's Seed* and *Triumph or Tragedy: Reflections on Vietnam*.]

The issue of power—who shall have it and how it shall be exercised—is the overwhelming political issue of modern times. In fact, it is far more than a political issue; it penetrates our social, economic, and personal life. Nor is it simply an American problem; it plagues the entire affluent West. And if it is different in the developing countries, that is only because they are preoccupied with urgent difficulties of poverty and oppression which we have largely overcome. Thus, their politics reflect more traditional clashes between economic and social groups. This issue, more than any other, explains the appeal and the ascendancy of Senator McCarthy and, more ominously, the attraction of George Wallace. It is now a source of enormous turbulence, but it can become the cement of a new style of national unity.

* * * * * * * * * * * * * * * * *

It would be hard to overstate the extent to which the malaise of powerlessness has eaten its way into our society, evoking an aimless unease, frustration, and fury. It is probably least pervasive among the poor urban blacks, around whom so much of the surface debate about local control and Black Power now revolves. Their grievances are, for the most part, closer to the classic ills that the New Deal was designed to solve. They want jobs and decent homes, a higher standard of living, and freedom from the welfare bureaucracy. If a beneficent government were to provide these rudimentary components of the just life, it would meet most of the present demands of the black community. Of course, even among America's poor, questions of power are more important than they were thirty years ago. For the poor of today are inevitably caught up in the main currents of our society and partake of the general atmosphere of helplessness and drift, and the resistant nature of racial feelings is forcing black Americans toward a kind of separatism as an alternative to the assimilation that was their initial goal. However, these questions can be seen most acutely among those who are neither poor nor black—the American middle class, or the American majority. Their psychological plight is both worse and more dangerous than that of the black militant leading a slum riot. For he at least has a cause and a purpose, an enemy, and comrades in the struggle. No such outlets and no human connections so satisfying are available to the man who lives in a middle-class suburb or a lower-income city apartment. And his discontents, unlike those of the poor, have real political weight.

It is impossible to provide an accurate and uniform description of a group of people as large and varied as non-poor Americans. For the most part, such an American commutes to a job that he may like or hate but is most probably indifferent to—indifferent not to the income or status it provides but to the products of his labor. It is the job that counts, not the refrigerators or vacuum tubes he produces. He would be among a minority if he felt that his work made an improving difference to the life of his country or his neighbors. At home, he can either sit amid his many purchases or get back into his car and drive to visit friends. There is probably no place for him to talk, and, almost certainly, no neighborhood gathering place where he can meet with friends, discuss the day's events, and share in the satisfactions and concerns of community.

If he stays home, he probably watches television, wishing both that he had something better to do and that he could buy the goods that float alluringly across the screen. It is this increasingly atomized and insulated existence that we have created with our wealth. And if this is the suburban man's life, how much less exciting is that of his wife. Perhaps she has gone to college. Yet she does not have a job, nor are there many outlets for her intelligence or her energies. She is expected to stay home, care for children, and shop and clean house, even though hospitals and schools and many other vital services are deteriorating for want of the skills she could provide. What an incredible monster women's education has become. We spend decades instilling the same values of competition and achievement in girls as in boys, even though we can clearly foresee an ultimate collision with the socially imposed responsibilities of housewife and mother and with the mythic compulsions of lover and servant-helpmate. Some of the most ambitious women in the world hasten to confide that they have an "Oriental" streak, as well they may have. The society that sets up this clash of desires provides neither day-care centers for children nor opportunities for the use and development by women of their wasted skills. The frustrations thus generated are aggravated by the absence, especially in our better suburbs, of any communal park or neighborhood center where women can naturally meet and share experiences.

The life of the lower-income urban white shares many characteristics with that of the suburban citizen. However, the urban white is also trapped in a no-man's-land between black poverty and what he sees or imagines of middle-class affluence. He has the advantage of being able to express many of his wants in traditional economic terms. However, his discontent is fed both by envy of the more prosperous and by anger at the blacks—not just because he fears the blacks but also because their problems, and not his, seem to be the focus of national concern. That is why it was possible for many members of this group to support Wallace after having supported Robert Kennedy: both men, in very different ways, could be identified with their wants, and both conveyed a deeply emotional sympathy with the importance of their fears and their plight.

The unexciting and envy-producing tone of the non-poor citizen's private life is heightened by the growing remoteness of public life. The air around him is poisoned, parkland disappears under relentless bulldozers, traffic stalls and jams, airplanes cannot land, and even his own streets are unsafe and, increasingly, streaked with terror. Yet he cannot remember having decided that these things should happen, or even having wished them. He has no sense that there is anything he can do to arrest the tide. He does not know whom to blame. Somehow, the crucial aspects of his environment seem in the grip of forces that are too huge and impersonal to attack. You cannot vote them out of office or shout them down. Even the speeches of mayors and governors are filled with exculpatory claims that the problems are too big, that there is not enough power or enough money to cope with them, and our commentators sympathize, readily agreeing that this city or that state is really ungovernable. Even when a source of authority can be identified, it seems hopelessly detached from the desires or actions of individual citizens. Thus, the citizens of Boston woke up one day not very long ago to read that two hundred million dollars' worth of anti-missile missiles were scheduled to replace hundreds of acres of nearby woodland. And who could say no? And who was asked? More grotesque and more shattering, we find ourselves in a major war, and our young people shipped off to battle, without any formal expression of consent or support, even by the members of Congress. And we are also aware, in some dim psychic recess, that our President, along with a few people whose names we can't remember, can blow us all up.

This powerlessness, in large measure a product of the complexity and the sheer size of modern society, is a problem in itself. It is a problem in the same way that lack of money or of useful work is a problem. For individuals have a fundamental, instinctive need for a degree of personal mastery over their lives and their environment. The sense of powerlessness is, moreover, greatly aggravated by the failure of our institutions and our social processes to respond to more specific ills. If we were providing good schools, inspiring cities, and safe streets, the degree of public discontent would be far less. If the quality of individual life were being steadily raised, we would be less concerned that we had little share in the process. But that is not the case. The desire to increase our national wealth and distribute it more broadly—a desire that was idealistic in origin and welcome in its consequences—led us to create machinery for both stimulating and regulating the economy. It is not simply that power was withdrawn from private centers and brought to Washington. It is that the use of that power was judged in terms of economic growth, which meant that construction, technology, and expansion were made into self-sufficient virtues. Build a better mousetrap or a bigger housing development and you not only made money, you were a hero of the Republic. Added to this were the exigencies of the Cold War, which persuaded us of the necessity of a large standing army. This was a historic decision, constituting the first irrevocable departure from almost two centuries of compliance with the warning of the founding fathers that such a military force would be a danger to democracy. The military-budget cutting of President Truman marked the last effort to return to the earlier tradition, and the farewell speech of President Eisenhower was an echo of those early warnings. The half peace of the past twenty years has made military forces essential, yet we are victims of some of the consequences against which we were warned. The military establishment has assumed a life of its own, developing more weapons and new ones, often unrelated to rational considerations of security, and, more subtly, leading policy-makers to look at diplomatic problems in terms of force. After all, if you are the strongest kid on the block, any passionate argument is bound to evoke at least the passing thought that you could end it with a couple of blows.

Unfortunately, the policies and the institutions we evolved to make ourselves wealthy are not appropriate to the needs of a society in which lack of wealth is not the problem either for the country as a whole or for most of the people. It is not simply that we need new values but that our institutions are facing demands they were never shaped to meet. A classic example is the federal housing programs, which were designed to stimulate construction and avoid a postwar depression, and which have failed miserably under the pressure of social demands for slum clearance and the creation of livable neighborhoods. These programs can do a job, but it is not the job we now need done. Moreover, many of our institutions, including our political parties themselves, are led by men who developed their ideas in response to earlier demands, and are therefore unable to understand or cope with a newer set of problems. The worst of these men no longer care for anything except the power and influence they have won, and the best of them are angry because their beneficent and humane intentions are not appreciated. The occasional violence of their response to opposition shows their unawareness that time and change, not particular individuals, have been their remorseless critics.

Asking many of today's institutions to respond to new needs is a little like putting a man on a windowsill and asking him to fly. Not only was he not built for flight but if you keep insisting he's likely to turn around and punch you in the nose. When institutions and leaders are faced with demands they barely understand, their reaction is often to become rigid and defensive, and even angry. Perhaps the ultimate symbol of this reaction was the contorted fury of Mayor Daley at the Chicago Democratic Convention, lashing out at a group whose values and aims were totally alien to his experience. It is precisely this phenomenon that led Thomas Jefferson to assert the necessity of periodic rebellion. It seems almost inevitable that the repositories of power and control will react to changing circumstances and a changing environment by hardening their attitudes, narrowing the avenues of access for new ideas and men, and losing the flexibility that gave them their initial glow and effectiveness. What is even more ominous, beliefs that were once tentative and responsive to changes in circumstance tend to stiffen into dogma when confronted by conceptual challenge. When this happened in the nineteen thirties, we were fortunate enough to get Franklin Roosevelt and a peaceful revolution. When it happened in the eighteen fifties—a period like our own in many ways—the system collapsed in civil war. Unfortunately, the profound nature of modern change resembles the eighteen-fifties more than it does the nineteen-thirties, and there is no Roosevelt in sight.

The same stiffening of established patterns invades the relationship between private institutions and the public interest. The basic pattern of government regulation of business has hardly changed for decades, although much of it is irrelevant, some is oppressive, and many new abuses are unrestrained. The Internal Revenue Code of 1954, despite its grotesque inequities—some of which are actually harmful to wealth and business—appears to be engraved in marble. We cannot stop incredibly wasteful subsidies to groups like the shipbuilders and large-scale farmers, even though their political power has almost evaporated, while at the same time it is extraordinarily difficult to supplement the income of more needy and numerous groups. No demonology of power and wealth can explain a rigidity that is part of a general resistance to new assertions of what is desirable and good. When we understand the fact that what now seems wrong may once have been right, then we can understand the fierceness of the defense.

Another example of this process in action is the Democratic party itself. It has clung to the ideas and attitudes that made it the country's leading party, and its leaders, once ensconced, have clung to positions of control, often closing the door behind them. The result is that the governors of eight out of the ten largest states are Republican, and much of the vigorous new talent in the Congress is Republican. Increasingly, "new Democrats" are coming from underpopulated states like Idaho, South Dakota, and Iowa, where they do not run up against rigidified party structures. More harmful in the long run is the shift in the locus of intellectual debate. It seems that almost all the ideological ferment and the passionate clash of new ideas come either from the alienated left or from the alienated right. The once fertile soil of liberal and Democratic thought finds it difficult to produce new concepts or institutions, and its Presidential candidate could only—and with the best of intentions—point to the liberal past and promise more and better of the same.

This phenomenon is not just political. In almost every aspect of life, men are confronted by institutions and processes that seem unresponsive to their needs. There is, for example, no way in which the citizen can even begin to create a community—a place where he can both work and play in some kind of shared fellowship with neighbors. Our society is simply not equipped to deal with such a demand, and our political leaders are not even able to articulate it, since it transcends their own professional assumptions.

Powerlessness is made more acute by the seeming opposite of rigidity—by the swirling inconstancies of modern life. We are like boats tied to a riverbank with the rapid waters constantly seething beneath us while rope after rope breaks away. It is now commonplace to observe the weakening of the ties of family and community. However, it is not merely that we are being deprived of important values. These institutions, and others, gave us a resting spot, an association within which we could have some secure sense of our own value and place regardless of our fate in the world outside. In a more subtle and profound way, the increasing incredibility of religious doctrines and the complexities of science, which have made it impossible to understand the natural world, have deprived us of anchors against the storm of events. Even our physical environment has betrayed our memories. The other day, I drove through Harvard Square, where I had gone to school ten years before. There were new buildings, shops, and roads. The familiar place of law-school days had changed beyond recognition. In fact, it did not exist. There was no place for the past, and the present, one knew, would also fade. Yet man has nearly always anchored his sense of reality, his sense of himself, to a fixed place, amid familiar landmarks. Our world has become nomadic as the scenery of our life is constantly shifted. It is small wonder if we sometimes feel as unreal as actors moving from part to part.

To all this is added the torrent of events: wars and riots, inventions and spaceships. One day we are informed that we must fear a man called Castro, on the next day that our security requires the end of strife in the Congo, and on the next that de Gaulle menaces the grandeur of our nation. And we pass through all this tumult, great and small, seated before the inexorable shadows of a television set—certainly the greatest psychic disturber ever created

ing consensus is in rejection of the present, and that was the decisive asset of Mr. Nixon's candidacy. In fact, many people are prepared to rebel against the entire system that has brought us to our present state of affairs. Part of McCarthy's appeal and much of Wallace's lay in the fact that these men appeared to stand outside the system. They did not talk in the increasingly hollow and banal rhetoric of most politicians. They spoke with candor, discussed new issues, offered fresh approaches. In different ways, each of them defied the traditional party structure, ignored the customary political rites, and incurred the hostility of party regulars. In McCarthy's case, his manner and language, although often abstract, conveyed a hope of beneficial change. Robert Kennedy's strength also derived not from his specific programs but from his manner, which radiated a passionate commitment to change. For the United States is prepared to move, and rather rapidly, either to the right or to the left. Or, in terms better suited to our time, it is prepared to move either toward repression or toward liberation.

. . . .

This is because you cannot simply soothe the discontent of today with traditional remedies. It is not only that many problems—the black ghettos, for example—will require immense efforts toward solution but that the forces that disrupt the mental peace of the more affluent have deep roots in our institutional structure and our historical circumstances. Race and Vietnam contribute, but we see a similar unrest all across the affluent West, in countries neither at war nor in the midst of racial conflict. In outlining some of the more subtle causes, I compared our present condition to that of the eighteen fifties. The United States was then turning away from expansionist goals and responsibilities; the conquest of the continent was complete, and, for almost the first time in our history, we had no significant external ambitions or threats. In our time, we are similarly turning away from Cold War globalism, and, if we are lucky, Vietnam may prove the last, convulsive gasp of that policy. In any event, we are now looking to

ourselves more intently than before. Far more important
in the eighteen fifties was that, underlying all the crises and
the violent turmoil, a new industrial age was making its
glacial advance on the values of an earlier period, uproot-
ing fixed ways of life, traditional institutions, and customary expectations. America was never to be the same again
—a change that was not caused by the Civil War but,
rather, was undoubtedly productive of the rigidity of leadership and the human uncertainty that led to that war. In
our time, also, a new type of society is tearing into the
now settled patterns of the industrial age. It has not been
given a name, for that is the historian's job. However,
economic and population growth and changing technology
and beliefs are creating a different kind of world, whether
it is called the computer age, the atomic age, the media
age, or simply the postindustrial age. This is a dislocation
of a kind that is common to all periods of history but that
happens only at long intervals in the life of a particular
society.

It is a rhetorical cliché to point out that our world has
grown small. That is obviously true in a technical sense.
We can travel rapidly and communicate instantly. It is also
true in terms of the concerns of foreign policy, although
much of our feeling that we must necessarily be affected by
events in every corner of every continent is surely a product of the simple fact that we know what is happening
there, rather than of any ideological preconception or any
concrete national interest. Yet for the individual the opposite is true. Our world is too big—too crowded, too abstract, too remote. Everywhere we go, the crowd of strangers goes with us, clogging our streets and our parks. Cities
spread, computers perform their mysteries, world leaders
cast their shadows and disappear. The comforting walls
that set off a host of little worlds have been broken open,
exposing to us a limitless and kaleidoscopic vista—one
that is reflected in our fragmentary and borderless art and
in the world of drugs. How many of us in turning inward
to escape or make sense of a turbulent environment simply
recreate external disorder, almost as if our time were now
beyond intellectual grasp? That feeling in itself contributes
to powerlessness. For understanding is a form of control,

if often illusory, and when we cannot understand how things work or why they happen—whether laws of nature or the television pictures that are corrupting us—we feel helpless. Perhaps one can no longer understand the world—only experience it. If that is true, politics can offer no real answer. And we must also face the possibility that there are too many people—that only through organization, and its counterpart, coercion, can we maintain civilized order among so vast a throng.

Such philosophical reflections, however, are irrelevant to politics, which must assume that problems can be dealt with, and also, in our own national context, that individual liberty can be maintained. If the forces feeding discontent are as profound and powerful as I have suggested, then political thinking and, ultimately, national policy must move toward an entirely new dimension. The last time the American establishment thought seriously about national goals was during the late Eisenhower and early Kennedy years. The formulations from this period of the more enlightened and liberal politicians are already out of date. A strong domestic defense establishment, economic growth, NATO, and so on, though they are still with us, barely touch the principal sources of our dissatisfaction. Other goals of that very recent time—such as the frantic desire to measure every national program, from education to overseas propaganda, in terms of competition with the Russians—are now irrelevant, and some are forgotten. Yet almost all our political leaders seem rooted in the old rhetoric, even if it is clothed in new facts and circumstances, and thus have lost their hold on the popular sensibilities.

The material out of which relevant national objectives can be shaped is at hand in the work of some social critics and a few economists, and even in the insights of a few of the more sensitive politicians. In the process, we must focus not only on solving "problems" as defined in the usual sense—education, pollution, and the rest—but also on the *ways* in which we solve them. This is a familiar idea within a democratic tradition that has, for example, valued many individual liberties above the alluring, if often illusory, efficiency of coercive techniques.

We have always placed certain abstract values—those

which cannot be measured or weighed—above economic, logical, or physically tangible goals. Confronted with the overwhelming and uncertain complexities of modern life, and informed by a greatly increased awareness of our limited ability to predict or control the forces loosed by our obsessive industry and invention, we must add to the list of such values. They have traditionally included not only the rights mentioned in the Bill of Rights and allied civil liberties but equality of opportunity, the freedom to develop individual talent, and, more recently, freedom from starvation and destitution. And all these, imperfectly realized though they may be, still exert a powerful hold on our national thinking and shape our political rhetoric and policy. I have no wish to coin a new set of slogans, but certainly the individual must also have the freedom to share in those public decisions which affect his private life beyond merely casting a vote in periodic elections. This does not mean a plebiscite on every problem but, rather, a distinct prejudice in favor of community and neighborhood control. We should also be guided by a desire to preserve freedom from isolation, which means, at least, that environmental decisions should be shaped to re-create the possibilities of community and neighborhood life. It is equally important that the individual be given freedom to participate in the important enterprises of our society, from working in the underdeveloped world to improving the life of the ghettos. If citizens are to find a purpose beyond their daily lives, it will come from having a personal share in important public causes, and the causes must be large and worthy enough to tap moral will and energy. Only in this way can we combat the increasing isolation and remoteness that are eroding the moral drive of our society.

Much of this resolves itself into a widening of one of the oldest staples of political language: freedom of choice. For all the talk about our permissive society, that freedom has steadily narrowed. In fact, much of the release of inhibitions on private behavior is surely a reaction to the confinements imposed by our ideology and social structure. (Successful revolutions tend to be puritanical.) When a young man sees no alternative to spending his youth in a classroom and his manhood in a modern suburb, he may want to assert himself by growing a beard. Conversely, the students who turned out to work for McCarthy cut their hair and shaved not because of adult dictates but through self-organization and self-discipline. They were involved in something more important than this kind of assertion. These are trivial things, but they are tokens of the fact that much frantic liberation of private behavior is a futile effort to alter or escape the hardening mold that envelops social man. We virtually demand, for example, that a young man go to college, and beyond, if he is to have a job that uses his abilities. At one time, a boy could go to sea or go West or start working in a factory and still aspire to success in a wide range of demanding tasks. The fact is that a lot of young men would develop more fully outside the regular educational system. The answer is not simply providing more and better schools but making alternative institutions, training, and experience available, and making them acceptable to those who guard the gates to achievement. Similarly, by huddling industry, commerce, and even intellectual life together in great urban areas we have seriously limited the kinds of places in which a man can live. Much of this is a product of the obsessive urge toward system and order, and of the fact that as systems grow larger they swiftly outpace the individual imagination or intelligence and assume a conforming life of their own. It is almost as if our society were afflicted with some kind of compulsive neatness, which it equated with efficiency or high purpose.

The fact is that organizational neatness and central control not only limit human scope but are often inefficient. Government programs break down or prove inadequate not merely because they are badly conceived but because the problems they seek to deal with are far too large for the limited abilities of a few administrators. Even a genius philosopher-king equipped by IBM could not hope to deal with the varied complexities of dozens of American cities. Central direction is inefficient in a more profound way, too. Given human nature in the context of our society, such oppressive structures are bound to breed discontent. This discontent necessarily impairs our ability to solve problems and maintain traditional values. Restless and unhappy people cannot easily be persuaded to join in enterprises of high purpose, especially those involving sacrifice.

Unless we are to move toward repression, the political platform of the future must contain words still alien to serious public dialogue—words such as "community," "power," and "purpose." This does not mean we will no longer worry about matters like economic policy and defense. For large elements of our population, economic questions are still critical, although they are increasingly fused with other desires. However, since poverty or a low standard of living is not the root of much of our unhappiness, wealth and its distribution do not point the way toward a solution. Words like "community," "power," and "purpose" seem rather abstract and vague, but then so do more traditional goals, such as "liberty" and "opportunity." And, like these more familiar terms, they can be given concrete content, yielding specific and tangible programs. Effective government action toward these ends will respond to the demands of the subject matter, and not to any master plan for their attainment, just as devotion to liberty does not tell you what kind of speech can be restricted or whether the State Department can limit travel to Cuba. Without trying to anticipate a report by the future Presidential task force, I would like to discuss some specific examples, simply to show that they do exist.

Many of the programs designed to re-create community will concern the physical environment, although the power to act as a community and the consequent sense of shared purpose are also critical. This will require that we concentrate not on the quantity of construction but on assembling the components of daily living within an area that a man can comprehend and easily traverse. Along with housing should go hospitals and government services, recreation and meeting centers, parks, and, to the extent that this is possible, places of work. This does not mean breaking up our cities but restoring the concept of neighborhood under modern conditions—a place where a man can live with other men. Some of this is happening by itself under pressures of growth, as shopping centers move to the suburbs and industry seeks sites outside the city. This beginning can proliferate and expand through programs ranging from tax incentives for businesses resettling in residential areas to the construction of new satellite cities. Much can be done, for example, simply by changing and enforcing zoning ordinances, building codes, and tax laws, without a cent of public expenditure. There is a lot more to community than this. Its roots go into the powerful cementing emotions of pride, belonging, friendship, and shared concern, yet these, in turn, depend on the physical possibilities. Not only is it within our power to create those possibilities but it is probably a more practical course than our present unthinking and hopelessly scattered mixture of government programs and private enterprise.

Increasing the individual's power over the conditions of his life involves the blended methods of transferring authority, creating it where it does not exist, and lessening the coercive weight of the state. At other times, I have discussed the need for decentralizing the operations of government—allowing communities, private groups, cities, and states to make public decisions that are now vested in the central government. Although the Constitution contains a prescriptive mandate for a federal system, the actual distribution of authority and responsibility has been worked out over two centuries and is constantly changing. Today, for example, the federal government exerts a power over the economy that would have been inconceivable only a few decades ago. Decentralization is another remodelling of the federal system, and to achieve it will require a patient pragmatism. The state may be the logical unit for dealing with river pollution, the metropolitan area for transportation programs, the neighborhood for schools and even post offices. *The general guide should be to transfer power to the smallest unit consistent with the scale of the problem.* Many conservatives have welcomed the idea of decentralization, hearing in it comforting echoes of old battle cries about states' rights. They are mistaken, for decentralization, if it is to work, will require even larger public programs and even more money for public needs. Otherwise, the momentum on which local interest and involvement depend will be lost. Nor does decentralization mean the absence of rigorous national standards for the use of national revenues. For example, money given for education must in fact be used for education open to all. Such standards are necessary to protect citizens against unresponsive government, and local government against the pressures of private interests. Of course, even with decentralization, most people will not actually make decisions. Still, those who do make them will be within reach of their fellow residents of the community, and thus will be far more familiar and readily accessible than federal officials. This, in itself, will yield at least the potential of influence and effective protest, which may be as close as we can come to the ideal of the town meeting.

Power is conferred in other ways: by a government that feels compelled to explain its policies and intentions with candor, that seeks the counsel of informed private groups and citizens, and that adheres to an honorable observance of the separation of powers. It will also be yielded by increased citizen control over the private institutions and processes that often determine the quality of our private lives. It is incredible, for example, that private builders, acting out of purely economic considerations, should be allowed to determine the shape of our urban environment —that individuals unresponsive to the public will should decide how the public will live. In addition, the expanding machinery of secret police, investigation, bugging, and wiretapping must be halted and dismantled. Fear and suspicion are the most paralyzing agents of all, and the most likely to provoke unrest.

The use of power is also an expression of purpose. All acts have their intention. But you can share in purpose without sharing in power. As a member of a society, the individual's pride and sense of well-being are inevitably enhanced or diminished by the purpose of his nation—what it stands for and where it is going. If money and power, self-indulgence and self-protection are the goals of our society, they will become the goals of its citizens, with damaging consequences. Nothing would do more for our national health than a feeling that we were engaged in enterprises touched with some kind of nobility and grandeur. It is this feeling that enriches the life of social man. Even the most pessimistic and critical literature written in other countries during their periods of greatness is infused with a sense of <u>pride in the nation</u>, despite doubts about, or even fierce opposition to, its contemporary acts. This sense of a noble destiny infused our country from the beginning, and in terms of our potential not only as a home for freedom and opportunity but as a guiding force in world affairs. Jefferson looked upon the United States as an example that would undermine despotism and monarchy; some of our other early leaders took a more direct hand by helping South American revolutionaries. This does not mean we must succumb to the naïve belief that it is possible to create a Great Society or a New Deal–style democracy among the varied cultures of the world, or that we should actively intervene to impose values bred of the American experience. However, our wealth and military power give us an unavoidable weight in world affairs. Therefore, it is unnecessary to decide the critical questions surrounding the wisdom of intervention in order to recognize that our acts are important to others. For example, when a military dictatorship takes over in an allied country, we can recognize it or not, suspend aid or continue it, continue preferential trading or interrupt it. There is no way to avoid decision, since failure to act will have its own meaning. The issue is whether we base our policies on unthinking reflex and an immediate mixture of attitudes and interests or whether our acts are consistent with a long-range purpose. We may decide to adopt a less active and ambitious foreign policy, but we cannot do without any policy at all. And a foreign policy actively devoted to social justice, increased liberty, and the institutionalization of peace on a worldwide scale can enlist the best impulses of the American people. Such a policy often collides with the thinking of global "realists," who led us into Santo Domingo and Vietnam; who failed to maintain a constructive common purpose among the Atlantic nations while contriving such monstrosities as the Multilateral Force; who allowed the United Nations to become trivialized; who supported Batista and ended up with Castro; and who have been unable to bring about the control of nuclear arms, which is clearly in the interests of both great powers. In fact, "realistic" policy now seems to have become no policy at all, aside from maintaining the territorial status quo with the Soviet Union and China, and hoping that Israel will survive. It is a policy virtually without long-range goals or any clear perception of the social and political forces at work on other continents, and—what is more dangerous—without any guiding concept of the kind of world community in which we will be safest and most comfortable. This is the ultimate romanticism of the ostrich.

. . . .

A foreign policy founded on traditional American values not only is wise but is essential to our domestic well-being, since shared purpose is the only enduring cement of national unity. In it lies our only hope of finding a moral equivalent of war—or, in this case, a partial alternative to domestic unrest and division. Of course, there is much within our own borders to capture the imagination and inspire worthy effort, but only for some, and, even then, probably not on a sufficiently large or lasting scale. We are so significant a nation that the nature of our role in world affairs must pervade every man's sense of himself as a citizen. John Kennedy's appeals to greatness and sacrifice evoked so strong a response not because they were expressions of a self-deceptive idealism but because they led toward the only realistic path for maintaining individual pride.

There are, of course, grave problems that do not fit easily into the rubric of power and purpose. One can add little to the interminable discussion of the race problem except to observe that politically there is no black problem at all—only a white problem. We can easily command the resources to meet the immediate needs and demands of black Americans. But we cannot do this until white Americans are persuaded of their responsibility to act. That will require more than public education and Presidential speeches. Unless we move to remedy the afflictions and grievances of white Americans, they will never consent to a concentrated effort in the ghettos. This is particularly true of the lower-income whites, who feel trapped in a relatively shabby material existence and a scorned social position. (A Chicago policeman said, pointing to the hippies in Grant

Park, "I had to work for a living, and so did my mother, and look at those kids. They do nothing and they got an education." Then he joined the charge.) It is little wonder that this group turns its wrath impartially on Negroes and college students—a perfect combination for the Wallace appeal. Its members feel scorned by the upper middle class, and, at the same time, they are deeply envious. Meanwhile, the Negro is a constant object of national discussion and attention, and a recipient of special programs. Racial feelings are very resistant, but many obstacles would fall before a national policy directed at enriching the life of *all* our citizens. Without it, the barriers will continue to rise.

The agency through which we can hope to formulate new policies is that strange American contraption the political party. My own repository of hopes for change is the Democratic party, for the Republicans seem unlikely to discard their historical role as defenders of things as they are. Since Nixon's victory, political men have begun to discuss the future of the Democratic party. Such discussion must come to grips with one essential fact: there is no Democratic party. There is the party of Daley in Illinois and the party of the county leaders in New York. There is the fragile alliance of liberals and leaders in California, and there is Kennedy in Massachusetts. In the South, there is almost nothing left at all. It is a truism to state that American political parties are not ideological in nature, since they embrace many diverse groups. Still, in the past most elements of the Democratic party agreed on certain broad goals and assumptions. There was, with some dissent, general agreement on the economic goals of the New Deal. It was broadly assumed that the Democratic party represented the disadvantaged and the poor against the great interests, and that it stood for alliance and tolerance in world affairs. There was, in other words, a base of generally accepted belief and emotional attitude. That this has largely dissolved becomes clear when we compare the parties of Daley, Meany, McCarthy, and Kennedy. The cause of the dissolution is that the issues of the past thirty years have lost their vitality. The consequence is that the Democratic party is little more than an institutional mechanism through which individuals hope to acquire public office. If the

Democratic party has a future, it will come not by raising more money or by hiring better advertising agencies but by developing a purpose and a program. I have outlined some of the possible elements of purpose and policy in support of which it might be possible to create a new, progressive coalition to replace the alliance of minorities, labor, and the South which has now fragmented and dissolved. The South has left; labor no longer exists as a coherent electoral force, having divided into upper and lower middle class; and the minorities are often at each other's throat. A new coalition will have to be made up of the populations of the inner cities, including some lower-income whites, and of the new suburbs inhabited by those who work in offices, electronics factories, and so on. This is the coalition that both Kennedy and McCarthy were trying to build, with McCarthy moving inward from the suburbs and Kennedy outward from the inner city. Neither quite got across the bridge, but the fact that their divergent constituencies responded to men who stood for enlightened and progressive change is evidence that the possibilities of coalition are there. However, the issues that will unite these groups are not only traditional economic concerns—although there are specific economic problems that must be met—but issues of the type I have set forth. For example, both in the ghettos and in the suburbs there is a desire for increased control and power over local affairs and public policy. If I am right in the belief that such desires respond to deeply felt national needs, then failure to move in this direction will leave public-spirited men with no alternative but to try to form a new party to combat the forces of repression.

Beyond such concrete and practical acts, there is a need to explore the deeper causes of our discontent. Again, as in the eighteen fifties, we can sense that we are at the beginning of a new age—or, rather, a new way of living—which is forcing its values and demands on a society not equipped to cope with them. This kind of dislocation, this gap between realities and custom, is characteristic of revolutionary historical periods. To pursue this analogy, the insulation and barrenness of the modern suburb are counterparts of the misery that enveloped the mid-nineteenth-century factory, and Mayor Daley is at one with the Southern agrarian in defending a system that history will find not to have been an unmixed evil. Without judging the efforts of men like Marshall McLuhan to abstract a single, seminal cause from the complexities of social change, we can agree with many that the ascendancy of technology is a principal feature of modern society. To that we must add growth, both of population and of our physical artifacts, such as houses, factories, and roads. The problem, however, is not technological but ideological. We are threatened not by our creations but by our beliefs. In another place, I have written, "All nations . . . are governed on the basis of ideas and values . . . which are not derived either from the necessities of nature or the command of God. If a man snatches his hand from a hot stove, that is not ideological. If he then decrees there shall be no more hot stoves in order to prevent burning, he has imposed an ideology (and one wholly alien to our own)." There is, for example, nothing in the development of the automobile which makes the clogging of our cities and the poisoning of our air logically inevitable. It is simply that we have preferred these consequences—perhaps without anticipating them—to restrictions on the use of automobiles.

No one has more bluntly stated the inward passion of the time than Lewis Strauss, who summed up the faith of two centuries when he was asked if nuclear physics might not have overstepped itself. "No," he answered. "I would not wipe out any part of it, not the bomb nor any other part of it, if I could. I believe everything man discovers, however he discovers it, is welcome and good for his future. In me this is the sort of belief that people go to the stake for." This is not a reasoned formula but an affirmation of an ideological belief verging on the mystical. Guided by such a belief, our society has developed virtually no mechanism for weighing technological change against the social consequences and enforcing its judgment. Only the great religious institutions engage in a similar process, and then, as in the case of Pope Paul and the pill, they are condemned because the values they seek to defend have lost their hold on men. This is not the place to pursue such philosophical abstractions. Yet they are at the heart of the problem. In political terms, we are barred from much effective action because we have not regarded human values—except for those related to survival, civil liberty, and prosperity—as appropriate objects of public protection. This reluctance to allow government to become concerned with the quality of individual life has its historical roots in a healthy fear of the state and a desire to insure secular liberty. It now works against us, having been outdistanced by our material circumstances. Thus, traditional principles of private enterprise join with modern construction technology to create suburban blight. But there is no inherent reason a builder should not be under as much compulsion to provide open spaces, parks, and community centers as he is to provide safe wiring and sound structures. We can also maintain that clear air and freedom of movement are as important to us as the economic advantages of urban concentration. On a broader scale, we need to reexamine all our institutions in order to determine whether what they do *for* people is worth what they do *to* them. This is not an easy job, especially since we must often match abstract or felt values against the formulations of logic and numbers. How, for example, does one explain an instinctive revulsion against the idea of a national computer center to store all the available information about every citizen, except to say that neatness and system and organization can be oppressive in themselves, and to draw upon our experience of human weakness to assert that increasing the capacity for control will increase the likelihood of control?

This kind of ideological reformation will not be easy for a people as little inclined to theory as our own. It will come, if it does come, in the context of relieving particular afflictions. Still, there is no other way that we can guide ourselves between the twin perils of uncontrollable turbulence and repression. We will be strengthened by the fact that such change corresponds to deeply felt human wants, many of which are manifesting themselves in our present disorders.

DECENTRALIZATION

Paul Goodman

[Political action should aim to achieve not simply new programs, but basic changes in the way society is organized. Paul Goodman argues that drastic decentralization is both feasible and necessary if individual autonomy is to be reasserted.

[Paul Goodman is the author of *Growing Up Absurd, The Community of Scholars, Compulsory Mis-Education,* and *People or Personnel.*]

Throughout society, the centralizing style of organization has been pushed so far as to become ineffectual, economically wasteful, humanly stultifying, and ruinous to democracy. There are overcentralized systems in industry, in government, in culture, and in agriculture. The tight interlocking of these systems has created a situation in which modest, direct, and independent action has become extremely difficult in every field. The only remedy is a strong admixture of decentralism. The problem is where, how much, and how to go about it.

Let me give some rough definitions. In a centralized enterprise, the function to be performed is the goal of the organization rather than of persons (except as they identify with the organization). The persons are personnel. Authority is top-down. Information is gathered from below in the field and is processed to be usable by those above; decisions are made in headquarters; and policy, schedule, and standard procedure are transmitted downward by chain of command. The enterprise as a whole is divided into departments of operation to which are assigned personnel with distinct roles, to give standard performance. This is the system in Mr. Goldwater's department store, in the federal government and in the state governments, in General Motors and in the UAW, in the New York public schools and in many universities, in most hospitals, in neighborhood renewal, in network broadcasting and the Associated Press, and in the deals that chain grocers make with farmers. The system was devised to discipline armies; to keep records, collect taxes, and perform bureaucratic functions; and for certain kinds of mass production. It has now become pervasive.

The principle of decentralism is that people are engaged in a function and the organization is how they cooperate. Authority is delegated away from the top as much as possible and there are many accommodating centers of policy-making and decision. Information is conveyed and discussed in face-to-face contacts between field and headquarters. Each person becomes increasingly aware of the whole operation and works at it in his own way according to his capacities. Groups arrange their own schedules. Historically, this system of voluntary association has yielded most of the values of civilization, but it is thought to be entirely unworkable under modern conditions and the very sound of it is strange.

. . . .

In a historical view, one can see cyclical swings from decentralized to centralized and overcentralized and back. Swings are in the nature of the case, since there are always forces in both directions. Concentrating power and rationalizing administration and production weld peoples into a centralized system by coercion or because there are real efficiencies and advantages. But a central authority can become too willful or taxes too high; lines of communication become too long or the distribution of imperial products too costly. Then people rebel, build their own factories, and try to rationalize production according to their own local customs, and they make shift decentrally because there are real efficiencies and advantages.

Especially when there is a radically new opportunity, there is a decentralizing trend, for the central style is old-fashioned with respect to it, and the persons who understand it and are good at it want to cut loose and proceed on their own. This can go as far as revolution. But the revolution, according to the modern theory, succumbs to the "bureaucratization of the prophetic" or the "iron law of oligarchy." (Not accidentally, the theorists of our century are good at proving that revolutions cannot "really" succeed.) On the other hand, there are routinized systems of prestigious authority, like the Catholic Church, where plenty of life goes on as if the central authority did not exist. Also, small "neutral" countries carry on peaceably for generations, once they have gotten over trying to be Powers.

All this is familiar. But formal historians usually concentrate on the centralizing swing, for that is where the history is: the concentration of power and growth of grandeur are more likely to have names and official chronicles. Small neutral nations are neglected in history books, though their citizens are adequately represented in the history of civilization. And historians would almost never use the word "decentralizing" to describe an important countermovement. If their judgment of the decentralization is negative, they call it "decline and fall"; if it is positive, they call it "liberation from the old regime." In either case they hurry on to recover from the dark ages or to erect the new regime out of the disorder. Or sometimes millions of persons suddenly drop out of world history, for things have ceased to "happen" with them.

I am reminded of the indignant question of Coleridge when an economist declared that a village that did not take part in the national trade was of no importance. "What, sir, are five hundred Christian souls of no importance?"

To anarchist writers, it seems as if academic and Marxist writers are always describing the failure of a revolution, namely the new regime, when they think they are describing a revolution. Wolin calls his book on the Russian Revolution *The Unknown Revolution;* the "real" revolution, he says, was effected by peasants, guerrillas, and mutinous sailors; it was systematically crushed by both foreign im-

perialists and Bolshevists. The same has been said of the
Spanish Civil War; a revolution was being made by peasants and miners, but it was stopped by liberals, communists, and fascists. In writing on the French Revolution,
Kropotkin wants to tell how provincial towns managed
to organize society when freed from the incubus of Paris.
I myself am evidently more interested in the politics of
the Articles of Confederation than of the Constitution.

The escape of the serfs from the feudal domains to the
growing towns of the eleventh and twelfth century—"town
air makes free"—is best regarded as a great swing to decentralization. The new opportunity was the revival of
trade, and the fugitives became craftsmen. In the framework of a fairly uniform law and a common religion, the
town societies managed to organize themselves locally in
multitudes of voluntary craft and professional associations,
and they organized themselves across the languages of
Europe in formal and informal federations of trade and
science. In his history of the commune of Florence, Machi-
avelli calls this decentral town constitution of the Middle
Ages the highest achievement of human politics, more glori-
ous than the simplicity of early Rome. (So the author of
The Prince! Karl Marx, similarly, said that the highest
achievement of humanity had so far been the Elizabethan
yeomanry!)

In fact, these towns—associations of associations, some
of which were hierarchical, some democratic—invented
modern technology, founded the modern university, hit
on modern corporate law, and by and large created modern civilization.

This is the bread and butter of social and cultural historians. Yet most political historians, in describing this
period, *prospectively* lay their emphasis on the feudal wars
and the emergence of the national sovereigns who took
the towns over, destroyed their freedoms, standardized and
took the life out of the culture, destroyed the interlanguage
community, emasculated the universities and bureaucrat-
ized the guilds, nationalized the religion, and turned centers
of civilization into capital headquarters for the old business of tax collecting, policing, and warring on a grander
scale.

In the seventeenth and eighteenth century, the development of the Enlightenment and the Industrial Revolution was a swing to decentralization. This time, the voluntary associations were friend-groups, partnerships, and companies of individuals rather than corporate bodies. They banded together to enterprise in their own way, free of royal monopolies, mercantilist regulations, and the ossified relics of guilds, universities, and feudalism. Scientists and scholars tended to go it alone, by correspondence, and in independent academies. Stockholders in joint-stock companies were vigilant of management. And these groups federated across national boundaries for trade, science, technical innovation, and political action. Out of it came political economy and modern social theory, the first colonial revolutions, the Bill of Rights, the limitation of absolute power, the critical philosophy, the theory of perpetual peace—in brief, everything that we now think of as our best.

Yet the emphasis of both social and political historians is again prospective: they talk about cash economics and absentee ownership, enclosure, national aggrandizement and imperialism, the proletarianization of labor, all of which were antithetic to the Enlightenment, political economy, and the French Revolution. Typical is the astonishing one-sided stress on Calvinism and divisive individualism in explaining seventeenth- and eighteenth-century rationalism ("rationalization"), as if the age had not also been mad for mathematics and inventions, and yearning for natural man, equality, and fraternity, which were spontaneous factors in rationalizing. The Enlightenment version of the neoclassic style is highly standard and communicable, but it is not at all centralist; on the contrary, it was again a common framework in which intellectual groups could satirize and go their own way.

Sometimes the prospective reference is not even one-sided but simply inaccurate. For instance, a scholarly dedication and energy are attributed to the centralized German universities after the unification, which had really developed during a brilliant hundred years before, in autonomous academies and city-state universities, and which indeed the centralized universities succeeded in transforming into pedantry and chauvinistic *Kultur*.

Our modern centralization is unique in that it pervades so many details of life, like an intensely ritualistic religion or a garrison state (it has aspects of both). So I have singled out the *style* of it, rather than protesting that it impedes some particular liberty, like free trade or free speech, or that it involves excessive public and corporation taxation. But recently every writer has criticized it in particular—*The Tastemakers, The Insolent Chariots, The Lonely Crowd, The Organization Man, The Hidden Persuaders, The Tyranny of Testing, Mass Leisure, The Exurbanites, Compulsory Mis-Education, The Status Seekers, The Affluent Society, Growing Up Absurd, The Paper Economy, Silent Spring, The Child Worshipers, The Death and Life of Great American Cities, The American Way of Death*—all these books, good or bad, are about the same thing: the irrelevance and destructiveness of a system running for its own sake and sometimes running wild.

Unfortunately, a corollary of dealing with a pervasive style is that it is hard to think not in the style. Voltaire could simply say *Écrasez l'Infâme* because he could conceive of simply doing without *l'Infâme*. For us, it is only after we have gotten out of the interlocking system that we will be able to see how much of it was unnecessary.

Certainly the surplus productivity requires a basic overhauling of economic concepts. Accumulated wealth and new technology are now so productive and plastic that they can no longer plausibly be managed on classical economic principles of allocating scarce human and material resources. But the dominant system can only repeat its routine motives and routine method—reinvesting, expanding the Gross National Product. And with this goes the grotesque disproportion between the "hard" money that many unfortunate people work for and reliefers starve on, and the giveaway money of fringe benefits, expense accounts, foundation grants, inflated salaries, and other tax dodges. In these circumstances, political economy and moral economics are impossible.

So psychologists, sociologists, and moral philosophers are busy reanalyzing basic economic concepts like "work," "unemployment," "property," "standard of living," "incentive," "security," etc. And they seem to end up by proposing everything on land or sea or in the air, from Dr. Skinner's universal operant conditioning to Dr. Leary's universal use of psychedelic drugs—both at Harvard. In my opinion, more significant than the content of these philosophies are two characteristics of their form: in them, the world seems open again to choice, we can choose how to live; yet they are curiously unpragmatic and lacking in news with regard to daily life and common mores. That is, arbitrary choice is taken seriously in the most far-out proposals, just when it is entirely vanishing in simpler matters like schoolgoing, looking for a job, working at a job, the layout of streets, housing, shopping, being informed, politics. Just so, Donald Michael, in *The Next Generation*, predicts that our society will continue as at present, only more interlocked and more abstract, but there will be plenty of asylums for the sensitive and intelligent to express themselves, like Indians on a reservation.

Since I am conservative by disposition, I am not quite so ready to remake human nature (even according to my own blueprint), nor to scuttle the culture of the Western world. In my opinion, precisely the simpler matters—housing, shopping, being informed, and making a living—are the most important matters, and I set a high value on democratic initiative and deciding. Thus, if we have choices, I am led to speak for decentralizing—"where it is feasible." This modest philosophy may be utopian, but it *is* pragmatic.

The idea of building-in decentralization is full of dilemmas, if not contradictions. Let me [discuss] . . . some of the dilemmas and some of the opportunities.

First, in community development. There is a realization, which has penetrated even government agencies, that urban anomie and the hopelessness of rural areas that have lost their economies cannot be manipulated away by simply importing social and medical services, or even money. Somehow the remedies do not add up to the whole that has been lost. Delinquency and addiction do not succumb to clinics any more than to policing and reformatories; retraining gets few takers; and my guess is that we shall find that dropout and youth unemployment are not materially helped by "better" schools. Instead, people become further dependent on precisely the remedial services.

The new wisdom is that the neighborhood or depressed area must "participate" in its own reconstruction. So urban extension agents, youth workers, and community developers are commissioned to help groups to help themselves. But what is "administered participation"?—the phrase is from a fine study of the dilemma by Martin Cohnstaedt. The techniques are decentral: to call local meetings and charter local boards; to go along with the youth ideology in gang or high school; to work side by side with the natives. But the goals, alas, are from headquarters: to get tenants to consent to relocation; to get kids to make less trouble or do their lessons; and to get the natives to see that Americans are good Joes. It is too early to judge, but I doubt that this rather immoral pattern can work when the chips are down. Certainly, Negroes have been expressing fierce resentment of liberals who know the answers for them.

Not surprisingly, an effective means of temporary community reintegration has been to help depressed people just to vent their spite, for spite is the vitality of the powerless. Protesting and circumventing arouse spirit. And all the better if there are also tangible positive results, like bringing to court the short-measure grocer, as in Woodlawn, or rent striking, as in Harlem. But this kind of activity, too, does not add up. It blows off steam rather than creates a community.

The more sophisticated philosophy of community development is to have no "goal" at all, but to be a "catalyst." As William Biddle analyzes it, the professional who wants to help must morally commit himself to the community and offer what knowledge he has, but he must expect that any solution that emerges will be different from anything he expects. In one of Biddle's reports of work in a depressed area, there is a striking incident of the community suddenly *remembering* that long ago it used to thrive on a different economic base from the later industry that had moved out; having remembered it, people were able to return to it in a new and viable form. This sounds like excellent psychotherapy.

But finally, the best means of creating community is to delegate power. Participation means initiating, deciding, acting. If we mean to restore health—in psychotherapy, too —we must give back the power to function in the areas that are still vital. Consider an important current problem: There is bitter complaint of police brutality and venality in depressed urban neighborhoods, and as a remedy, the leaders of minority groups ask for civilian review boards; with typical liberalism, they add on a new level of administration, in which the neighborhood is "included" and has a voice. But surely a more direct remedy would be, as far as possible, to _give back_ the administration and personnel of the police to the neighborhood itself. Then both the enforcement and the _interpretation_ of the law would be in accordance with local public sentiment. The aim of police law is to keep the peace; it is not to enforce an impossible conformity on millions of people of all conditions. (As it is, graft is more relevant and less damaging than attempts at reform.)

• • • • • • • • • • • • • • • • • • • •

In this context, there is an excellent use for the public underwriting of "advocates," as proposed by Edgar Cahn of the Office of Economic Opportunity. These are persons trained in law and administration who, when called on, can teach poor people the ropes and represent them if necessary. Thus, instead of being ruled by experts who know what is good for them, poor people—like rich people—can have available experts whom they can use. This must lead to new confidence.

Similar dilemmas occur in industry and business. It is now the fashion to try to make workers less alienated, more "belonging," and generally happier, by profit sharing, insurance benefits, recreation facilities, and the improvement of psychological conditions of work. The purpose of these devices is to prevent labor disputes and increase efficiency, and they somewhat work. But the evidence is that they do _not_ create identity with the rational goals of the organization, but rather increase dependency on the organization.

That is, the men are treated like children and they become childish.

(It seems to me that this is the significant interpretation of the "Hawthorne effect," that people respond to participating in the experiment, to being paid attention to, no matter what the content or ultimate purpose of the experiment. It is dismaying that adults on a job should be so infantile and so little able to further their own objective interests.)

Researching job attitudes, Frederick Herzberg of Western Reserve has developed a valuable psychiatric distinction between the health-producing and the merely protective or hygienic. The health-producing, says Herzberg, is inner-motivated, task-engaged, outgoing; it is, finally, that which enables a man to exercise power. The hygienic is that which avoids anxiety or emotional stress. A workman is happy on the job when the work is interesting, when he uses his capacities, when he can use initiative; he is "not unhappy" when conditions are pleasant, when he has security, when his dignity is not insulted.

Let us draw an obvious moral. Bosses and managers could far more directly improve the conditions of work if, instead of indulging in paternalism, they would cut out the unnecessary authoritarianism and time controlling that in fact make people dependent and spiritless. In any big office, for example, a good part of the day is spent by a good many people doing nothing and trying to look busy. In such an office it is a big deal and a subject of gratitude if, on a hot day, the boss dismisses people early. Isn't this childish? As adults, the workers have agreed to do a job for a wage; then why cannot they themselves tailor the schedule to the job, including doing work at home when that is just as efficient? Think of it, grown people phone in lying excuses about not coming in.

When a man applies at a plant and there are several open stations requiring equivalent skill, it would certainly be intelligent to let him try them and choose. If the attempt to make him "belong" were authentic, a workman would be encouraged to change his station and get to know various parts of the operation; that is, he would be treated like the boss's son. Instead, he has to compete and be well-behaved in order to be "promoted" to a higher bracket, as though he were still in grade school.

A good arrangement for treating men as responsible agents is the collective contract. . . . The gang makes its own schedule and rules and hires and fires. Presumably the men in the gang know their own skills and interests better than a production manager does.

In automatic production it is plausible . . . that model changes and retooling might also best be devised by teams working decentrally. This would allow much fresher perspective. And it is all the more appropriate since in such production there must be a great increase of the highly skilled and ingenious, as designers and programmers, who also know more about the whole operation than formal management is likely to.

To be sure, all these suggestions involve, in one way or another, the possibility of workmen taking part in management, and this is the point at which American management balks, and American unions do not press. Yet it is hard to see why any of them would be less productively efficient or even necessarily diminish profits.

The American educational system is easier to decentralize, sweepingly, from bottom to top, since teaching and learning consist entirely in face-to-face and community relations, and the present overcentralization has no authentic functions at all. The schools are being used as universal baby-sitter and time-occupier, and as apprentice training for a few industries. But there are simpler, more enjoyable, and more efficient ways to perform these functions. (The other great present use of the schools, for the aggrandizement of school systems and universities, is better just forgotten.)

It is claimed by the National Science Foundation that since the new technology requires more specialized skills, the schools must generally be more tightly geared to centrally improved curricula. This argument is singularly wrong-headed. If a relatively few will work in that technology, it is senseless to waste the general time on specialist skills. It would be far more just and more efficient for the relevant industries to pay for and administer special training, rather than getting half-apprentices at the public and parents' expense. That is, at present we need *less* centralized schooling than we did.

Colleges, high schools, and primary schools could all usefully be cut down in size and run by their faculties and staff. The present framework of administration and outside social pressuring are merely distracting and wasteful. The whole extrinsic rigmarole of credits, prescribed syllabus, competitive grading, and promotion up the ladder is pedagogically destructive and should simply be scrapped. There is little evidence that a student learns anything of value if he has learned it merely to pass; and those who want to learn a subject at their own time and according to their own interest are interrupted by the schedule and misled by extrinsic motivation.

But more important, the concept that all "education" should be administered by school people is a delusion of overcentralization. It is impossible that long, continuous years of sitting in schoolrooms is the appropriate means of educating most people to be useful to themselves and society. Yet we are now trying to keep 100 percent in school till eighteen, and by 1970 50 percent will be in colleges. Very many youngsters, including very many of the bright, are stupefied by the methods and language of the academic setting. Given the variety of conditions and talents, we should be exploring and experimenting many settings to educate, and pay as much attention as possible to individual differences and signs of choice.

The centralizing approach is to abstract from the functions of society, whatever they happen to be, and to put the abstractions in a school-box as the curriculum. The decentralist approach would be to turn directly to the functions of society that might be educated for, and to open in them opportunities for the young to take part. Academic learning is for the academically talented. We have just mentioned the responsibility of the corporations to provide schooling for their own apprentices, and also their workmen. (In this respect, by the way, the armed services are not a bad model, not only for teaching radar but also for teaching to read. School money could be used to help finance worthwhile activities that will otherwise be neglected, e.g., some public works, independent broadcasting and newspapers, little theaters; these provide educational opportunities and immensely broaden the range of choice. Also, it is reasonable to extend the idea of the GI Bill to the high schools: to give the school money directly to the student to pursue any course he chooses that is plausibly educational. This would have the advantage of multiplying experimental schools, sorely needed in our present mono-lithic system.

Another gross defect of the tightly interlocked, contin-uous system is that it discourages leaving and reentry, whereas these are in the essential nature of the educational process. There must be moratoria in growing up, and one must accumulate other experiences and scenes than doing lessons. Young people now come to college who are too young, who have never done or seen anything, and who are ineducable in university subjects. On the other hand, there are times when mature people need and want aca-demic learning and could profit immensely by it; but they are stymied by the bureaucratic system of credits and diplomas irrelevant to their actual situation.

Decentralizing the interlocking communications is im-perative, to make democracy possible. . . . But there is no doubt that writers and artists could do much more for themselves than they do, to countervail homogenization and brainwashing. The mass media cannot do without original and highly talented people; if even a few score of these would band together, they could importantly liberate edi-torial policy. (It seems to me that the same holds for the chief scientists of all countries, in forcing disarmament.) Just as the AAUP protects academic freedom by publiciz-ing and boycotting, we could defend against wiping out and editing our tapes, against format that kills free ex-pression, against rewriting that takes the life out of style, and against blacklisting. A barrage of exposure, satire, and orneriness would do the trick.

When I have made feeble efforts to awaken such con-certed action, however, I have been appalled at the lack of community of art and letters in this country as contrasted with France or England. Intellectuals will combine to pro-test a particular abuse or censorship, but they seem unable to regard themselves as a uniquely responsible corporation, though we have constitutional powers. Of course, competitiveness and envy are strongly divisive among artists and writers, and many are chary about "joining" anything, whether for economic advantage or reasons of ideology. Yet we are unanimous about freedom of expression and autonomy of style, and we alone understand the problems. We could cooperate.

In the face of mass values in publishing, it is surprising that cooperative houses do not arise. A few disgruntled editors and a few well-known authors could make a go of it independently; they have the skills and the guaranteed sales. (The costs of publishing are about the same for small houses and big houses.) But well-known writers are economically satisfied where they are. They would need a new notion of their social function in order to want to publish their own way. The problem has been more acute for advance-guard writers or those who do not use the salable genres. Occasionally, a fairly big house—I shall name no names—has specialized in this new and noncommercial writing, but it is as with off-Broadway: the house is looking, prospectively, for "successes." (Typically, Beckett is rejected; then, when he has made a success, he is sought out.)

Smaller advance-guard publishers, like Jonathan Williams or Ferlinghetti, are more authentic, but cliquish and marginal. It seems to me that there could be a federation of such houses, that would increase promotion and put them all in a more powerful position. Certainly there should be federations of little magazines. The irregular and short-lived careers of little magazines destroy the chance for circulation to grow; a federation could guarantee that a subscriber will regularly receive something or other for his money. As I have pointed out, different little magazines of one tendency get their material from exactly the same pool of artists and writers anyway; a federation would express this continuity. There have been efforts to form such federations, but apparently no one has yet hit on the right formula; or, more likely, no one with a good head for business has yet put it to this good use.

Probably the most characteristic of all our dilemmas is the "problem of leisure," as it is called. It is feared, alternatively, that with the maturation of automatic and computer technology, either people won't *have* to work and will degenerate; or there won't be anything for them to work *at*, and they will be unhappy spending their time in trivial leisure activities. (Indeed, culturally, the prospect of a great nation playing golf and folk-dancing is dismaying.)

The fear of degeneracy is mentioned mostly by our Conservatives, and is of the same vintage as the argument that unemployment insurance and Social Security must lead to general goofing off and milking the public treasury. (Similarly, a hundred years ago it was solemnly argued that the general public could not be trusted to have open access to the shelves of libraries.) In fact, everywhere that a detailed checkup of cheating has been made, the cost of the checkup has been many times the amount saved on cheaters. The bother has been the other way: when hours of work are cut, there is too much moonlighting.

The other fear, of having nothing to do with oneself, is expressed rather by Liberals. It has substance, but the problem is an artifact. It is an expression of the same spirit of dependency that we have noticed in depressed neighborhoods and in business and industry. If people have not been rendered stupid and powerless, by schools and liberals among others, they will no doubt know what to do with themselves. Psychologically, boredom is not a deprivation, the want of something to do; it is a positive act of repressing what is attractive but forbidden, and *then* there is nothing interesting to do.

The remedy of thoughtful Liberals is also typical, that we must get rid of our lust for productive activity and for being functional. The Aristotelian notion that happiness consists in activity is now considered "Calvinistic"; rather, we must learn "how to have a good time" or "self-development" and "self-actualization." (Liberals do not go as far as the psychedelic drugs—the *soma* of *Brave New World*— but some of them toy with satori.) What a remarkable sign of a system running for its own sake!—they are willing to entertain these extraordinary changes in the character of people rather than thinking of altering the way we do things, organizationally, economically, or technologically.

The paradoxes of surplus are pathetic. We can buy an assortment of beautiful hand power tools: they are lusted for—the sale is tremendous; yet they are mostly put to only trivial uses—the users cannot repair them—they are for Christmas presents and they lie broken like Christmas toys. At present, with the splendid equipment, the cars, and TV, the conditions of small farming are rather paradisal; judged all around, it is probably the most attractive way of life now available in the United States; even economically, it can be combined in many ways with cottage industry and factory jobs to earn enough cash. Yet the heart and community have vanished out of it, and nine out of ten youths will leave it. It is simply never entertained as one possibility of diminishing urban overcrowding and squalor. Again, there is a fantastic amount of schooling; we are flooded with profound books, in paperback, that correctly analyze the conditions of society and are a guide to life. Yet in fact almost no one is a free agent able to use his wits and act on what he knows, so the education and reading have no point.

Return now to the proposal for a guaranteed decent income. As I have said, I agree with this, for nothing else is moral. If goods are available, they must not be withheld from need and use. And I predict that—*as applied to the United States*—people will soon grasp this, and we shall have the guaranteed income. Besides, the guaranteed income is probably far more economical than our present welfare procedures. It would cost less in money, effort, and suffering than our social-work and means-test methods of coping with poverty, unemployment, and much of delinquency and crime. (Curiously, this kind of arithmetic is what the public can never grasp.)

Nevertheless, it will be a pity if this important change in our conditions of life is, as urged by the economists, simply tied to the expanding Gross National Product, and is not used as an opportunity toward a more mixed and open system. The freedom from unwanted and alienated work, and from "unemployment," should be accompanied by the opportunity for wanted and engaged work. The problem of guaranteed income is not whether the income should be given, but how it should be given.

In the first place, guaranteed income could be used as an occasion for dividing the subsistence economy from the general market economy, and directly and independently producing the subsistence. (Let us assume that subsistence constitutes half of the "decent income.") The advantage of segregating the production and distribution of subsistence is to remove this crucial universal necessity from the fluctuations and pressures of the rest of the economy; thus, to take care of first things first and so make the whole both more flexible and more secure. When we wrote *Communitas* twenty years ago, my brother and I estimated that maximum mass production and free distribution of "minimum" (American standard) subsistence would require about one-tenth of the labor force, each person working a forty-hour week one year in ten. I have no idea what the ratio would dwindle to with automation, but my guess is that to produce subsistence for society would be a job wanted by many more people than there would be places available.

[There are] . . . neglected community services and improvements that an affluent society cannot afford, but that would willingly be performed by people happy to live in decent poverty if they could do the work they wanted. Such work also could be regarded as "working for" the guaranteed income. (This would perhaps satisfy the scruples of those who do not think that people, especially serious people, should get something for nothing.) But note that this kind of world is *not* the "public sector"—housing, schools, highways, transit—that the economists talk about. It would not exist in the same system of union labor, public appropriations, contracting, and promotion. It would be voluntary and often exempt from central administration. (E.g., a neighborhood improvement, like the playground of the Harlem Education Project . . . , is entirely a local affair. But a concerted voluntary effort to clean up a river requires central administration.) It would be a use of the guaranteed income to make the country lovely and its "leisure" meaningful.

Further, the economic motives of a new generation would inevitably be profoundly influenced by the pluralism of educational opportunity described in the last section. If young people grew up accustomed to try out where they could be useful and engaged, very many would be immune from the plague of extrinsic rewards; they would have found vocations and would *know* what they wanted to do with themselves. This is a more interesting proposition than

the "good time" or the "self-actualization" of the anti-
Calvinists. (Other people, perhaps the majority, who
would still find their chief excitement in the things that
money can buy, might then work to get rich at least by
choice and not because of anxiety.)

Finally, the necessary sharp distinction that we must
ultimately make between those goods and services that are
appropriately automatic and those from which automation
and computing should be expunged, will reopen many occupations. Instead of the skimping that now occurs in employment for human service, whether waiting on table or
teaching school or caring for the insane, we may come
to see that people are useful after all. Even indispensable.
A beneficent, though unintended, result of the mass production and economic centralization of two centuries may yet
be to give us the freedom to understand what needless
sacrifices we have made for that mass production and centralization.

Surplus productivity, however, exists—or could soon
exist—only in technologically advanced parts of the world,
the United States, Europe, Japan; the relative poverty, and
sometimes absolute poverty, of many other regions is
sharply increasing. Thus, a strong political and moral case
can be made for continuing to expand our economy and
pouring the products into overseas aid; that is, it is not
yet time, in the One World, for a guaranteed income in the
United States. (Needless to say, this is not the thinking of
the worshipers of the GNP.)

In my opinion, there are important distinctions to be
made:

1. It is immoral, and certainly politically unwise, not
to try to wipe out disease, hunger, and drudgery wherever
they exist in the world. Such an effort involves exporting
a certain amount of consumers' goods, especially in emergencies, but mostly community development, expert ad-
vice, education, and a very limited kind of producers'
goods, namely the technology of basic subsistence, where
it is necessary and usable. Given health and some education and leisure, a people can "take off" into a higher

standard at its own pace. This is implicitly the philosophy of the Friends, UNICEF, the Peace Corps, and other service organizations.

2. It is an entirely different matter, however, to try to export the high standard and elaborate capital of technologically advanced nations, a process that necessarily results in a total change of local mores, the disruption of communities, forced urbanization, political bondage, and often tribal wars. Plus fantastic waste and overcommitment to mistakes. Inevitably, the Western-trained élite of backward peoples desire this kind of foreign capitalization; but it is also the philosophy espoused both by well-intentioned Westerners like C. P. Snow and by capitalists who have equipment to sell (often outmoded).

3. By and large, the export of our own high standard is a form of neo-imperialism, and has invariably turned underdeveloped regions into battlegrounds of the Cold War between Great Powers. It makes it impossible, for instance, for the United Nations to neutralize a region so that it can come to its own peace and government. Nor does this new kind of wealth, if any survives, filter down to the mass of the people. On the contrary, they are often reduced to a degradation worse than their worst poverty.

4. On the other hand, in our own country, the peaceful disposition, free of the taint of profits and power, and the personal friendliness, willingness to serve, and adventurousness necessary for the intercourse of peoples and the creation of a really equal One World, depend, it seems to me, on resolving our frantic domestic hang-ups, quieting down, learning to work for community use and not for money and status. In the fairly short run, the mass of the poor peoples of the world will get more help from happy young Americans than from harried ones.

Ultimately, let me say in a sentence, the lesson of decentralizing is the formation of the world community on a basis of functional regions rather than national states.

These, then, are the considerations that I present to college students who want to talk about decentralization, urging them to make the empirical studies that I am incompetent to make. It seems to me that they are interested.

. . . .

When the first thousand volunteers of the Peace Corps returned and were asked what they liked best about the experience, "The most common response is the same, whether you ask a development worker in Latin America, a teacher in Africa, or a farmer in Asia. 'The freedom and autonomy I enjoyed.' 'The opportunities for self-expression and creativity in my assignment.' 'The responsibility I was given for my age.'" (David Pearson, Deputy Information Director of the Peace Corps.) If this is the value they have learned, they have their work cut out for them in the United States.

FREEDOM AND DEMOCRACY

Erich Fromm

[Richard Goodwin and Paul Goodman have considered
political and social changes, but there is another dimension to the problem of individualism. Erich Fromm
focuses on the psychological aspects of individualism
and indicates how and why men must change their
attitudes toward themselves and toward society.

[Erich Fromm is a psychoanalyst and the author of
*Escape from Freedom, The Art of Loving, The Sane
Society*, and *The Heart of Man.*]

. . . Certain factors in the modern industrial system in
general and its monopolistic phase in particular make for
the development of a personality which feels powerless
and alone, anxious and insecure . . . There is no greater
mistake and no graver danger than not to see that in our
own society we are faced with the same phenomenon that
is fertile soil for the rise of Fascism anywhere: the insignificance and powerlessness of the individual.

This statement challenges the conventional belief that by
freeing the individual from all external restraints modern
democracy has achieved true individualism. We are proud
that we are not subject to any external authority, that we
are free to express our thoughts and feelings, and we take
it for granted that this freedom almost automatically guarantees our individuality. *The right to express our thoughts,*
however, *means something only if we are able to have
thoughts of our own;* freedom from external authority is a
lasting gain only if the inner psychological conditions are
such that we are able to establish our own individuality.

Have we achieved that aim, or are we at least approaching it? . . . In discussing the two aspects of freedom for modern man, we should point out the economic conditions that make for increasing isolation and powerlessness of the individual in our era; in discussing the psychological results we believe that this powerlessness leads either to the kind of escape that we find in the authoritarian character, or else to a compulsive conforming in the process of which the isolated individual becomes an automaton, loses his self, and yet at the same time consciously conceives of himself as free and subject only to himself.

It is important to consider how our culture fosters this tendency to conform, even though there is space for only a few outstanding examples. The suppression of spontaneous feelings, and thereby of the development of genuine individuality, starts very early, as a matter of fact with the earliest training of a child.[1] This is not to say that training must inevitably lead to suppression of spontaneity if the real aim of education is to further the inner independence and individuality of the child, its growth and integrity. The restrictions which such a kind of education may have to impose upon the growing child are only transitory measures that really support the process of growth and expansion. In our culture, however, education too often results in the elimination of spontaneity and in the substitution of original psychic acts by superimposed feelings, thoughts, and wishes. (By original I do not mean that an idea has not been thought before by someone else, but that it originates in the individual, that it is the result of his own activity and in this sense is *his* thought.) To choose one illustration somewhat arbitrarily, one of the earliest suppressions of *feelings* concerns hostility and dislike. To start with, most children have a certain measure of hostility and rebelliousness as a result of their conflicts with a surrounding world that tends to block their expan-

---

[1] According to a communication by Anna Hartoch (from a forthcoming book on case studies of Sarah Lawrence Nursery School children, jointly by M. Gay, A. Hartoch, L. B. Murphy) Rorschach tests of three- to five-year-old children have shown that the attempt to preserve their spontaneity gives rise to the chief conflict between the children and the authoritative adults.

siveness and to which, as the weaker opponent, they usually have to yield. It is one of the essential aims of the education process to eliminate this antagonistic reaction. The methods are different; they vary from threats and punishments, which frighten the child, to the subtler methods of bribery or "explanations," which confuse the child and make him give up his hostility. The child starts with giving up the expression of his feeling and eventually gives up the very feeling itself. Together with that, he is taught to suppress the awareness of hostility and insincerity in others; sometimes this is not entirely easy, since children have a capacity for noticing such negative qualities in others without being so easily deceived by words as adults usually are. They still dislike somebody "for no good reason"—except the very good one that they feel the hostility, or insincerity, radiating from that person. This reaction is soon discouraged; it does not take long for the child to reach the "maturity" of the average adult and to lose the sense of discrimination between a decent person and a scoundrel, as long as the latter has not committed some flagrant act.

On the other hand, early in his education, the child is taught to have feelings that are not at all "his"; particularly is he taught to like people, to be uncritically friendly to them, and to smile. What education may not have accomplished is usually done by social pressure in later life. If you do not smile, you are judged lacking in a "pleasing personality"—and you need to have a pleasing personality if you want to sell your services, whether as a waitress, a salesman, or a physician. Only those at the bottom of the social pyramid, who sell nothing but their physical labor, and those at the very top do not need to be particularly "pleasant." Friendliness, cheerfulness, and everything that a smile is supposed to express, become automatic responses which one turns on and off like an electric switch.[2]

---

[2] As one telling illustration of the commercialization of friendliness I should like to cite *Fortune's* report on "The Howard Johnson Restaurants" (*Fortune*, September 1940, p. 96). Johnson employs a force of "shoppers" who go from restaurant to restaurant to watch for lapses. "Since everything is cooked on the premises according to standard recipes and measurements issued by the home office, the inspector knows how large a portion of steak he should

To be sure, in many instances the person is aware of merely making a gesture; in most cases, however, he loses that awareness and thereby the ability to discriminate between the pseudo feeling and spontaneous friendliness.

.   .   .   .

In our society emotions in general are discouraged. While there can be no doubt that any creative thinking—as well as any other creative activity—is inseparably linked with emotion, it has become an ideal to think and to live without emotions. To be "emotional" has become synonymous with being unsound or unbalanced. By the acceptance of this standard the individual has become greatly weakened; his thinking is impoverished and flattened. On the other hand, since emotions cannot be completely killed, they must have their existence totally apart from the intellectual side of the personality; the result is the cheap and insincere sentimentality with which movies and popular songs feed millions of emotion-starved customers.

There is one tabooed emotion that I want to mention in particular, because its suppression touches deeply on the roots of personality: the sense of tragedy. . . . The awareness of death and of the tragic aspect of life, whether dim or clear, is one of the basic characteristics of man. Each culture has its own way of coping with the problem of death. For those societies in which the process of individuation has progressed but little, the end of individual existence is less of a problem since the experience of individual existence itself is less developed. Death is not yet conceived as being basically different from life. Cultures in which we find a higher development of individuation have treated death according to their social and psychological structure. The Greeks put all emphasis on life and pictured death as nothing but a shadowy and dreary continuation of life. The Egyptians based their hopes on a belief in the indestructibility of the human body, at least of

---

receive and how the vegetable should taste. He also knows how long it should take for the dinner to be served and he knows the exact degree of friendliness that should be shown by the hostess and the waitress."

those whose power during life was indestructible. The Jews admitted the fact of death realistically and were able to reconcile themselves with the idea of the destruction of individual life by the vision of a state of happiness and justice ultimately to be reached by mankind in this world. Christianity has made death unreal and tried to comfort the unhappy individual by promises of a life after death. Our own era simply denies death and with it one fundamental aspect of life. Instead of allowing the awareness of death and suffering to become one of the strongest incentives for life, the basis for human solidarity, and an experience without which joy and enthusiasm lack intensity and depth, the individual is forced to repress it. But, as is always the case with repression, by being removed from sight the repressed elements do not cease to exist. Thus the fear of death lives an illegitimate existence among us. It remains alive in spite of the attempt to deny it, but being repressed it remains sterile. It is one source of the flatness of other experiences, of the restlessness pervading life, and it explains, I would venture to say, the exorbitant amount of money this nation pays for its funerals.

In the process of tabooing emotions modern psychiatry plays an ambiguous role. On the one hand its greatest representative, Freud, has broken through the fiction of the rational, purposeful character of the human mind and opened a path which allows a view into the abyss of human passions. On the other hand psychiatry, enriched by these very achievements of Freud, has made itself an instrument of the general trends in the manipulation of personality. Many psychiatrists, including psychoanalysts, have painted the picture of a "normal" personality which is never too sad, too angry, or too excited. They use words like "infantile" or "neurotic" to denounce traits or types of personalities that do not conform with the conventional pattern of a "normal" individual. This kind of influence is in a way more dangerous than the older and franker forms of name-calling. Then the individual knew at least that there was some person or some doctrine which criticized him and he could fight back. But who can fight back at "science"?

The same distortion happens to original *thinking* as happens to feelings and emotions. From the very start of education original thinking is discouraged and ready-made thoughts are put into people's heads. How this is done with young children is easy enough to see. They are filled with curiosity about the world, they want to grasp it physically as well as intellectually. They want to know the truth, since that is the safest way to orient themselves in a strange and powerful world. Instead, they are not taken seriously, and it does not matter whether this attitude takes the form of open disrespect or of the subtle condescension which is usual toward all who have no power (such as children, aged or sick people). Although this treatment by itself offers strong discouragement to independent thinking, there is a worse handicap: the insincerity—often unintentional—which is typical of the average adult's behavior toward a child. This insincerity consists partly in the fictitious picture of the world which the child is given. It is about as useful as instructions concerning life in the Arctic would be to someone who has asked how to prepare for an expedition to the Sahara Desert. Besides this general misrepresentation of the world, there are the many specific lies that tend to conceal facts which, for various personal reasons, adults do not want children to know. From a bad temper, which is rationalized as justified dissatisfaction with the child's behavior, to concealment of the parents' sexual activities and their quarrels, the child is "not supposed to know" and his inquiries meet with hostile or polite discouragement.

The child thus prepared enters school and perhaps college. I want to mention briefly some of the educational methods used today which in effect further discourage original thinking. One is the emphasis on knowledge of facts, or I should rather say on information. The pathetic superstition prevails that by knowing more and more facts one arrives at knowledge of reality. Hundreds of scattered and unrelated facts are dumped into the heads of students; their time and energy are taken up by learning more and more facts so that there is little left for thinking. To be sure, thinking without a knowledge of facts remains empty and fictitious; but "information" alone can be just as much of an obstacle to thinking as the lack of it.

Another closely related way of discouraging original

thinking is to regard all truth as relative.[3] Truth is made out to be a metaphysical concept, and if anyone speaks about wanting to discover the truth, he is thought backward by the "progressive" thinkers of our age. Truth is declared to be an entirely subjective matter, almost a matter of taste. Scientific endeavor must be detached from subjective factors, and its aim is to look at the world without passion and interest. The scientist has to approach facts with sterilized hands as a surgeon approaches his patient. The result of this relativism, which often presents itself by the name of empiricism or positivism or which recommends itself by its concern for the correct usage of words, is that thinking loses its essential stimulus—the wishes and interests of the person who thinks; instead, it becomes a machine to register "facts." Actually, just as thinking in general has developed out of the need for mastery of material life, so the quest for truth is rooted in the interests and needs of individuals and social groups. Without such interest the stimulus for seeking the truth would be lacking. There are always groups whose interest is furthered by truth, and their representatives have been the pioneers of human thought; there are other groups whose interests are furthered by concealing truth. Only in the latter case does interest prove harmful to the cause of truth. The problem, therefore, is not that there is *an* interest at stake, but *which kind* of interest is at stake. I might say that inasmuch as there is some longing for the truth in every human being, it is because every human being has some need for it.

This holds true in the first place with regard to a person's orientation in the outer world, and it holds especially true for the child. As a child, every human being passes through a state of powerlessness, and truth is one of the strongest weapons of those who have no power. But the truth is in the individual's interest not only with regard to his orientation in the outer world; his own strength depends to a great extent on his knowing the truth about himself. Illu-

[3] Cf. to this whole problem Robert S. Lynd's *Knowledge for What?* (Princeton University Press, Princeton: 1939). For its philosophical aspects cf. M. Horkheimer's *Zum Rationalismusstreit in der Gegenwärtigen Philosophie.* Zeitschrift für Sozialforschung, Vol. 3 Paris: Alcan, 1934.

sions about oneself can become crutches useful to those who are not able to walk alone; but they increase a person's weakness. The individual's greatest strength is based on the maximum of integration of his personality, and that means also on the maximum of transparence to himself. "Know thyself" is one of the fundamental commands that aim at human strength and happiness.

In addition to the factors just mentioned there are others which actively tend to confuse whatever is left of the capacity for original thinking in the average adult. With regard to all basic questions of individual and social life, with regard to psychological, economic, political, and moral problems, a great sector of our culture has just one function—to befog the issues. One kind of smokescreen is the assertion that the problems are too complicated for the average individual to grasp. On the contrary it would seem that many of the basic issues of individual and social life are very simple, so simple, in fact, that everyone should be expected to understand them. To let them appear to be so enormously complicated that only a "specialist" can understand them, and he only in his own limited field, actually—and often intentionally—tends to discourage people from trusting their own capacity to think about those problems that really matter. The individual feels helplessly caught in a chaotic mass of data and with pathetic patience waits until the specialists have found out what to do and where to go.

The result of this kind of influence is a twofold one: one is a scepticism and cynicism toward everything which is said or printed, while the other is a childish belief in anything that a person is told with authority. This combination of cynicism and naïveté is very typical of the modern individual. Its essential result is to discourage him from doing his own thinking and deciding.

Another way of paralyzing the ability to think critically is the destruction of any kind of structuralized picture of the world. Facts lose the specific quality which they can have only as parts of a structuralized whole and retain merely an abstract, quantitative meaning; each fact is just *another* fact and all that matters is whether we know more or less. Radio, moving pictures, and newspapers have a devastating effect on this score. The announcement of the bombing of a city and the death of hundreds of people is shamelessly followed or interrupted by an advertisement for soap or wine. The same speaker with the same suggestive, ingratiating, and authoritative voice, which he has just used to impress you with the seriousness of the political situation, impresses now upon his audience the merits of the particular brand of soap which pays for the news broadcast. Newsreels let pictures of torpedoed ships be followed by those of a fashion show. Newspapers tell us the trite thoughts or breakfast habits of a debutante with the same space and seriousness they use for reporting events of scientific or artistic importance. Because of all this we cease to be genuinely related to what we hear. We cease to be excited, our emotions and our critical judgment become hampered, and eventually our attitude to what is going on in the world assumes a quality of flatness and indifference. In the name of "freedom" life loses all structure; it is composed of many little pieces, each separate from the other and lacking any sense as a whole. The individual is left alone with these pieces like a child with a puzzle; the difference, however, is that the child knows what a house is and therefore can recognize the parts of the house in the little pieces he is playing with, whereas the adult does not see the meaning of the "whole," the pieces of which come into his hands. He is bewildered and afraid and just goes on gazing at his little meaningless pieces.

What has been said about the lack of "originality" in feeling and thinking holds true also of the act of *willing*. To recognize this is particularly difficult; modern man seems, if anything, to have too many wishes and his only problem seems to be that, although he knows what he wants, he cannot have it. All our energy is spent for the purpose of getting what we want, and most people never question the premise of this activity: that they know their true wants. They do not stop to think whether the aims they are pursuing are something they themselves want. In school they want to have good marks, as adults they want to be more and more successful, to make more money, to have more prestige, to buy a better car, to go places, and so on. Yet when they do stop to think in the midst of all this frantic activity, this question may come to their minds: "If I do get this new job, if I get this better car, if I can take this trip—what then? What is the use of it all? Is it really I who wants all this? Am I not running after some goal which is supposed to make me happy and which eludes me as soon as I have reached it?" These questions, when they arise, are frightening, for they question the very basis on which man's whole activity is built, his knowledge of what he wants. People tend, therefore, to get rid as soon as possible of these disturbing thoughts. They feel that they have been bothered by these questions because they were tired or depressed—and they go on in the pursuit of the aims which they believe are their own.

Yet all this bespeaks a dim realization of the truth—the truth that modern man lives under the illusion that he knows what he wants, while he actually wants what he is *supposed* to want. In order to accept this it is necessary to realize that to know what one really wants is not comparatively easy, as most people think, but one of the most difficult problems any human being has to solve. It is a task we frantically try to avoid by accepting ready-made goals as though they were our own. Modern man is ready to take great risks when he tries to achieve the aims which are supposed to be "his"; but he is deeply afraid of taking the risk and the responsibility of giving himself his own aims. Intense activity is often mistaken for evidence of self-determined action, although we know that it may well be no more spontaneous than the behavior of an actor or a person hypnotized. When the general plot of the play is handed out, each actor can act vigorously the role he is assigned and even make up his lines and certain details of the action by himself. Yet he is only playing a role that has been handed over to him.

The particular difficulty in recognizing to what extent our wishes—and our thoughts and feelings as well—are not really our own but put into us from the outside, is closely linked up with the problem of authority and freedom. In the course of modern history the authority of the Church has been replaced by that of the State, that of the State by that of conscience, and in our era, the latter has been replaced by the anonymous authority of common sense and public opinion as instruments of conformity. Because we have freed ourselves of the older overt forms of authority, we do not see that we have become the prey of a new kind of authority. We have become automatons who live under the illusion of being self-willing individuals. This illusion helps the individual to remain unaware of his insecurity, but this is all the help such an illusion can give. Basically the self of the individual is weakened, so that he feels powerless and extremely insecure. He lives in a world to which he has lost genuine relatedness and in which everybody and everything has become instrumentalized, where he has become a part of the machine that his hands have built. He thinks, feels, and wills what he believes he is supposed to think, feel, and will; in this very process he loses his self upon which all genuine security of a free individual must be built.

The loss of the self has increased the necessity to conform, for it results in a profound doubt of one's own identity. If I am nothing but what I believe I am supposed to be—who am "I"? We have seen how the doubt about one's own self started with the breakdown of the medieval order in which the individual had had an unquestionable place in a fixed order. The identity of the individual has been a major problem of modern philosophy since Descartes. Today we take for granted that we are we. Yet the doubt about ourselves still exists, or has even grown. In his plays Pirandello has given expression to this feeling of modern man. He starts with the question: Who am I? What proof have I for my own identity other than the continuation of my physical self? His answer is not like Descartes'—the affirmation of the individual self—but its denial: I have no identity, there is no self excepting the one which is the reflex of what others expect me to be: I am "as you desire me."

This loss of identity then makes it still more imperative to conform; it means that one can be sure of oneself only if one lives up to the expectations of others. If we do not live up to this picture we not only risk disapproval and increased isolation, but we risk losing the identity of our personality, which means jeoparidizing sanity.

By conforming with the expectations of others, by not being different, these doubts about one's own identity are silenced and a certain security is gained. However, the price paid is high. Giving up spontaneity and individuality results in a thwarting of life. Psychologically the automaton, while being alive biologically, is dead emotionally and mentally. While he goes through the motions of living, his life runs through his hands like sand. Behind a front of satisfaction and optimism modern man is deeply unhappy; as a matter of fact, he is on the verge of desperation. He desperately clings to the notion of individuality; he wants to be "different," and he has no greater recommendation of anything than that "it is different." We are informed of the individual name of the railroad clerk we buy our tickets from; handbags, playing cards, and portable radios are "personalized," by having the initials of the owner put on them. All this indicates the hunger for "difference" and yet these are almost the last vestiges of individuality that are left. Modern man is starved for life. But since, being an automaton, he cannot experience life in the sense of spontaneous activity, he takes as surrogate any kind of excitement and thrill: the thrill of drinking, of sports, of vicariously living the excitements of fictitious persons on the screen.

What then is the meaning of freedom for modern man?

He has become free from the external bonds that would prevent him from doing and thinking as he sees fit. He would be free to act according to his own will, if he knew what he wanted, thought, and felt. But he does not know. He conforms to anonymous authorities and adopts a self which is not his. The more he does this, the more powerless he feels, the more he is forced to conform. In spite of a veneer of optimism and initiative, modern man is overcome by a profound feeling of powerlessness which makes him gaze toward approaching catastrophes as though he were paralyzed.

Looked at superficially, people appear to function well enough in economic and social life; yet it would be dangerous to overlook the deep-seated unhappiness behind that comforting veneer. If life loses its meaning because it is not lived, man becomes desperate. People do not die quietly from physical starvation; they do not die quietly from psychic starvation either. If we look only at the economic needs as far as the "normal" person is concerned, if we do not see the unconscious suffering of the average automatized person, then we fail to see the danger that threatens our culture from its human basis: the readiness to accept any ideology and any leader, if only he promises excitement and offers a political structure and symbols which allegedly give meaning and order to an individual's life. The despair of the human automaton is fertile soil for the political purposes of Fascism.

FREEDOM AND SPONTANEITY

So far I have dealt with one aspect of freedom: the powerlessness and insecurity of the isolated individual in modern society who has become free from all bonds that once gave meaning and security to life. We have seen that the individual cannot bear this isolation; as an isolated being he is utterly helpless in comparison with the world outside and therefore deeply afraid of it; and because of his isolation, the unity of the world has broken down for him and he has lost any point of orientation. He is therefore overcome by doubts concerning himself, the meaning of life, and eventually any principle according to which he can direct his actions. Both helplessness and doubt paralyze life, and in order to live man tries to escape from freedom, negative freedom. He is driven into new bondage. This bondage is different from the primary bonds, from which, though dominated by authorities or the social group, he was not entirely separated. The escape does not restore his lost security, but only helps him to forget his self as a separate entity. He finds new and fragile security at the expense of sacrificing the integrity of his individual self. He chooses to lose his self since he cannot bear to be alone. Thus freedom—as freedom from—leads into new bondage.

Does our analysis lend itself to the conclusion that there is an inevitable circle that leads from freedom into new dependence? Does freedom from all primary ties make the individual so alone and isolated that inevitably he must escape into new bondage? Are *independence* and freedom identical with *isolation* and fear? Or is there a state of positive freedom in which the individual exists an an independent self and yet is not isolated but united with the world, with other men, and nature?

We believe that there is a positive answer, that the process of growing freedom does not constitute a vicious circle, and that man can be free and yet not alone, critical and yet not filled with doubts, independent and yet an integral part of mankind. This freedom man can attain by the realization of his self, by being himself. What is realization of the self? Idealistic philosophers have believed that self-realization can be achieved by intellectual insight alone. They have insisted upon splitting human personality, so that man's nature may be suppressed and guarded by his reasons. The result of this split, however, has been that not only the emotional life of man but also his intellectual faculties have been crippled. Reason, by becoming a guard set to watch its prisoner, nature, has become a prisoner itself; and thus both sides of human personality, reason and emotion, were crippled. We believe that the realization of the self is accomplished not only by an act of thinking but also by the realization of man's total personality, by the active expression of his emotional and intellectual potentialities. These potentialities are present in everybody; they become real only to the extent to which they are expressed. In other words, *positive freedom consists in the spontaneous activity of the total, integrated personality.*

We approach here one of the most difficult problems of psychology: the problem of spontaneity. An attempt to discuss this problem adequately would require a volume. However, on the basis of what we have said so far, it is possible to arrive at an understanding of the essential quality of spontaneous activity by means of contrast. Spontaneous activity is not compulsive activity, to which the individual is driven by his isolation and powerlessness; it is not the activity of the automaton, which is the uncritical adoption of patterns suggested from the outside. Spontaneous activity is free activity of the self and implies, psychologically, what the Latin root of the world, *sponte,* means literally: of one's free will. By activity we do not mean "doing something," but the quality of creative activity that can operate in one's emotional, intellectual, and sensuous experiences and in one's will as well. One premise for this spontaneity is the acceptance of the total personality and the elimination of the split between "reason" and "nature"; for only if man does not repress essential parts of his self, only if he has become transparent to himself, and only if the different spheres of life have reached a fundamental integration, is spontaneous activity possible.

While spontaneity is a relatively rare phenomenon in our culture, we are not entirely devoid of it. In order to help in the understanding of this point, I should like to remind the reader of some instances where we all catch a glimpse of spontaneity.

In the first place, we know of individuals who are—or have been—spontaneous, whose thinking, feeling, and acting were the expression of their selves and not of an automaton. These individuals are mostly known to us as artists. As a matter of fact, the artist can be defined as an individual who can express himself spontaneously. If this were the definition of an artist—Balzac defined him just in that way—then certain philosophers and scientists have to be called artists too, while others are as different from them as an old-fashioned photographer from a creative painter. There are other individuals who, though lacking the ability—or perhaps merely the training—for expressing themselves in an objective medium as the artist does, possess the same spontaneity. The position of the artist is vulnerable, though, for it is really only the successful artist whose individuality or spontaneity is respected; if he does not succeed in selling the art, he remains to his contemporaries a crank, a "neurotic." The artist in this matter is in a similar position to that of the revolutionary throughout history. The successful revolutionary is a statesman, the unsuccessful one a criminal.

Small children offer another instance of spontaneity. They have an ability to feel and think that which is really *theirs;* this spontaneity shows in what they say and think, in the feelings that are expressed in their faces. If one asks what makes for the attraction small children have for most people I believe that, aside from sentimental and conventional reasons, the answer must be that it is this very quality of spontaneity. It appeals profoundly to everyone who is not so dead himself that he has lost the ability to perceive it. As a matter of fact, there is nothing more attractive and convincing than spontaneity whether it is to be found in a child, in an artist, or in those individuals who cannot thus be grouped according to age or profession.

Most of us can observe at least moments of our own

spontaneity which are at the same time moments of genuine happiness. Whether it be the fresh and spontaneous perception of a landscape, or the drawing of some truth as the result of our thinking, or a sensuous pleasure that is not stereotyped, or the welling up of love for another person— in these moments we all know what a spontaneous act is and may have some vision of what human life could be if these experiences were not such rare and uncultivated occurrences.

Why is spontaneous activity the answer to the problem of freedom? We have said that negative freedom by itself makes the individual an isolated being, whose relationship to the world is distant and distrustful and whose self is weak and constantly threatened. Spontaneous activity is the one way in which man can overcome the terror of alone-ness without sacrificing the integrity of his self; for in the spontaneous realization of the self man unites himself anew with the world—with man, nature, and himself. Love is the foremost component of such spontaneity; not love as the dissolution of the self in another person, not love as the possession of another person, but love as spontaneous affirmation of others, as the union of the individual with others on the basis of the preservation of the individual self. The dynamic quality of love lies in this very polarity: that it springs from the need of overcoming separateness, that it leads to oneness—and yet that individuality is not eliminated. Work is the other component; not work as a compulsive activity in order to escape aloneness, not work as a relationship to nature which is partly one of dominat-ing her, partly one of worship of and enslavement by the very products of man's hands, but work as creation in which man becomes one with nature in the act of creation. What holds true of love and work holds true of all spon-taneous action, whether it be the realization of sensuous pleasure or participation in the political life of the com-munity. It affirms the individuality of the self and at the same time it unites the self with man and nature. The basic dichotomy that is inherent in freedom—the birth of individuality and the pain of aloneness—is dissolved on a higher plane by man's spontaneous action.

In all spontaneous activity the individual embraces the world. Not only does his individual self remain intact; it becomes stronger and more solidified. *For the self is as strong as it is active.* There is no genuine strength in possession as such, neither of material property nor of mental qualities like emotions or thoughts. There is also no strength in use and manipulation of objects; what we use is not ours simply because we use it. Ours is only that to which we are genuinely related by our creative activity, be it a person or an inanimate object. Only those qualities that result from our spontaneous activity give strength to the self and thereby form the basis of its integrity. The inability to act spontaneously, to express what one genuinely feels and thinks, and the resulting necessity to present a pseudo self to others and oneself, are the root of the feeling of inferiority and weakness. Whether or not we are aware of it, there is nothing of which we are more ashamed than of not being ourselves, and there is nothing that gives us greater pride and happiness than to think, to feel, and to say what is ours.

This implies that what matters is the activity as such, the process and not the result. In our culture the emphasis is just the reverse. We produce not for a concrete satisfaction but for the abstract purpose of selling our commodity; we feel that we can acquire everything material or immaterial by buying it, and thus things become ours independently of any creative effort of our own in relation to them. In the same way, we regard our personal qualities and the result of our efforts as commodities that can be sold for money, prestige, and power. The emphasis thus shifts from the present satisfaction of creative activity to the value of the finished product. Thereby man misses the only satisfaction that can give him real happiness—the experience of the activity of the present moment—and chases after a phantom that leaves him disappointed as soon as he believes he has caught it—the illusory happiness called success.

If the individual realizes his self by spontaneous activity and thus relates himself to the world, he ceases to be an isolated atom; he and the world become part of one structuralized whole; he has his rightful place, and thereby his doubt concerning himself and the meaning of life disappears. This doubt sprang from his separateness and from the thwarting of life; when he can live, neither compulsively nor automatically but spontaneously, the doubt disappears. He is aware of himself as an active and creative individual and recognizes that *there is only one meaning of life: the act of living itself.*

If the individual overcomes the basic doubt concerning himself and his place in life, if he is related to the world by embracing it in the act of spontaneous living, he gains strength as an individual and he gains security. This security, however, differs from the security that characterizes the preindividualist state in the same way in which the new relatedness to the world differs from that of the primary ties. The new security is not rooted in the protection which the individual has from a higher power outside of himself; neither is it a security in which the tragic quality of life is eliminated. The new security is dynamic; it is not based on protection, but on man's spontaneous activity. It is the security acquired each moment by man's spontaneous activity. It is the security that only freedom can give, that needs no illusions because it has eliminated those conditions that necessitate illusions.

Positive freedom as the realization of the self implies the full affirmation of the uniqueness of the individual. Men are born equal but they are also born different. The basis of this difference is the inherited equipment, physiological and mental, with which they start life, to which is added the particular constellation of circumstances and experiences that they meet with. This individual basis of the personality is as little identical with any other as two organisms are ever identical physically. The genuine growth of the self is always a growth on this particular basis; it is an organic growth, the unfolding of a nucleus that is peculiar for this one person and only for him. The development of the automaton, in contrast, is not an organic growth. The growth of the basis of the self is blocked and a pseudo self is superimposed upon this self, which is —as we have seen—essentially the incorporation of extraneous patterns of thinking and feeling. Organic growth is possible only under the condition of supreme respect for the peculiarity of the self of other persons as well as of our own self. This respect for and cultivation of the uniqueness of the self is the most valuable achievement of human culture and it is this very achievement that is in danger today.

The uniqueness of the self in no way contradicts the principle of equality. The thesis that men are born equal implies that they all share the same fundamental human qualities, that they share the basic fate of human beings, that they all have the same inalienable claim on freedom and happiness. It furthermore means that their relationship is one of solidarity, not one of domination-submission. What the concept of equality does not mean is that all men are alike. Such a concept of equality is derived from the role that the individual plays in his economic activities today. In the relation between the man who buys and the one who sells, the concrete differences of personality are eliminated. In this situation only one thing matters, that the one has something to sell and the other has money to buy it. In economic life one man is not different from another; as real persons they are, and the cultivation of their uniqueness is the essence of individuality.

Positive freedom also implies the principle that there is no higher power than this unique individual self, that man is the center and purpose of his life; that the growth and realization of man's individuality is an end that can never be subordinated to purposes which are supposed to have greater dignity. This interpretation may arouse serious objections. Does it not postulate unbridled egotism? Is is not the negation of the idea of sacrifice for an ideal? Would its acceptance not lead to anarchy? . . .

To say that man should not be subject to anything higher than himself does not deny the dignity of ideals. On the contrary, it is the strongest affirmation of ideals. It forces us, however, to a critical analysis of what an ideal is. One is generally apt today to assume that an ideal is any aim whose achievement does not imply material gain, anything for which a person is ready to sacrifice egotistical ends. This is a purely psychological—and for that matter relativistic—concept of an ideal. From this subjectivist viewpoint a Fascist, who is driven by the desire to subordinate himself to a higher power and at the same time to overpower other people, has an ideal just as much as the man who fights for human equality and freedom. On this basis the problem of ideals can never be solved.

We must recognize the difference between genuine and fictitious ideals, which is just as fundamental a difference as that between truth and falsehood. All genuine ideals have one thing in common: they express the desire for something which is not yet accomplished but which is desirable for the purposes of the growth and happiness of the individual.[4] We may not always know what serves this end, we may disagree about the function of this or that ideal in terms of human development, but this is no reason for a relativism which says that we cannot know what furthers life or what blocks it. We are not always sure which food is healthy and which is not, yet we do not conclude that we have no way whatsoever of recognizing poison. In the same way, we can know, if we want to, what is poisonous for mental life. We know that poverty, intimidation, isolation are directed *against* life; that everything that serves freedom and furthers the courage and strength to be oneself is *for* life. What is good or bad for man is not a metaphysical question, but an empirical one that can be answered on the basis of an analysis of man's nature and the effect which certain conditions have on him.

.   .   .   .

One last objection is to be met: If individuals are allowed to act freely in the sense of spontaneity, if they acknowledge no higher authority than themselves, will anarchy be the inevitable result? Insofar as the word "anarchy" stands for heedless egotism and destructiveness, the determining factor depends upon one's understanding of human nature. I can only refer to what has been pointed out [before]. . . , that man is neither good nor bad; that life has an inherent tendency to grow, to expand, to express potentialities; that if life is thwarted, if the individual is isolated and overcome by doubt or a feeling of aloneness and powerlessness, then he is driven to destructiveness and craving for power or submission. If human freedom is established as *freedom to,* if man can realize his self fully and uncompromisingly, the fundamental cause for his

---

[4] Cf. Max Otto, *The Human Enterprise* (New York: T. S. Croft, 1940), Chaps. IV and V.

asocial drives will have disappeared and only a sick and abnormal individual will be dangerous. This freedom has never been realized in the history of mankind, yet it has been an ideal to which mankind has stuck even if it was often expressed in abstruse and irrational forms. There is no reason to wonder why the record of history shows so much cruelty and destructiveness. If there is anything to be surprised at—and encouraged by—I believe it is the fact that the human race, in spite of all that has happened to men, has retained—and actually developed—such qualities of dignity, courage, decency, and kindness as we find them throughout history and in countless individuals today.

If by anarchy one means that the individual does not acknowledge any kind of authority, the answer is to be found in what has been said about the difference between rational and irrational authority. Rational authority—like a genuine ideal—represents the aims of growth and expansion of the individual. It is, therefore, in principle never in conflict with the individual and his real, and not his pathological, aims.

It has been my thesis that freedom has a twofold meaning for modern man: that he has been freed from traditional authorities and has become an "individual," but that at the same time he has become isolated, powerless, and an instrument of purposes outside of himself, alienated from himself and others; furthermore, that this state undermines his self, weakens and frightens him, and makes him ready for submission to new kinds of bondage. Positive freedom on the other hand is identical with the full realization of the individual's potentialities, together with his ability to live actively and spontaneously. Freedom has reached a critical point where, driven by the logic of its own dynamism, it threatens to change into its opposite. The future of democracy depends on the realization of the individualism that has been the ideological aim of modern thought since the Renaissance. The cultural and political crisis of our day is not due to the fact that there is too much individualism but that what we believe to be individualism has become an empty shell. The victory of freedom is possible only if democracy develops into a society in which the individual, his growth and happiness,

is the aim and purpose of culture, in which life does not
need any justification in success or anything else, and
in which the individual is not subordinated to or manipulated by any power outside of himself, be it the State or
the economic machine; finally, a society in which his
conscience and ideals are not the internalization of external
demands, but are really *his* and express the aims that result from the peculiarity of his self. These aims could not
be fully realized in any previous period of modern history; they had to remain largely ideological aims, because
the material basis for the development of genuine individualism was lacking. Capitalism has created this
premise. The problem of production is solved—in principle at least—and we can visualize a future of abundance,
in which the fight for economic privileges is no longer
necessitated by economic scarcity. The problem we are
confronted with today is that of the organization of social
and economic forces, so that man—as a member of organized society—may become the master of these forces
and cease to be their slave.

I have stressed the psychological side of freedom, but I
have also tried to show that the psychological problem
cannot be separated from the material basis of human
existence, from the economic, social, and political structure
of society. It follows from this premise that the realization
of positive freedom and individualism is also bound up with
economic and social changes that will permit the individual to become free in terms of the realization of his
self. It is not the aim of this essay to deal with the
economic problems resulting from that premise or to give
a picture of economic plans for the future. But I should not
like to leave any doubt concerning the direction in which
I believe the solution to lie.

In the first place this must be said: We cannot afford
to lose any of the fundamental achievements of modern
democracy—either the fundamental one of representative
government, that is, government elected by the people and
responsible to the people, or any of the rights which the Bill
of Rights guarantees to every citizen. Nor can we compromise the newer democratic principle that no one shall be
allowed to starve, that society is responsible for all its members, that no one shall be frightened into submission and

lose his human pride through fear of unemployment and starvation. These basic achievements must not only be preserved; they must be fortified and expanded.

In spite of the fact that this measure of democracy has been realized—though far from completely—it is not enough. Progress for democracy lies in enhancing the actual freedom, initiative, and spontaneity of the individual, not only in certain private and spiritual matters, but above all in the activity fundamental to every man's existence, his work.

What are the general conditions for that? The irrational and planless character of society must be replaced by a planned economy that represents the planned and concerted effort of society as such. Society must master the social problem as rationally as it has mastered nature. One condition for this is the elimination of the secret rule of those who, though few in number, wield great economic power without any responsibility to those whose fate depends on their decisions. We may call this new order by the name of democratic socialism but the name does not matter; all that matters is that we establish a rational economic system serving the purposes of the people. Today the vast majority of the people not only have no control over the whole of the economic machine, but they have little chance to develop genuine initiative and spontaneity at the particular job they are doing. They are "employed," and nothing more is expected from them than that they do what they are told. Only in a planned economy in which the whole nation has rationally mastered the economic and social forces can the individual share responsibility and use creative intelligence in his work. All that matters is that the opportunity for genuine activity be restored to the individual; that the purposes of society and of his own become identical, not ideologically but in reality; and that he apply his effort and reason actively to the work he is doing, as something for which he can feel responsible because it has meaning and purpose in terms of his human ends. We must replace manipulation of men by active and intelligent cooperation, and expand the principle of government of the people, by the people, for the people, from the formal political to the economic sphere.

The question of whether an economic and political system

furthers the cause of human freedom cannot be answered in political and economic terms alone. The only criterion for the realization of freedom is whether or not the individual actively participates in determining his life and that of society, and this not only by the formal act of voting but in his daily activity, in his work, and in his relations to others. Modern political democracy, if it restricts itself to the purely political sphere, cannot sufficiently counteract the results of the economic insignificance of the average individual. But purely economic concepts like socialization of the means of production are not sufficient either. I am not thinking here so much of the deceitful usage of the word "socialism" as it has been applied—for reasons of tactical expediency—in National Socialism. I have in mind Russia, where "socialism" has become a deceptive word; for although socialization of the means of production has taken place, actually a powerful bureaucracy manipulates the vast mass of the population; this necessarily prevents the development of freedom and individualism, even if government control may be effective in the economic interest of the majority of the people.

. . . .

Obviously, one of the greatest difficulties in the establishment of the conditions for the realization of democracy lies in the contradiction between a planned economy and the active cooperation of each individual. A planned economy of the scope of any big industrial system requires a great deal of centralization and, as a consequence, a bureaucracy to administer this centralized machine. On the other hand, the active control and cooperation by each individual and by the smallest units of the whole system requires a great amount of decentralization. Unless planning from the top is blended with active participation from below, unless the stream of social life continuously flows from below upwards, a planned economy will lead to renewed manipulation of the people. To solve this problem of combining centralization with decentralization is one of the major tasks of society. But it is certainly no less soluble than the technical problems we have already solved and which have brought us an almost complete

Freedom and Democracy 319

mastery over nature. It is to be solved, however, only if we clearly recognize the necessity of doing so and if we have faith in the people, in their capacity to take care of their real interests as human beings.

In a way it is again the problem of individual initiative with which we are confronted. Individual initiative was one of the great stimuli both of the economic system and also of personal development under liberal capitalism. But there are two qualifications: It developed only selected qualities of man, his will and rationality, while leaving him otherwise subordinate to economic goals. It was a principle that functioned best in a highly individualized and competitive phase of capitalism which had room for countless independent economic units. Today this space has narrowed down. Only a small number can exercise individual initiative. If we want to realize this principle today and enlarge it so that the whole personality becomes free, it will be possible only on the basis of the rational and concerted effort of a society as a whole, and by an amount of decentralization which can guarantee real, genuine, active cooperation and control by the smallest units of the system.

Only if man masters society and subordinates the economic machine to the purposes of human happiness and only if he actively participates in the social process, can he overcome what now drives him into despair—his aloneness and his feeling of powerlessness. Man does not suffer so much from poverty today as he suffers from the fact that he has become a cog in a large machine, an automaton, that his life has become empty and lost its meaning. The victory over all kinds of authoritarian systems will be possible only if democracy does not retreat but takes the offensive and proceeds to realize what has been its aim in the minds of those who fought for freedom throughout the last centuries. It will triumph over the forces of nihilism only if it can imbue people with a faith that is the strongest the human mind is capable of, the faith in life and in truth, and in freedom as the active and spontaneous realization of the individual self.

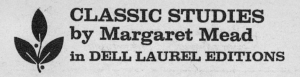

CLASSIC STUDIES
by Margaret Mead
in DELL LAUREL EDITIONS

COMING OF AGE IN SAMOA 95c

With a new preface by Dr. Mead
Foreword by Franz Boas
Margaret Mead's lucid study of youth in a primitive society is
rightly regarded as a classic scientific study.

GROWING UP IN NEW GUINEA 95c

With an expanded preface by the author
Introduction by Franz Boas
Provides perceptive analysis of family life in a primitive community on the South Pacific Island of Manus—their attitudes
toward sex, marriage, the raising of children, and the supernatural.

SEX AND TEMPERAMENT IN 95c
THREE PRIMITIVE SOCIETIES

In this study of three primitive tribes living within a hundred-
mile area in New Guinea, Dr. Mead explores the distinctions
between sexual and temperamental differences and the effect
of cultural conditioning on both.

MALE AND FEMALE: 1.25

A Study of the Sexes in a Changing World
Drawing upon the author's studies of peoples of the Pacific
Islands, this book discusses how some of the basic relationships
between men and women are obscured by our modern way of
life in the United States.

NEW LIVES FOR OLD 1.25

With a new preface by the author
An account of the cultural transformation that has taken place
among the Manus in the twenty-five years since the author
visited them to write *Growing Up in New Guinea*.

By the author of
TERRITORIAL IMPERATIVE . . .
ROBERT ARDREY

AFRICAN
GENESIS

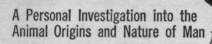

A Personal Investigation into the
Animal Origins and Nature of Man

AFRICAN GENESIS presents a fascinating array of new scientific evidence, largely accumulated over the past thirty years, on the origins of man. It is the author's unorthodox and intriguing theory that **Homo sapiens** developed from carnivorous, predatory killer apes and that man's age-old affinity for war and weapons is the natural result of this inherited animal instinct.

AFRICAN GENESIS will long continue to be read and remembered not only for the startlingly radical ideas which it champions, but also for the exceptional clarity of its style and the sense of mounting excitement which it vividly generates.

". . . the most enjoyable and stimulating book on the evolution of man . . . that has been published for some time."
—*The Nation*

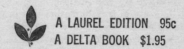

A LAUREL EDITION   95c
A DELTA BOOK $1.95